EVERYTHIN

YOU NEED TO KNOW ABOUT...

Managing
Stress

EVERYTHING
YOU NEED TO KNOW ABOUT...
Managing Stress

EVE ADAMSON

David & Charles

A DAVID & CHARLES BOOK

David & Charles is a subsidiary of F+W (UK) Ltd.,

an F+W Publications Inc. company

First published in the UK in 2004

First published in the USA as The Everything® Stress Management Book,

by Adams Media Corporation in 2002

Project Manager Ian Kearey

Cover Design Ali Myer

A catalogue record for this book is available from the British Library.

ISBN 0 7153 2061 0

Printed in Great Britain by CPI Bath

for David & Charles

Brunel House   Newton Abbot   Devon

Visit our website at www.davidandcharles.co.uk

David & Charles books are available from all good bookshops;

alternatively you can contact our Orderline on (0)1626 334555 or

write to us at FREEPOST EX2110, David & Charles Direct,

Newton Abbot, TQ12 4ZZ (no stamp required UK mainland).

Contents

Introduction

So you think you're stressed? At least you're in good company! Stress seems to have reached epidemic proportions, but knowing that everyone else around you is suffering as much as you are isn't much help when your muscles are tense, your mind is racing, your palms are sweaty, your stomach hurts and you can't concentrate on any of the many items on your monumental to-do list.

Although you know what the experts say about stress, you don't have time for a bubble bath, you can't justify the expense of a weekly massage, you wouldn't know how to begin meditating and, as far as a healthy diet and exercise are concerned, if you don't stop to pick up a takeaway on the way home, nobody in the family is going to eat tonight. Is there any hope for you?

Of course there is. You just need a little training in managing stress, and you've come to the right place. This book explains how to work through all the information floating around out there about what stress is, what it is doing to your health and happiness, and why you need to do something about it today. You'll find simple descriptions of many stress management techniques, from 'mindfulness' to de-cluttering, from easy exercise suggestions to advice on how to finally take control of your finances.

You'll also find quizzes and prompts to help you explore your own tendencies for accumulating and reacting to stress, and personalized methods for managing your individual stress. You can keep track of your stress and of the effectiveness of different stress-management techniques by using the charts in the book and a tip-filled stress management journal. It's all here.

You *can* manage your stress, and you don't have to do it alone. With guidance, inspiration and a commitment to help yourself to be your best possible self, you can be feeling better soon. So relax, take a deep breath, put your feet up on your desk or table and start reading this book. Stress doesn't stand a chance.

CHAPTER 1
Stress Unmasked

You know you're under stress when you bump into the car in front of you on the way to work (ouch!), make it to work three hours late and are sacked (no!), then have your wallet stolen on the bus home (oh, that's the final straw!). But what about when you get engaged to the love of your life? Or when you finally get the promotion of your dreams? What about when you have hay fever, or move into a new home or adopt a dog? Is it stressful to finish education, start an exercise routine or binge on chocolate biscuits? You bet it is.

What Is Stress?

What's so stressful about eating a few chocolate biscuits? Nothing, if you eat two chocolate digestives every day as part of a well-balanced diet. Plenty, if you deprive yourself of desserts for a month, then eat an entire packet of chocolate biscuits. You aren't used to all those biscuits, your body isn't used to all that sugar, and that's stressful. Not as stressful as writing off your car or being transferred to your employer's equivalent of Siberia, but stressful nonetheless.

According to a survey in October 2003, 70 per cent of the UK population believe themselves to be suffering from stress. This increases to 88 per cent among 25–34-year-olds, 83 per cent for 35–44-year-olds and 81 per cent for 45–54-year-olds.

Stress is the body's reaction to a certain degree of stimulation. Anything out of the ordinary that happens to you causes your body to experience stress. Some of that stress feels good, even great. Without any stress at all, life would be unexciting. Stress isn't, by definition, necessarily bad, but it certainly isn't always good, either. In fact, it can cause dramatic health problems if it happens to you too often and for too long.

Stress isn't just caused by out-of-the-ordinary things, however. It can also be deeply embedded and hidden in your life. What if you can't stand your job in middle management but continue to go to work every day because you're afraid of starting your own business and giving up a regular salary? What if your family has serious communication problems, or if you live in a place where you don't feel safe? Perhaps everything *seems* just fine, but nevertheless you feel deeply unhappy. Even when you are accustomed to certain things in your life – dirty washing in the sink, family members who don't help out, 12-hour days at the office – those things can still be stressful. You might even feel stressed out when something goes right. Perhaps someone is nice to you and you become suspicious, or you feel uncomfortable if your house is too clean. You can be so used to things being difficult that you don't know how to adjust. Stress is a strange and highly individual phenomenon.

Unless you live in a cave without a television (actually, not a bad way to eliminate stress from your life), you've probably heard quite a lot about stress from radio and TV, around the photocopier at work or from magazines and newspapers. Most people have a preconceived notion of what stress is in general, as well as what it means to them personally. What does stress mean to you?

· Discomfort?
· Pain?
· Worry?
· Anxiety?
· Excitement?
· Fear?
· Uncertainty?

All the above cause stress and are also often conditions stemming from stress. But stress is such a broad term, and there are so many different kinds of stress, affecting so many people in so many different ways, that the word *stress* itself may seem to defy definition. Just to complicate things further, what is stressful to one person might be exhilarating to another. So, what exactly is stress?

Stress comes in several guises, some more obvious than others. Stress can be acute, episodic or chronic. Let's take a closer look at each kind of stress and how it affects you.

When Life Changes: Acute Stress

Acute stress is the most obvious kind of stress, and it's fairly easy to spot if you associate it with one thing:

ACUTE STRESS = CHANGE

Yes, that's all it is. Change. Things you're not used to. And that can include anything, from a change in your diet to a change in your exercise habits to a change in your job to a change in the people involved in your life, whether you've lost them or gained them.

In other words, acute stress is something that disturbs your entire equilibrium. You get used to things as they are, physically, mentally, emotionally, even chemically. Your body clock is set for sleep at certain times, your energy rises and falls at certain times and your blood glucose levels change in response to the food you eat at certain times each day. As you go along your merry way in life, entrenched in your routines and habits and 'normal' way of living, your body and mind know pretty well what to expect.

All of the following are stressful to your mind and body: serious illness (either your own or that of a loved one), divorce, bankruptcy, too much overtime at work, a promotion, the loss of a job, marriage, graduation and a winning lottery ticket.

When something happens to *change* our existence, whether that something is a physical change (such as a cold virus or a sprained ankle), a chemical change (the side effects of a medication or the hormonal fluctuations following childbirth, for example), or an emotional change (a marriage, a child leaving home, the death of a loved one), our equilibrium is altered. Our life changes. Our bodies and minds are thrown out of the routine they've come to expect. We've experienced change, and with that comes stress.

Change is hard on our bodies and our minds because people tend to be creatures of habit. Even the most spontaneous and routine-resistant among us have our habits, and that doesn't just mean enjoying a morning cup of coffee or sleeping on a favourite side of the bed. Habits include minute, complex, intricate interworkings of physical, chemical and emotional factors on our bodies.

Say you get up and go to work five days a week, rising at 6:00 AM, grabbing a piece of toast and a cup of coffee, then plunging into the rush hour. Once a year you go on holiday, and for two weeks you sleep until 11:00 AM, and on waking eat a full cooked breakfast. This is stressful, too, because you've changed your habits. You probably enjoy it, and in some ways, a holiday can soften the chronic stress caused by sleep deprivation. But if you are suddenly sleeping late and eating different foods, your body clock will have to readjust, your blood chemistry will have to readjust, and just when you've readjusted, you'll probably have to go back to waking up at 6:00 AM and foregoing the bacon and eggs for that piece of toast, eaten in a rush again.

That's not to say you shouldn't go on holiday, and you certainly shouldn't avoid all change. Without it, life wouldn't be very interesting. Humans desire and need a certain degree of change – it can be exciting and memorable. Change can be fun... up to a point.

But here's the tricky part: how much change you can take before the stress of changes starts to have a negative effect on you is a completely individual matter. A certain amount of stress is fine, but too much is unhealthy, unsettling and unbalancing. There is no single formula to calculate what 'too much stress' is for everyone, because everyone differs. The level of acute stress you can tolerate is likely to be very different from the level of stress your friends and relatives can stand (although a low level of stress tolerance does appear to be inheritable).

Pushing yourself to work too hard, staying up too late, eating too much (or too little), or worrying constantly is not only stressful for your mind but also for your body. Many medical professionals believe that stress can contribute to heart disease, cancer, and an increased chance of accidents.

When Life Is a Roller Coaster: Episodic Stress

Episodic stress means lots of acute stress – in other words, lots of life changes – occurring over an extended period of time. People who suffer from episodic stress always seem to be in the midst of a crisis. They tend to be overwrought, sometimes tense, often irritable, angry or anxious.

If you've ever been through a week, a month or even a year when you seemed to suffer personal disaster after personal disaster, you know what it's like to experience episodic stress. First, your central heating breaks down, then one of your cheques bounces, then you get a speeding fine, then your entire extended family decides to come and stay with you for four weeks, then your sister-in-law crashes into your garage with her car, and then you get flu. For some people, episodic stress goes on for so long that they become used to it, and the stress state is obvious to others. 'Oh, that poor woman. She has terrible luck!' 'Did you hear what happened to Jerry *this* time?'

Episodic stress, like acute stress, can also come in more positive forms. First, a whirlwind courtship, then a big wedding, a honeymoon in Bali, buying a new home and moving in with your partner for the first time – all this in the same year would be an extremely stressful sequence of events. Fun, of course. Romantic, yes. Even thrilling. But still an excellent example of episodic stress in its sunnier, though no less punishing, manifestation.

Sometimes the cause of episodic stress is more subtle – for example, 'worrying'. Worrying creates stress *before* anything changes, and often when there is little chance of the feared change happening. Excessive worry can be linked to a specific anxiety disorder, but even when it is less severe than that, it saps the body's energy, usually for no good reason.

Worrying doesn't solve problems – in fact it usually involves the contemplation of horrible things that are extremely unlikely to happen. Worrying puts your body under stress by creating imaginary changes in the equilibrium of life – changes that haven't actually happened!

Are you a worrier? How many of the following describe you?

- You find yourself worrying about things that are extremely unlikely to happen, such as having an accident out of the blue or developing an illness you have no real reason to believe you would develop. (Read the first part of *Three Men in a Boat* for a comical and reassuring extreme version of this.)
- You often lose sleep worrying about what would happen if you lost a loved one, or what would happen to your loved ones if they lost you.
- You have difficulty falling asleep because you can't slow down the frantic worrying process in your head.
- When the phone rings or the post arrives, you always imagine you are about to receive bad news.

- You feel compelled to try to control others because you worry that they can't take care of themselves.
- You are extremely cautious about taking part in any activity that could possibly result in harm to you or to those around you, even if the risk is small (such as driving a car, flying in an aeroplane or visiting a big city).

Even if just one of these worrier characteristics applies to you, you probably worry more than you need to. If most or all of the statements apply to you, worry is probably having a distinctly negative effect on you. Worry and the anxiety it produces can cause specific physical, cognitive, and emotional symptoms, from heart palpitations, dry mouth, hyperventilation, muscle pain and fatigue to fear, panic, anger and depression. Worry is a major cause of episodic stress.

Like many other things we think we can't control, worry is largely a matter of habit. So how do you stop worrying? By retraining your brain! One way to do this is to get moving. It's hard to worry when your energy is directed towards following an exercise video or breathing in fresh air as you go for a run through the park.

When Life Stinks: Chronic Stress

Chronic stress is very different from acute and episodic stress, although its long-term effects are much the same. Chronic stress has nothing to do with change. Chronic stress is long-term, constant, unrelenting stress on the body, mind or spirit. For example, someone living in poverty for years and years is under chronic stress. So is someone with an illness such as arthritis, or with migraine or other conditions that result in constant pain. Living in a dysfunctional family or working at a job you hate is a source of chronic stress. So is deep-seated self-hatred or low self-esteem.

The causes of some chronic stress are obvious. People live in horrible conditions or have to endure terrible abuse. They are in prison, live in a war-torn country or are part of a minority in a place where minorities suffer constant discrimination. Other causes are less obvious. A person who despises her job and feels she can never realize her dreams is under chronic stress. So is a person who feels trapped in a bad relationship.

Sometimes, chronic stress is the result of acute or episodic stress. An acute illness can result in chronic pain. An abused child can grow up filled with self-loathing and low self-esteem. The problem with chronic stress is that people become so used to it they can't begin to see a way to change things. They come to believe life can only be unremittingly painful, unrewarding or miserable.

All forms of stress can result in a downward spiral of illness, depression and anxiety, leading to breakdown – physical, emotional, mental and spiritual. Too much stress is dangerous. It not only saps the joy from life, it can kill, whether through a heart attack, a stroke, an act of violence, suicide or, as some research suggests, as a cause of cancer.

According to a January 2001 article in *Time* magazine, scientists have discovered that a sedentary 40-year-old woman who starts walking briskly for 30 minutes four times per week will have about the same low risk of a heart attack as a woman who has exercised regularly for her entire life. It's never too late to start taking care of yourself!

Who Has It?

So who is affected by all this stress? You? Your partner? Your parents? Your grandparents? Your children? Your friends? Your enemies? The person at the next desk? The woman in the lift? The head of the company? The people in the postroom?

Yes, all of them.

Everyone has experienced some kind of stress at some point, and many people experience chronic – i.e. constant, regular – stress every day of their lives. Some people handle stress fairly well, even when it is extreme. Others fall apart under stress that seems negligible to everyone else. What's the difference? Some may have learned better coping mechanisms, but many researchers believe that people have an inherited level of stress tolerance. Some people can take a lot and still feel great – in fact, they often do their best work under stress. Other people require very low-stress lives to function productively.

So we all experience stress some of the time, and these days more and more people seem to experience stress all the time. And it isn't just individuals who are affected, either. According to research by the Health and Safety Executive:

- About 500,000 people in the UK experience work-related stress at a level they believe is making them ill.
- Up to 5,000,000 people in the UK say they feel 'very' or 'extremely' stressed by their work.
- Work-related stress costs UK society about £3.75 billion every year, and the costs are set to increase even further.
- Well over 50 per cent of industrial accidents are thought to be due to some form of stress.
- Every year in the UK, about 150,000 people take at least a month off work for ailments caused by stress. This results in a loss of some 6,500,000 working days.
- Compensation claims for workplace stress, once rare, are on the increase, and more are successful.

But although stress has become an integral part of life for many, this doesn't mean we should sit back and accept its insidious effects on our bodies, minds and spirits. While you probably can't do much about the stress experienced by others (unless you're the cause of the stress), you can certainly tackle the stress in your own life (and that's a good way to stop being stressful to others!).

 Chronic stress can trick our bodies into thinking they are in equilibrium. Even if an unhealthy habit becomes part of your daily routine and you think your body has adjusted to, say, working late, eating junk food or not getting enough sleep, the stress of not giving your body what it requires to be healthy will eventually catch up with you.

Where Does It Come From?

Stress can come from inside. It can be caused by your perception of events, rather than by the events themselves. A new job might be a great cause of stress to one person, and a magnificent opportunity to another. A lot depends on attitude.

But even when the stress is undeniably external – if you have been defrauded of all your money, for example – there will be a host of changes inside your body. More specifically, stress in any form interferes with the body's production of three hormones that help you feel balanced and healthy:

1. *Serotonin* is the hormone that helps you get a good night's sleep. Produced in the pineal gland deep inside your brain, serotonin controls your body clock by converting into melatonin and then converting back into serotonin over the course of a 24-hour day. This process regulates your energy, body temperature and sleep cycle. The serotonin cycle synchronizes with the cycle of the sun, regulating itself according to exposure to daylight and darkness. This is why some of those who are rarely exposed to the sun, people who live in northern climates for example, experience seasonal depression during the long, dark winter months – their serotonin production falls below adequate levels. Stress can have an effect, too, and one result is the inability to sleep well. People under stress often experience a disturbed sleep cycle, manifesting itself either as insomnia or as an excessive need to sleep because the regular sleep is of poor quality.

2. *Noradrenaline* is a hormone produced by your adrenal glands. It is related to the adrenaline that your body releases in emergencies to give you an extra chance of survival. Noradrenaline affects your daily cycle of energy, and too much stress can disrupt its production, leaving you with a profound lack of energy and motivation to do anything. It's the feeling you get when you just want to sit and stare at the television, even though you have a long list of things that you absolutely have to do. If your noradrenaline production is disrupted, you will probably just keep sitting there, watching television, as you simply won't have the energy to do anything else.

3. *Dopamine* is a hormone linked to the release of endorphins in your brain. Endorphins help to reduce pain and are chemically related to opiate substances such as morphine and heroin. If you are injured, your body releases endorphins to reduce pain and allow you to function. When stress compromises your body's ability to produce dopamine, it also compromises your body's ability to produce endorphins, so you become more sensitive to pain. Dopamine is also responsible for the wonderful feeling you have when you achieve things. But too much stress leads to too little dopamine, and nothing seems fun or pleasurable anymore. You feel flat and depressed.

Stress can disrupt your body's production of serotonin, noradrenaline and dopamine. When the disruption of these hormones results in depression, your doctor may prescribe antidepressants. Many antidepressants are designed to regulate the production of serotonin, noradrenaline and dopamine, and to re-establish the body's equilibrium. If stress management techniques don't work for you, you may require medication. See your doctor.

So stress can come from inside your head, as well as from outside you. Your perception of events, combined with other influences (such as your health) on your body and mind, actually cause chemical changes within your body. Anyone who has ever doubted the intricate connection between mind and body need only look at what happens when people worry and feel stress. It's all connected (and therein lies a clue to what you can do about stress!).

When Do You Get It?

There are many causes of stress, and they can happen at any time. Stress is inevitable when you experience a major life change, so expect it when you move house, lose someone you love, get married, change jobs or experience a big change in financial status, diet, exercise habits or health.

But you can also expect stress when you have a minor illness such as a cold, argue with a friend, go on a diet, join a gym, stay out too late, drink too much, or even spend the day at home with your children when school is cancelled due to sudden blizzards. Remember, stress can result from *any* kind of change to normal routine. It also results from living a life that doesn't make you happy: if that includes you, your life may be one long episode of stress. You need stress management now!

When people don't take care of themselves, this results in stress on the body. Smoking, obesity and lack of exercise all contribute to physical stress. According to the World Health Organization, Type 2 diabetes has become one of the major causes of premature death in most countries. In 2000, there were 171,000,000 people with diabetes worldwide. This figure is expected to more than double by 2030.

Why, Why, Why?

What is the point of stress? Stress is a relatively complex interaction of external and internal processes caused by something relatively simple: the survival instinct, which is still important, even today!

Life is full of stimuli. We enjoy some of them, and don't enjoy others. But our bodies are programmed by millions of years of learning to survive and react in certain ways to extreme stimuli. We've evolved so that if you suddenly find yourself in a dangerous situation – in front of a speeding car, teetering on the edge of a cliff, calling your boss a troglodyte when he is standing right behind you – your body will react in the way that will best ensure your survival. You might move very quickly, suddenly pitch yourself back to safety, or think on your feet and be able to talk your way out of trouble.

Whether you are being chased around the savanna by a hungry lion or around a car park by an aggressive motorist, your body recognizes an emergency and pours stress hormones, including adrenaline and cortisol, into your bloodstream. Adrenaline produces what scientists call the 'fight or flight' response (which will be discussed further in the next chapter).

This gives you an extra boost of strength and energy so that you can turn around and fight the lion, if you think you will win (you're probably better off up against the motorist), or run like mad (also effective against irate motorists), if that seems the more sensible option.

Adrenaline increases your heart rate and breathing rate, and sends blood straight to your vital organs to improve their efficiency – faster muscle response, quicker thinking and so on. It also helps your blood to clot faster and draws blood away from your skin (if you are swiped by the lion's claw, you won't bleed as much) and from your digestive tract (so you won't be sick – no, it doesn't always work). Cortisol flows through your body to keep the stress response responding for as long as the stress situation continues.

But even cavemen weren't being chased by hungry lions all day long, every day, for weeks on end (or, if they were, they really should have considered moving to a different cave). Extreme physical reactions aren't meant to occur all the time. They are undeniably helpful during emergencies and in other extreme but fun situations such as performing in a play or making a speech at your best friend's wedding. The stress reaction can help you to think more quickly and react more accurately, including responding with clever, witty repartee and just the right joke to keep the audience entranced by your sparkling performance.

If your life seems stressful even though nothing seems to have changed, the culprit may be sleep deprivation. Even if your serotonin cycle isn't so disrupted that you can't sleep, plenty of people simply don't sleep because they stay up late watching television. Most of us really do need seven to eight hours sleep a night to feel refreshed and handle everyday stress.

But if you were to experience the release of adrenaline and cortisol every day, eventually the feeling would become tiresome, quite literally. You'd start to feel exhaustion, physical pain, a decrease in your ability to concentrate and remember, frustration, irritability, insomnia and possibly even violent episodes. Your body would become out of balance, because we aren't designed to be in a crisis all the time.

But life moves so quickly these days, and as technology allows us to do ten times more work in a fraction of the time, everybody wants everything yesterday, so we feel the strain. Too much stress will negate the benefits of all that great technology – you won't get much work done if you have no energy and no motivation, and are ill most of the time.

So How Do You Get Rid of It?

You may not feel that the stress in your life is really that bad just yet. After all, you aren't on the verge of a heart attack or a breakdown... are you?

But what will happen if you *don't* begin to manage the stress in your life? How long will you allow stress to compromise your quality of life, especially knowing that you don't have to? That's where stress management comes in, and stress management is the focus of this book.

As pervasive as stress may be in all its forms, stress management techniques that really work are equally pervasive. You *can* manage, even eliminate, the negative stress in your life. All you have to do is find the stress-management techniques that work best for you. Learn them and turn your life around.

And that's the purpose of this book. You'll learn about stress management in its many forms so that you can design a management programme that works for you.

CHAPTER 2

What Is Stress Doing to Me?

We have lots of ways to describe how we feel when stressed. Keyed up, wound up, geared up, fired up – all those expressions contain the word '*up*' because the stress response is, indeed, an 'up' experience. Muscles are pumped for action, senses are heightened, awareness is sharpened. And these feelings are useful, unless they are too frequent. Constant stress exacts a heavy toll on the mind, body and emotional well-being. Your health and happiness depend on responding to stress appropriately.

Stress on Your Body

You can control some potential stress on your body. For example, you can determine what and how much you eat and how much you exercise. These stresses fall into the physiological stressor category. Then there are environmental stressors, such as pollution.

1. *Physiological stressors.* These are the stressors within your own body. For example, hormonal changes during pregnancy or the menopause put direct physiological stress on your system, as does premenstrual syndrome (PMS). Hormones may also cause indirect stress because of the emotional changes they bring about. In addition, bad health habits, such as smoking, drinking too much, eating junk food, substance abuse or being sedentary put physiological stress on your body. So does illness, whether it's the common cold or something more serious like heart disease or cancer. Injury also puts stress on your body – a broken leg, a sprained wrist or a slipped disc are all stressful.

2. *Environmental stressors.* These are things in your immediate environment that put constant stress on your body. They include air pollution, polluted drinking water, noise pollution, artificial lighting, bad ventilation, and allergens, whether pollen from the field outside your bedroom window, or in the fur of the cat who likes to sleep on your pillow.

One of the most common reactions to stress is compulsive eating. The best way to handle this impulse is to find a healthier way to deal with your feelings at times of stress. Drinking a large glass of water, taking a walk outside, or phoning a friend might be just what you need. Remember, you can control your life.

Just as potent are the indirect stressors that affect your body by way of your mind. For example, being caught in a traffic jam may stress your body directly because of the air pollution you are exposed to, but it will also stress your body indirectly if you get so worked up and irritated sitting in your car in the middle of the traffic that your blood pressure rises, your muscles tense and your heart beats faster. If you were to view the traffic jam differently – perhaps as an opportunity to relax and listen to your favourite CD before getting to work – your body might not experience any stress at all. Again, attitude plays a major role.

Pain is another cause of indirect stress. If you have a terrible headache, your body may not experience direct physiological stress, but your emotional reaction to the pain might cause your body significant stress. People tend to be afraid of pain, but it can be an important way of letting us know that something is wrong – for instance, injury or disease. However, sometimes we already know what's wrong. We get migraines, or have arthritis or period pains, or a bad knee that acts up when the weather changes. This kind of 'familiar' pain isn't useful in terms of alerting us to something that needs immediate medical attention.

But whether the pain is something new or something we are used to, we still tend to become tense. 'Oh no, not another migraine! No, not today!' Our emotional reaction to the pain causes the physiological stress. So although stress-management techniques will not stop the pain, they can stop the physiological stress associated with pain.

Therapies designed to help people manage chronic pain counsel patients to explore the difference between pain and the negative interpretation of pain. People living with chronic pain learn meditation techniques for confronting pain as an alternative to the brain's interpretation of pain as a source of suffering.

When your body is experiencing this stress response, whether caused by direct or indirect physiological stressors, it undergoes some very specific changes. Around the beginning of the 20th century, the physiologist Walter B. Cannon coined the phrase 'fight or flight' to describe the biochemical changes brought about in the body by stress, preparing it to flee or to confront danger more safely and effectively. These are the changes that happen in your body every time you feel stressed, even if running away or fighting are not real options (for example, if you're about to give a speech, take a test, or confront your father-in-law about his constant unsolicited advice, neither fight nor flight are particularly helpful responses).

When you feel stress:

1. Your cerebral cortex sends an alarm message to your hypothalamus, the part of your brain that releases the chemicals that create the stress response. Anything your brain *perceives* as stress will cause this effect, whether or not you are in any real danger.
2. Your hypothalamus releases chemicals that stimulate your sympathetic nervous system to prepare for danger.
3. Your nervous system reacts by raising your heart rate, respiration rate and blood pressure. Everything is turned 'up'.
4. Your muscles tense, preparing for action. Blood moves away from your extremities and digestive system, and into your muscles and brain. Blood glucose is mobilized to travel to where it will be needed most.
5. Your senses get sharper. You can hear better, see better, smell better, taste better. Even your sense of touch becomes more sensitive.

That sounds pretty powerful, doesn't it? Imagine the high-powered executive, stunning clients with a superb presentation and sharp, clever answers to every question. Imagine the football player in the vital championship game, scoring a hat trick. Imagine the student sitting her finals, all the answers coming immediately to mind, the perfect words coming from her pen for an A+ paper. Imagine yourself at the office party, sparkling and witty, attracting crowds who hang on your every word. Stress can be great – no wonder it's addictive.

You can make yourself relax by associating relaxation with a cue. Make yourself comfortable, breathe deeply, and repeat out loud for one minute a word or sound that has positive associations (for example, 'love', 'yellow', 'ahhh'). As you do this, concentrate on relaxing. Repeat the exercise several times a day for a week. Then try saying the word whenever you feel stress mounting, and feel your body relax automatically.

But the problem is that the stress response, while beneficial in moderate amounts, is harmful in excessive amounts, as are most things. It can cause problems in different systems throughout your body. Some problems are immediate, such as digestive trouble or a racing heartbeat. Other are more likely to occur as a result of longer-term stress. Some of stress's less desirable symptoms, directly related to the immediate increase of adrenaline in the body, include the following:

· Sweating
· Cold extremities
· Nausea, vomiting, diarrhoea
· Muscle tension
· Dry mouth
· Confusion
· Nervousness, anxiety
· Irritability, impatience
· Frustration
· Panic
· Hostility, aggression

Long-term effects of stress can be harder to correct, and include such things as depression, loss of or increase in appetite resulting in undesirable weight changes, frequent minor illnesses, increased aches and pains, sexual problems, fatigue, loss of interest in social activities, increased addictive behaviour, chronic headaches, acne, chronic backache, chronic stomach ache, an impaired immune system, increased sensitivity to pain and worsened symptoms associated with medical conditions such as asthma and arthritis.

Brain Stress

We already know that stress causes your cerebral cortex to begin a process that results in the release of chemicals to prepare your body to handle danger. But what else goes on in your brain when you are under too much stress? At first, you think more clearly and respond more quickly. But after you've reached your stress tolerance point, your brain begins to malfunction. You forget things. You lose things. You can't concentrate. Your willpower declines and you indulge in bad habits such as drinking, smoking or eating too much.

Some people begin to experience increased forgetfulness in their forties and fifties, and worry that they are developing Alzheimer's disease. In most cases, however, increased forgetfulness is often linked to stress, which can be at its peak for parents of teenagers and those experiencing career and relationship changes.

The problem is that production of the chemicals for the stress response is directly related to the depletion of chemicals that, under too much stress, prevent you from thinking effectively or reacting quickly. At first the answers to the test were coming without hesitation. However, three hours later you can barely remember which end of the pencil you are supposed to write with. If your brain is to keep working at its optimal level on a daily basis, stress can't be allowed to overwhelm your circuits!

Tummy Trouble

One of the first things that happens during the stress response is that blood is diverted away from your digestive tract to your large muscles. The stomach and intestines may empty their contents, preparing the body for fast action. Many people experiencing stress, anxiety and nervousness also experience stomach ache, nausea, vomiting or diarrhoea. (Doctors used to call this 'a nervous stomach'.)

Long-term episodic and chronic stress have been linked to a number of digestive maladies, from irritable bowel syndrome and colitis to ulcers and chronic diarrhoea.

Cardiovascular Connection

If your heart races or skips a beat when you are nervous, or have drunk a few too many cups of coffee or tins of fizzy drink, you know what it feels like to have your heart affected by stress. But stress can actually inhibit the activity of your entire cardiovascular system. Some scientists believe that stress contributes to hypertension (high blood pressure), and the nervous, anxious, irritable and pessimistic are constantly being told that they'll put themselves into an early grave. In fact, people who are inclined to see events as stressful do seem to have an increased rate of heart disease.

Stress can also contribute to bad health habits that can in turn contribute to heart disease. A high-fat, high-sugar, low-fibre diet (the fast-food, junk-food syndrome) contributes to fat in the blood and, eventually, clogged arteries and a heart attack-prone heart. When coupled with lack of exercise, the risk factors for heart disease increase – and all because you were too stressed to eat a salad and go for a walk (day after day after day).

 Polluting your body with too much saturated fat and highly processed, low-fibre food has a direct effect on health. Just as a polluted river soon cleans itself when the pollution stops, so will your coronary arteries begin to clear when your body is freed from having to process foods that are damaging to good health.

Stressed-out Skin

Skin problems such as acne are usually related to hormonal fluctuations, which in turn can be exacerbated by stress. Women in their twenties, thirties and forties may experience outbreaks during a particular time in their menstrual cycle. If there is an emotional reaction to the outbreak, stress can extend the duration of the outbreak. And a compromised, stressed immune system can mean an increased length of time for the damage to be repaired.

Men aren't immune, either. Stress can result in chemical imbalances that may cause or worsen adult acne in men. Teenagers, undergoing the dramatic hormonal fluctuations of adolescence, are prone to acne anyway, but stressed-out teenagers may have a much more difficult time getting acne under control. Remember the spot that always appeared before a big date? It wasn't a coincidence, it was the result of stress.

Long-term stress can lead to chronic acne. And it can contribute to psoriasis, hives, and other forms of dermatitis.

Chronic Pain

An impaired immune system and increased sensitivity to pain can worsen conditions that involve chronic pain. Migraine, arthritis, fibromyalgia, multiple sclerosis, degenerative bone and joint diseases, and old injuries all feel worse when the body is under stress. Stress management techniques and pain management techniques can not only help to ease chronic pain, but they can also help the mind to deal with pain so that the pain doesn't make the stress worse.

Stress and Your Immune System

How does stress compromise the immune system's effectiveness? When the body's equilibrium is disturbed due to the long-term release of stress hormones, the immune system can't work efficiently. Imagine trying to finish an important report during an earthquake!

Many studies reveal that patients given a placebo, such as a sugar pill, experience improved self-healing, significant symptom relief and a strengthened immune system. This suggests that the brain has formidable healing powers. Other studies suggest that patients can use this power consciously to help themselves heal.

Under optimal conditions, the immune system is able to help the body heal itself. However, there are those who believe that when conditions are not optimal, guided meditation or focused inner reflection can help the conscious mind perceive what the immune system requires the body to do to facilitate healing. While some doubt such intra-body experiences, the mind–body interaction is far from understood. There is widespread testimonial evidence that managing stress and listening to the body are essential elements in the promotion of self-healing.

The Stress–Disease Connection

While experts do not agree on which diseases are caused by stress and which are attributable to other factors, such as infections or genetics, an increasing number believe that the interrelatedness of the body and mind means that stress can contribute to, if not actually cause, almost any physical problem. And physical illness and injury can contribute to stress.

The result is a spiral of stress–disease–more stress–more disease, which can ultimately cause serious damage to the body, mind and spirit. The 'which came first' question may be irrelevant, as may quibbling about which conditions are or are not caused by stress. Managing stress – whether it is the cause or the result of physical problems – will put the body into a more balanced state, and a body that is more balanced is in a better position to heal itself. It will also help the mind to deal with physical injury or illness, reducing suffering. Managing stress may not necessarily heal you, but it will make your life more enjoyable.

That said, please remember that stress-management techniques should never be used instead of professional medical advice. Stress management is best used as a complement to the care you are already receiving – or should seek – for your physical illness or injury. Follow the advice of your doctor, and give your body's natural healing mechanisms an extra boost by getting debilitating stress out of the way.

Stress on Your Mind

Stress can also cause or be caused by a variety of mental and emotional conditions. Working too hard, pushing yourself too far, spreading yourself too thin, taking on too much or living in a state of unhappiness or anxiety is very stressful. Like physical stress, mental stress makes life difficult, and the harder things are, the more stress they cause. You are caught in another downward spiral.

Perhaps you are having difficulties with a personal relationship. This is stressful, but rather than deal with the problem – perhaps there seems to be no solution – you throw yourself into your job, working long hours and taking on too much extra responsibility. This new obsession with work adds more mental stress to your life, while long hours, lost sleep and the poor dietary habits that you've developed add to your physical stress. Your body begins to suffer, and so does your mind. At first you may find you have an extra edge at work because you are channelling energy from your personal life into your work. But eventually you will reach your stress tolerance point. Your will start to show a lack of judgment. You won't be able to concentrate or pay attention. You'll become more emotional or irritable, or both. You'll begin to think badly of your work performance, and of yourself. Frustration, anxiety, panic or depression will set in.

Don't get caught in stress's vicious cycle. If you feel stressed by an event that is supposed to be positive, the guilt or confusion you may feel about your stress will make the stress worse. Try to see your stress for what it is – a natural human reaction to change.

Mental stress comes in lots of forms. Social stressors include pressure at work; an impending important event; relationship problems, with a partner, child or parent, for example; or the death of a loved one. Any major change in life can result in mental stress, and even when an event is positive – a marriage, a graduation, a new job, a Caribbean cruise – the changes it involves, even if they are no more than temporary, can ultimately be overwhelming.

Mental stress can result in low self-esteem, a negative outlook on life, cynicism or the desire for isolation, as the mind tries to justify and stop the stress by any means possible. If you've ever had an extremely stressful week and want nothing more than to spend the entire weekend alone in bed with a good book and the remote control, you've experienced the mind trying to regain its equilibrium. Too much activity and change can create a desire for zero activity and reversion to comfortable, familiar rituals. (After a row with your best friend, a large bar of fruit and nut may be just the thing.)

If you allow stress to continue for too long, you could suffer burnout, losing all interest in your job as your sense of lack of control increases. You could begin to experience panic attacks, severe depression, or even a nervous breakdown, which is a temporary state of mental illness that can occur suddenly or slowly over a long period of time.

Mental stress is insidious because you can ignore it more easily than a physical illness. Yet it is just as powerful and just as harmful to the body and to your life. Identifying sources of mental stress is essential to managing your stress. Life will become more enjoyable when you respect your mental as well as your physical stress tolerance level.

Signs of burnout include a loss of joy, motivation and interest in life; an escalating sense of a loss of control; constant negative thinking; detachment from personal or work relationships; and a general loss of focus and purpose.

Stress on Your Spirit

Spiritual stress is more nebulous. It can't be measured directly, but it remains a potent and harmful form of stress that is inextricably linked to physical and mental stress. What is spiritual stress? It is the neglect and eventual loss of our spiritual lives, or the part of us that hopes, loves, dreams, plans and reaches for something greater and better in humanity and in life. It is the noncorporeal in us, the soul. Whether or not you have religious beliefs, you still have a spiritual side. Think of it as the part of you that can't be measured, calculated, or wholly explained – the part of you that makes you *you*.

When we ignore our spiritual side, we throw our bodies out of balance. When our spiritual lives are further compromised because of the effects of physical and mental stress – low self-esteem, anger, frustration, pessimism, the destruction of relationships, the loss of creativity, hopelessness, fear – we can lose our sense of the energy and joy of life.

Signs of a nervous breakdown include personality changes, uncontrolled behaviour, irrational thinking, excessive anxiety, obsessive behaviour, manic or depressive behaviour, severe depression, uncontrolled outbreaks of emotion or violence, severing of relationships, engaging in illegal acts, developing addictions, attempting suicide or the onset of a mental illness such as schizophrenia.

Have you ever known someone who, when faced with seemingly insurmountable obstacles, pain, trauma, tragedy or loss, continues to be happy? Such people have nurtured and nourished their spiritual sides, either through effort or because it comes to them naturally.

Of course, there are those who deny that people have a spiritual side or a soul. It's all down to chemicals, they say. Others of us prefer to believe that it's all related – intertwined like a dramatic and intricate web. Ultimately, if you manage your stress with the *whole* you in sight, you'll manage stress fully, effectively and in a way that really works for your unique self. Preserve, cherish, and nurture every strand of silk in the web of your self. If you do, you will preserve the miraculous artistry that is you, no matter how you happen to label the different parts.

CHAPTER 3

Stress and Your Self-Esteem

S tress and self-esteem are intricately linked in the same way that stress is linked to your physical and mental health. Not only does low self-esteem make you more vulnerable to stress, but chronic stress of all kinds – physical, emotional, environmental, social, personal and so on – can profoundly affect your self-esteem.

The Stress/Self-Esteem Cycle

Let's look at how stress can subtly undermine your self-esteem. It's often hard to pinpoint where the cycle begins, but imagine for a moment that you've had a very stressful day. (Maybe you don't have to imagine!) It seems as if everything has gone wrong. You banged your shin on the stairs. You spilled coffee on your jacket on your way out of the door. Your car wouldn't start. And then, at work, your boss dumped some work on you that will make the next two months extremely difficult. You envision working late for the foreseeable future. You have to miss lunch. A colleague tells you that you 'look terrible'. Then, when you get home at the end of the day, you scrap your plans to go to the gym, order a pizza instead and eat the whole thing. Then you feel guilty. You feel bad about skipping the gym, about giving in to junk food and about eating far too much. You feel so guilty that you get a tub of ice cream from the freezer and stay up late watching TV. Forget the dishes.

In the morning you wake up puffy-eyed and lacking energy. A messy kitchen greets you, you go to work exhausted, and you still have the same stress from the day before. So the cycle continues. You keep overeating, undersleeping and not doing anything about the things that are causing you stress – perhaps because you don't have the energy, or perhaps because you simply have no idea what you can do about it. You begin to feel worse and worse about yourself because you are so tired, so overwhelmed, and totally unable to exercise your willpower. The worse you feel about yourself, the more you are likely to continue in this destructive pattern.

What do you see when you look in the mirror?
Most people focus on external features first, but looking at your reflection in a mirror can be a form of meditation. Gaze into your eyes, deeper and deeper, until you no longer recognize your features but only the self behind the eyes. This is both an exercise for relieving stress through focus and a technique for pursuing self-knowledge.

Of course, this is just one example. Stress from a chronic condition such as arthritis, multiple sclerosis or chronic fatigue syndrome can take a heavy toll on your self-esteem. You wonder why you can't do all the things other people can do. You feel so ill all the time that you don't enjoy yourself anymore. Self-satisfaction seems a distant memory.

Similarly, stress that doesn't allow you any time for yourself makes you feel as if you don't deserve time to yourself, or that everyone else is more important than you are. Stress that keeps your mind racing and scattered can make you feel as if you aren't capable of focus.

 The stress cycle works in both directions. Stress can cause low self-esteem, but low self-esteem can be a major contributor to your stress level. If you don't feel good about yourself, lack confidence or doubt your ability to succeed, you'll be more likely to let stress overwhelm you.

So what are you supposed to do about this insidious cycle? Solutions often seem difficult to come by, especially when the problems don't seem to begin anywhere in particular. How do you jump in and slam on the brakes?

Build Self-Esteem by Demolishing Excess Stress

The first step in breaking the stress/self-esteem cycle is to identify one thing you can do something about, and it doesn't have to have anything to do with self-esteem. It's important to start with one thing, because a characteristic condition of stress is a lack of focus. If you have so many things going on in your life that you feel overwhelmed, you probably know what it is like to wander around in a daze, unable to do any of them. Perhaps you do some work on one project, but then get distracted by the pressing deadline on another project, so you move onto that one, but are distracted again by something else that needs attention. Before you know it, another day is gone and nothing has been finished.

So to repeat, the best way to break the cycle is to choose one single thing you can do something about, something you can finish. Lots of other things may need finishing, but they aren't going to get finished as long as you are feeling the way you are feeling. The only way to make a difference is to focus.

The way you focus is up to you. You may decide to complete one thing on your to-do list – so that you can actually cross it off. Or you may decide to have some enforced personal time. Meditation might be what it takes to stop the incessant buzzing in your head that is interfering with your productivity and making you feel so rotten about yourself.

What you choose to do also depends on the kind of stress that is overwhelming you. Let's look at some of the options for conquering stress that also specifically help you to fortify your self-esteem. Let's also look at how each strategy can be used most effectively.

Think of all the ways you could waste 30 minutes each day. Watching television. Queuing in line in an overcrowded supermarket. Surfing the Internet. Throwing a ball against the wall. Eating something you know you shouldn't be eating. Worrying. Talking on the phone. Being irritated at somebody who cut you up in traffic. Thinking about how much you have to do. Just think how much better 30 minutes could be spent doing any of the things listed in this chapter!

Your Self-Esteem-Building Strategies: Point A to Point B

The act of eliminating some of the excess stress in your life builds self-esteem simply by virtue of the fact that the elimination of stress makes you feel better. Thus, all of the stress management strategies in this book have the potential to build self-esteem. And working through these strategies with the specific purpose of building self-esteem can make them work even faster. But remember, you have to finish. You have to start at point A and work all the way to point B without stopping or getting distracted.

None of these strategies takes more than 30 minutes, so you don't have any excuse not to do them. Anybody can spare 30 minutes out of a busy day in the interest of feeling better and becoming more efficient. Isn't feeling better about who you are and how you are spending your life worth at least 30 minutes of your day?

Take a Reflection Walk

This strategy is for people who (a) don't get enough exercise on most days and (b) tend to worry too much or mentally obsess about negative things in their lives. You know who you are! A reflection walk is a way to take control of both your physical and mental states, at the same time, for one short, 30-minute period. If you worry all day, sit at a desk all day or feel rotten all day, then you need a daily reflection walk – badly. You may have to pretend to be an active optimist at first, but eventually, subtly, the effects of your 30-minute reflection walk will begin to take hold.

If there isn't a suitable or pleasant place to walk near you, or if the weather is really awful, have a walking back-up plan, such as walking in the gym or a shopping mall.

Although, as you probably know, exercise helps relieve stress, a reflection walk can help relieve stress and make you feel better about yourself at the same time. This is what you do: first, put on comfortable walking shoes and comfortable clothes that are appropriate for moderate exercise and also make you feel good about yourself. In other words, let your criteria be to dress so that if you meet someone you know, you won't feel self-conscious about what you are wearing. Brush or comb your hair. Wash your face, put on some sunscreen on a sunny day, and, if it makes you feel more human, put on some make-up. Go to the front door and take five deep, full breaths. Then, out loud, say: 'I'm ready to reflect upon all the good things in my life.'

Then go out and walk for 30 minutes at a moderate pace – just fast enough to feel as though you are getting some exercise, but not enough to wear you out or make you frustrated or your muscles ache.

As you walk, continue to take deep breaths and, most importantly, begin your mental list of all the things that are good in your life. Here are some questions you might consider:

· What is working for you?
· Which parts of your life make you feel great?
· Who are the people in your life that make your life better?
· Who do you love?
· What do you like about yourself?
· What are some of your fondest memories?
· Where do you love to go?
· What do you most like doing?
· Which foods make you feel really good?
· What is your favourite book?
· What do you love about your home, your pets, your car and your job?
· In what areas of your life are you successful?

Don't undermine your efforts at building up your self-esteem by telling yourself that any accomplishment isn't worth celebrating. If, for example, you finally completed your tax return, or vacuumed, or turned off the TV last night earlier than you usually do, that's great! Or perhaps you didn't eat a whole packet of biscuits or spend £30 on things you don't need. You can and should feel good about things like that.

You can be as general as 'I love my children' or as specific as 'I set up a system for paying my bills on time that works really well.' If you are having difficulty focusing or thinking of things, set a goal, such as adding one item to your mental list for every 25 steps or for every five breaths. If you get stuck, stop until you think of something, then move on.

The challenge of the reflection walk is to put aside for a full 30 minutes all the things that aren't working for you, the negativity, the things you think you should be doing. After the walk is over, you can get back to work, but for now, put all your stressful thoughts aside. They'll still be there when you get back, but they may not seem quite so overwhelming once you've begun to put them in perspective. After a reflection walk, your life will probably look a lot better, and you'll feel a lot better about yourself, too.

Clean Your Kitchen Sink

If you are housework-challenged, and if the state of messiness in your house is often directly related to the level of your stress, then there is a website you can visit. This website can transform the life of anyone who feels they are incapable of getting their housework under control – something that can severely undermine your self-esteem but that is a condition of life for thousands of people. Go to *www.flylady.net*. Read everything on there, and continue to read on many subsequent visits to the site.

This is an American-based website that buzzes with enthusiasm and encouragement, and contains a complete system for getting your house – and, by association, your life – in order, even if you've never been able to do it before. Flylady has a few ground rules, and complaining about them is not allowed. One of the most important Flylady rules is to keep your kitchen sink empty, clean and sparkling.

Another Flylady golden rule is that every single morning you must learn to get up, make your bed and get dressed all the way to your shoes. Many resist at first, but once they try it, they discover the miraculous effects of following the rule.

A clean sink has incredible stress-relieving power. As Flylady says, 'As the kitchen sink goes, so goes the rest of the house.' I would only add, 'As the kitchen sink goes, so goes the rest of your life!' The kitchen is the heart and soul of the house, and if one's house is symbolic of one's life (as it is in *feng shui*), then keeping the heart and soul in perfect order will resonate all over your life.

If you aren't one of those people who has difficulty keeping things clean, this step isn't for you. But, if you are like me, you may discover that the kitchen sink is a clear and direct reflection of how your life is going. When it sparkles, you feel great about yourself and everything in your life seems to be working. When it gets to the point where you won't let anybody in the kitchen unless they live in your house and insist on being fed, then the chances are that your life is in disarray.

The kitchen sink is an ideal jumping-in spot to break the stress cycle. No matter how busy you are, no matter how behind or overwhelmed, just take 30 minutes – or even 15 will do – to go into your kitchen. If you have a dishwasher, unload and put away all the clean plates from the dishwasher and load it up with dirty ones. If you don't have a dishwasher, or there is washing up that won't fit in the dishwasher, fill the sink with hot soapy water, and wash up, dry, and put away everything that is sitting around in the sink or on any other surface. Drain the sink, give it a good scrub using an appropriate cleaner, and a rinse and polish at the end. You won't believe the impact it will have on your self-esteem.

Do this every day, especially every evening, and the effect of walking into the kitchen in the morning to face a bright, shiny sink – as opposed to one piled high with dirty plates, making it impossible even to fill the kettle – will astound you. This really works. And if you need help from there, visit Flylady's website.

The best part about getting into the habit of keeping your sink clean is that the rest of the kitchen will soon follow. And once you are in the habit of keeping your kitchen clean, it only takes a few minutes a day to keep it like that.

Seeing Green

Some people can take or leave natural beauty – forests, mountains, gardens and suchlike – while others find that being in or even just looking at natural beauty has a profound effect on how they feel about their lives, the world, and themselves. Those who know something about Ayurveda may be aware that Pitta types are often these kinds of people. But you don't have to know anything about Ayurveda to know whether or not natural beauty has a deep effect on you.

Even if you live in a city, you can use natural beauty to help relieve stress and feel better about yourself. Surrounding yourself with images of natural beauty can give you little lifts all day long. Here are some ways to accomplish this:

· Use a computer wallpaper and/or screensaver that shows rotating images of stunning scenery. Sign up at Webshots, at *www.webshots.com*, for free daily photos to use as computer wallpaper and screensavers, hundreds of which are of beautiful scenery, animals, and natural phenomena such as storms and unusual cloud formations. Making your photo choice each morning can be like going on a mini holiday – well, perhaps not quite, but it can be revitalizing just to look at the pictures.

· Tonight, instead of watching soaps or police dramas on TV, see if a natural history programme is being shown. If you have satellite TV, try the National Geographic channel. This is good for your brain and healthy food for your soul.

· Spend 30 minutes pottering around your own microenvironment. (Even if you only have a yard, it probably contains some green things.) Meander about, examining each bush, flower, patch of grass or plantpot. Don't think about anything else. Just see how much you can observe.

· If there are trees on your property, get to know them. Some cultures believe the trees are spirit guardians. Look at and think about the trees surrounding your home. If the spirit moves you, you might even ask for their protection. Who knows?

· If you have no microenvironment to speak of (although even a single flower can be worth examining), walk, cycle or drive to somewhere close by, for example, a park or a nicely landscaped area. Walk around and look, look, look. Fill up your brain with natural beauty and there won't be room for anxiety, at least not during the 30 minutes you've reserved for this purpose.

· Grow herbs or flowers, either from seeds or by transferring purchased plants to a large pot or window box. Put the pot on the front step or back step, or in a sunny window. Check and tend it daily. It's like taking vitamins for your soul!

· Go to your local library or bookshop and browse through a book that contains large colour photographs of natural beauty. Perhaps you'll feel transported by a photo essay on Hawaii, or maybe the Alps or Urals are more your style. Or North America? Africa? The Central American rainforests? Let your imagination whisk you away for 30 minutes.

· Plan your next holiday in a place of natural beauty, such as the Lake District, or take a cruise to the Caribbean, or go camping in a national park or forest, or go to a beach in Cornwall. OK, this takes more than 30 minutes, but not if you average it out over the year.

Do One Thing All the Way

This one's for those who feel as if all the little things in life are out of control. If you have so many things to do that you can't seem to finish any of them, take 30 minutes and complete just one of the short tasks listed below. You'll get a feeling of accomplishment you could never get from half-finishing 20 different tasks. None of these tasks takes very long, but they are all things that a lot of people have difficulty getting round to. When they remain undone, they weigh on your mind and add to your stress and the sense that you aren't able to keep things under control.

Doing just one thing on this list each day can make a huge difference to how you feel about yourself. Try it for a week. You'll see.

· Clean out your car. Get rid of all the rubbish, put everything back in the house that belongs in the house, and attack the floor mats with the extension to the vacuum cleaner. Then clean the windows with glass cleaner.

· Sort out your purse or wallet. Throw away all the rubbish you don't need, file the receipts, put everything in the right place, flatten out your notes and make sure they all face the same way. Put any small change in a jar somewhere. (If you do this every day, you may soon have enough change to pay for a week's shopping.)

Spend some quality time with your pet, if you have one. Pets relieve stress, and because they seem to love us unconditionally, they can make us feel pretty good about ourselves, too.

- Sort out the coat cupboard. Take out all the things that don't belong elsewhere and put them away properly. Hang up all the coats properly on hangers. Store scarves, hats and gloves in a box. Give away all the things that don't fit any more or that nobody wants. Where did that space in there come from?
- Sort out your finances. Stop putting it off. Just do it.
- Make an appointment with the dentist – and keep it!
- Go to your desk and take one manageable pile from the many stacks of things that need to be filed or put away, and file or put away everything in that one pile.
- Drink a really big glass of water. Make sure you finish it all.
- Dust all the flat surfaces in your living room. This should only take five minutes, but it makes a perceptible difference.
- Make your bed.
- Take a bath or a shower, then put moisturizer on every square inch of your skin. Put on a dressing gown and relax for 15 minutes.
- Read a complete chapter of the book you've been trying to start.
- Sweep out the garage. Don't worry about everything else in there; just sweep the floor.
- Remember the call you've been meaning to make to sort out that problem with that company? Make that call.
- Groom any pets you have.
- You know the thing you've been meaning to tell that person but keep forgetting or putting off? Tell him.
- Set aside 15 minutes – just 15 minutes! – to start, experience and finish your own personal time. After instructing others you are not to be disturbed, go to a quiet room, set a timer and do something all on your own that you really want to do, and do it for 15 minutes solid. Read, listen to music, sew, whistle, whatever. Don't short-change yourself – do the whole 15 minutes, start to finish. Voilà! You're ready to continue with your day. I bet you feel better already.

Have a water day. For one day, don't drink anything but water. (If you are addicted to caffeine, you might need just one cup of black coffee or tea in the morning to avoid the inevitable headache.) If you drink about eight cups of water during the day, you'll feel lighter and airier, and you'll have much more energy.

Commit to Yourself

It's all very well wanting to manage your stress for the sake of others in your life, but you have to commit to yourself, too. Self-esteem, at its most basic level, is about recognizing that you are worth self-care. And, of course, that means you'll be better able to care for others. As the Buddha once said, 'Be a light unto yourself'. Seek self-knowledge, treat yourself well and care for yourself, and you'll learn to love, appreciate and esteem yourself.

Then, when stressful things happen, which they will, you'll understand that what happens outside you doesn't change who you are, what you are worth, how precious and individual and worthy of self-love you are. No one understands you like you do, and if you don't try to understand yourself, you can't expect others to. So make it a point to understand, study, nurture and honour yourself. The rest – including all those things that cause the stress in your life – will fall into place.

CHAPTER 4
Your Personal Stress Profile

You may have tried stress management techniques before, but perhaps the technique didn't work for you personally. Or perhaps you just haven't found a stress-management technique that fits your unique life. Your personality, the kind of stress you are trying to relieve, and the way you tend to handle stress are all factors in your success. So how do you know which techniques to try? First, you determine your Personal Stress Profile.

The Many Faces of Stress

As already mentioned, stress itself is a pretty simple concept – it's the body's reaction to a certain degree of stimulation. But how stress affects you is likely to be completely different from how it affects your best friend. Your bodies are both releasing adrenaline and cortisol in response to stress, but, while your stress might result from having a demanding boss, supervising some difficult employees and being required to meet impossible deadlines, your friend's stress might be caused by being at home with four young children and trying to stick to a tight budget. While one person is dealing with the stress of chronic osteoarthritis, another might be stressed by chronic relationship problems.

What should I do when I feel stressed?
Doodle! When something is worrying you and you find yourself obsessively trying to work out a logical solution, give your left brain a rest and exercise your right brain for a while. Doodling taps your creative side, which might come up with the solution you've been trying to find!

Because the word *stress* can mean so many different things to different people, it is essential at first to compile a Personal Stress Profile, before an effective stress-management plan can be put into practice.

Your Personal Stress Profile identifies:

· The stressors that are unique to your life.
· Your personality's stress-related tendencies.
· How you personally tend to cope with stress.

With this information, you can design a Stress Management Portfolio that works for you. For example, someone who is physically drained by too much interaction with people is unlikely to be helped by strategies that encourage increased social activities with friends. Someone else who is stressed by the lack of a support system might find profound benefit in increased social activity. Some people are deeply calmed by meditation; others find it excruciating. Some people find assertiveness training a relief, but a naturally assertive type might benefit more from learning to sit back and let other people take responsibility.

Think of your Personal Stress Profile, or PSP, as similar to a business proposal. You are the business, and the business isn't operating at peak efficiency. Your PSP is a picture of the business as a whole, including the specific nature of all the factors that are keeping it from performing as well as it could. With a PSP, you can effectively create your own Stress Management Portfolio. Before you know it, you'll be running smoothly, efficiently, productively and happily.

Drinking two to three cups of coffee will dose you with approximately 400 milligrams of caffeine. This chemical causes your body to release adrenaline, and can exacerbate the effects of stress.

The information you discover about yourself through the Personal Stress Test and prompts in this chapter will allow you to develop your own PSP. Your PSP has four parts:

1. Your Stress Tolerance Point
2. Your Stress Triggers
3. Your Stress Vulnerability Factor
4. Your Stress Response Tendencies

Once you understand how much stress you can handle, what things trigger stress for *you* (even if they don't trigger stress in a friend, a partner or a sibling), where your personal stress vulnerability lies, and how you tend to respond to stress, you'll be able to build your own unique Stress Management Portfolio. This is the 'business plan' – once you've identified where the trouble lies, you can start to make strategies: you can develop a plan for improving your life by managing your stress.

Your Stress Tolerance Point

Note that I say *managing* your stress, not eliminating it, because eliminating all stress is impossible. As I mentioned earlier, some stress is actually good for you. It can energize you just when you need a boost. It can make life more fun, more interesting, more exciting. Don't we all crave some stress? When we are bored with the daily routine, we long for an exciting holiday. We desire that feeling of falling in love, the thrill of meeting someone new, the challenge of a promotion, the excitement of learning a new subject, visiting a new place, even getting lost (for just a little while) in a new city or perhaps just an unfamiliar part of town.

So while too much stress is bad, some stress is good, and it doesn't make sense to eliminate all stress from your life. Although good stress can be great, eventually most of us like to get back to an equilibrium, whether that is a familiar, comforting routine, an earlier bedtime or a home-cooked meal.

You may have noticed that some people thrive on constant change, stimulation and a high-stress kind of life. Think about war reporters, international sales managers or people who can turn the most mundane everyday events into high dramas. Others prefer a highly regular, even ritualistic kind of existence. Think of the people who have rarely left their home towns and are perfectly happy about it. Most of us are somewhere in the middle. We like to travel, to experience the occasional thrilling event, but are usually fairly glad to be back at home or settle back into our normal routine (normal being the state of equilibrium where we function best).

Whichever type of person you are, the changes in your body that make you react more quickly, think more sharply, and give you a kind of 'high', or feeling of super accomplishment, only last up to a point. This point, when the stress response turns from productive to counterproductive, is different for each person. Stress feels great, and actually increases your performance until it reaches your Stress Tolerance Point. If stress continues or increases after that turning point, your performance will decrease, and the effects on your body will start to have a negative rather than a positive result.

According to a report from the Health and Safety Executive, one in five Britons describe their work as 'very' or 'extremely' stressful, while about half a million are suffering from work-related stress, anxiety or depression at levels that make them ill.

Your Stress Triggers

Stress Triggers are the things that cause you stress, and your Stress Tolerance Point determines how many stress triggers and what degree of stress you can tolerate while still remaining productive. Your combination of Stress Triggers is unique to you.

The way you get to your Stress Tolerance Point is highly individual. Everyone's life is different and filled with different kinds of Stress Triggers. Someone who has just been in a car accident has experienced a completely different Stress Trigger from someone who is about to take an important exam, but both may experience equal stress, depending on the severity of the accident and the perceived importance of the exam. Of course, since both people probably have a different Stress Tolerance Point, high stress to the exam taker may be moderate stress to the car accident victim, and both people may have higher stress tolerance than the person about to experience their third migraine in a week.

Your Stress Vulnerability Factor

The Stress Vulnerability Factor further complicates the picture. Some people have a high stress tolerance, *except* when it comes to their families. Others can ignore criticism and other forms of personal stress, *unless* it relates to their job performance. Some people can take all the criticism their friends and colleagues have to offer, but will be devastated by a pulled muscle.

Every individual, because of personality, past experiences, probably genetics and a host of other factors, will tend to be particularly vulnerable to certain stress categories while remaining impervious to others. The Stress Vulnerability Factor determines which events in your life will tend to affect you in a stressful way, and which ones may not stress you at all, even if they would be stressful to someone else.

Finding the stress management techniques that work best for you is essential for success. If keeping a stress diary or meditating causes you more stress, those techniques aren't working for you. A stress management technique should feel relaxing and be a positive experience. You should look forward to it. Don't force yourself to do things you don't want to do, or you are likely to make your situation worse.

Your Stress Response Tendencies

Add to this already complex picture your Stress Response Tendencies. This is the way you tend to react to stress. Do you reach for food or nicotine or alcohol whenever life gets difficult, or are you more likely to withdraw, sleep too much or lash out in irritation at friends? Perhaps you seek out friends to talk to, or perhaps you practise relaxation or meditation. Maybe you react in one particular way when it comes to your areas of greatest vulnerability, and in another when the stress is the kind you find easier to handle.

Through stress awareness, conscious tracking of stress triggers, commitment to managing the stress in your life in a personalized way, experimenting with stress management techniques to find those that work for you, and creating and implementing your Personal Stress Profile, you can handle the stress that is sapping your energy and draining your brain power.

Let's begin by discovering some things about you, the stressors in your life and the way you tend to cope with them. The following test will uncover the details of the stress in your life, and from it, you will develop your Personal Stress Profile.

Exceeding your Stress Tolerance Point on a regular basis can result in any or all of the following:

- Poor performance
- Lack of concentration
- Debilitating anxiety or depression
- A less effective immune system
- Illness

Your Personal Stress Test

Don't let this 'test' add to your stress. It isn't marked! Use it as an opportunity to reflect on yourself, your life and your personal tendencies. Take your time! And bear in mind that your answers and your entire stress profile will probably change sooner or later. This year, this month or this week might be particularly stressful, but next year, next month or next week might be easier. You can take the test again in the future, to assess how well you've implemented your Stress Management Portfolio. For now, answer the questions as they apply to you today.

Part I: Your Stress Tolerance Point

Circle the answers that most apply to you:

1. Which of the following best describes your average day?

    A. *Comfortingly regular* – I get up, eat, work and play at about the same time each day. I like my routines and orderly life.
    B. *Maddeningly regular* – I get up, eat, work and play at about the same time each day, and the boredom is killing me.
    C. *Regular in essence but not in order* – I get up, eat, work and play almost every day, but I never know when I'll do what, and if something new happens, then that's great – I like to go with the flow.
    D. *Highly irregular and stressful* – every day something disrupts my timetable. I long for routine, but life keeps foiling my efforts.

2. What happens when you don't eat or exercise regularly?

    A. I get either a cold, flu, an allergy attack or bloating, feel tired, or there is some other indication that my good habits have lapsed.
    B. I don't pay much attention to my diet or have an exercise routine, but seem to feel fine most of the time.
    C. Eat well? Exercise? Maybe I'll give it a try, if I ever have the time or energy to fit it into my packed schedule.
    D. I feel thrilled and emotionally heightened. I enjoy changing my routine and throwing myself into a different physical state.

3. When criticized by someone or reprimanded by an authority figure, how do you tend to feel?

    A. I feel panicky, hopeless, anxious or depressed, as if something terrible and beyond my control has happened.
    B. I feel angry and vengeful. I obsess about all the ways I could or should have responded. I make elaborate plans for revenge, even if I don't intend to carry them out.
    C. I feel irritated or hurt for a while, but not for long. I focus on how I could avoid another similar situation.
    D. I feel misunderstood by the masses. I know I was right, but that's the price of genius!

4. When preparing to perform in front of people for any reason (a concert, a speech, a presentation, a lecture), how do you tend to feel?

    A. I feel like being sick.
    B. I feel stimulated, thrilled, a little nervous, but full of energy.
    C. I avoid situations where I have to perform because I don't like it.
    D. I feel aggressive or boastful.

5. When in the middle of a crowd, how do you feel?

    A. Exhilaration!
    B. Panic!
    C. I feel like causing trouble. Wouldn't it be funny to set off the fire alarm?
    D. I feel OK for a while, but then I'm ready to go home.

According to a survey conducted by *Prima* magazine, 56 per cent of women have taken prescribed antidepressants or homeopathic alternatives because they feel stressed, overstretched and unhappy with their lives.

Part II: Your Stress Triggers

Circle the answers that most apply to you. If none apply – for instance, if you are perfectly satisfied with your working life and it doesn't cause you stress – don't circle any of the answers under that question:

6. What stresses you most about where you live?

    A. I feel stressed by city pollution/indoor allergens.
    B. I feel stressed by frequent quarrelling with someone in my home.
    C. I feel stressed by sleep deprivation. My living conditions (new baby, noisy flatmates) don't ever allow me to sleep as much as I feel that I need.
    D. I feel stressed by a sudden change in the people that live in my home, either because of an absence (someone has moved out, passed away) or a presence (someone has moved in, a new baby).

7. What habits should you change?

    A. I shouldn't stay indoors so much. I know I should get more fresh air regularly.
    B. I shouldn't constantly put myself down.
    C. I shouldn't smoke, drink or eat so much.
    D. I shouldn't be so concerned about what other people think of me.

8. What could make your life so much better?

    A. If only I could move out of the city/rural area/small town/ suburbs/this country!
    B. If only I felt better about who I am.
    C. If only I were healthier and had more energy.
    D. If only I had more power, prestige and money.

9. What do you truly dread?

    A. I dread holidays such as Christmas. All that 'festive cheer' everywhere gets me down.
    B. I dread failure.
    C. I dread illness and/or pain.
    D. I dread having to speak in front of people.

10. How do you feel about your life's work or career?

    A. I feel I would be happier in a completely different work environment.
    B. I feel dissatisfied. My skills aren't being fully utilized.
    C. I feel stressed. I've already had a lot of time off work caused by minor illnesses.
    D. I feel pressure to conform to the working practices of my colleagues or the expectations of my supervisor, even though I'm not comfortable working like that.

Lighten up – it just might save your health! According to a study presented at the American Heart Association's annual meeting in 2000, people with heart disease were 40 per cent less likely to laugh than those without cardiovascular problems.

Part III: Your Stress Vulnerability Factor

Circle the answers that best apply to you:

11. How do you describe yourself?

    A. I'm an extrovert, energized by social contact.
    B. I'm an introvert, energized by time alone.
    C. I'm a workaholic.
    D. I'm a carer.

12. What makes you tense?

    A. I feel tense when I think about my financial situation.
    B. I feel tense when I think about my family.
    C. I feel tense when I think about the safety of my loved ones.
    D. I feel tense when I think about what people think of me.

13. While plenty of areas of your life are under control, where do you suddenly lose control?

    A. I consume too much food and/or alcohol and/or spend too much money.
    B. I worry obsessively.
    C. I clean the house and/or organize constantly.
    D. I just can't keep my mouth shut! I often unintentionally anger and/or offend people.

14. How would you describe yourself at work?

    A. I'm highly motivated and ambitious.
    B. I'm just a cog in a wheel. Work is boring and unfulfilling.
    C. I'm satisfied but glad I've got a life outside my job.
    D. I'm deeply dissatisfied. I know I could accomplish something so much better than this if only I had the opportunity to try!

15. What are you like in personal relationships?

    A. I'm usually the one in control.
    B. I'm a follower.
    C. I'm always looking for something I don't have.
    D. I'm rather distant.

A passive attitude can drastically lower your stress level. Letting things go or deciding they don't matter may seem cold or unfeeling in certain circumstances, but often a passive attitude can counterbalance the feeling that things are out of control. If you can't control it, let it go. If you can't change it, accept it for what it is.

Part IV: Your Stress Response Tendencies

Circle the answer that best describes how you would be most likely to react to each of the following stressful situations:

16. What would you do if your life were really busy – you had too many social obligations and too much work, and it seemed as though your days consisted of nothing but frantic rushing around to complete your to-do list?

    A. I'd feel overwhelmed, anxious and out of control.
    B. I'd gain weight.
    C. I'd construct an elaborate and detailed system for keeping every aspect of my life in order, which I'd stick to for a few weeks before abandoning it.
    D. I'd cut back on current obligations and say 'no' to new ones.

17. What would you do if you woke with a nasty cold – a scratchy throat, a stuffy nose, chills and an all-over ache?

    A. I'd call in sick at work and spend the day resting and drinking hot lemon with honey.
    B. I'd take a cold remedy, go to work and try to pretend that I wasn't at all ill.
    C. I'd go to the gym and try to sweat it out by throwing myself into a kickboxing class or by running a few miles on the treadmill.
    D. I'd wonder how this could happen to me when I had so many important things to do. I'd worry about how many things in my life will be disrupted by my falling ill.

18. How would you handle a problem with a personal relationship?

    A. I'd pretend there wasn't a problem.
    B. I'd demand that we talk about it, and talk about it now.
    C. I'd get depressed, think it must be my fault and wonder why I always ruin relationships.
    D. I'd spend some time thinking about exactly what I would like to say so as not to sound critical, then approach the person to discuss some specific problems. If this didn't work, at least I could say I tried.

19. If your supervisor told you that a client had complained about you, then advised you not to worry about it, but suggested you be more careful about what you said to clients in the future, how would you feel?

    A. I'd feel extremely offended and obsess for days about who the client might have been, and how I might be able to take revenge for being made to look bad in front of my superior.
    B. I'd feel indifferent. Some people are oversensitive.
    C. I'd feel aghast if I thought I'd offended someone and wonder how it could have happened. I'd then be very polite and accommodating to everyone, but my confidence would definitely be dented.
    D. I'd feel hurt or perhaps a little angry, but would probably decide to take my supervisor's advice and not worry about it. I would then make a point of noticing how I spoke to clients.

20. If you had a big test or presentation in the morning and a lot depended on the result, how would you feel as you tried to get to sleep?

    A. I'd feel a little nervous, but also excited because I'd be well prepared. I'd plan to get a really good night's sleep so that I'd be at my best.
    B. I'd feel so nervous that I would probably be sick. I'd have a few drinks, eat some biscuits or smoke some cigarettes to calm myself down, even though that usually doesn't work very well. I'd sleep restlessly.
    C. I'd stay up all night going over my notes, even though I knew them by heart. My feeling would be that it can't hurt to look at them again... and again.
    D. Thinking about the test or presentation would make me nervous, so I'd pretend nothing was going on and do my best to not think about it.

That's the end of the questions. Now, for each section, add up your answers as follows.

Part I: Your Stress Tolerance Point Analysis

Circle your answers in the following chart, then see in which column you have the most answers:

	JUST RIGHT LOW	JUST RIGHT HIGH	TOO LOW	TOO HIGH
1.	A	C	B	D
2.	A	B	D	C
3.	C	D	B	A
4.	C	B	D	A
5.	D	A	C	B

Your Stress Tolerance Point shows how much stress you can take. In which category did you have the most answers? If your answers fell about equally in more than one category, that probably means either that you can take lots of stress when it comes to certain things and less in other areas, or that some parts of your life are too high in stress and others are just right or even too low. Here's how to interpret your Stress Tolerance Point score:

If you scored the most points under **JUST RIGHT LOW**, you don't tolerate too much stress, but you already know that and are good at taking measures to limit the stress in your life. You perform best and feel happiest when the comfortable routine you've created for yourself runs smoothly and nothing too unexpected happens. You can deal with stressful situations for short periods of time, but you are always happy to get home after a holiday – no matter how wonderful it was – and you are very attached to your rituals, whether daily (your morning workout, the evening news with supper), weekly (your every-Friday meeting for coffee with your best friend), or annually (preparing the same recipes each year at Christmas, giving an annual Valentine's Day party, your systematic spring cleaning).

You've constructed a routine that works for you, and when events disrupt this routine, you tend to experience stress. Having recognized your low stress tolerance, however, you've already got the mechanisms in place for keeping your life low-key and systematic whenever possible. Perhaps you are good at saying 'no' to things you don't have room for in your life. Perhaps you will go on holiday over Easter, but stay at home over Christmas because that is tradition.

The coping skills you need to cultivate are those that will help you to deal with the inevitable times when life changes dramatically or when you aren't able to stick to your routine due to circumstances beyond your control. If you or a family member becomes ill, if you are forced to change jobs or move to another town, if you start or leave school, things will, inevitably, change, whether you like it or not. Long-term or permanent changes will require you to make your routine flexible enough to accommodate new circumstances, either temporarily or permanently. Short-term changes may require a temporary suspension of your all-important routine.

Stress-management techniques can help you to cope with change more effectively by bending when you feel like breaking.

If you scored the most points under **JUST RIGHT HIGH**, you can take a fairly high level of stress, and you actually like life to be a bit more exciting. You perform better and feel happier when life isn't *too* routine. You are probably an easygoing person who enjoys seeing what lies around the next bend in life, and strict routines bore you. You like traditions and rituals in some areas of your life – for example, you may cherish your morning cup of tea, but you are just as likely to drink it watching children's TV as reading the *Financial Times* investment section. You might sip it at the kitchen table one day, out in the garden the next day, or you might buy a takeaway to drink on the train because you decided to stay in bed for an extra 45 minutes that morning.

You probably don't always eat or exercise at regular times, but that's how you like it. You've designed your life – whether consciously or not – around keeping yourself happily stimulated. You know you like things to be interesting, so you resist routines and let just enough stress into your life to keep you humming along efficiently. You may not always look efficient in your whirlwind of activity, but if stress makes you happy, then stress makes you happy. The peak point at which a certain amount of stress is satisfying may be higher for you than for someone else – you may enjoy a little more stress than your friends. But at some point, even for you, the stress will become too much and you'll start to compromise your mental, physical and spiritual health and happiness.

Not all change is pleasant, and the stress-management techniques you can master are those that will help you deal with the less welcome changes life sometimes has to offer – for example, illness, injury or the loss of a loved one. Even you can't go with the flow *all* the time.

You may also find it difficult to sit still and concentrate. Meditation and other techniques that cultivate inner as well as outer stillness could be of great benefit to you – they teach you self-discipline and how to slow down (because once in a while, we all need to slow down, whether we like it or not!). You may also benefit from learning *how* to live within a routine, even if you don't always choose to have one. When you are ill, have small children or live with people who have a lower stress tolerance point than you, knowing how to work with routines can be helpful. You are already a flexible person, but learning stress-management techniques of all kinds (not just the kinds that amuse you in the immediate moment) will make you even more flexible, disciplined and able to cope with all kinds of situations.

When your mind is overburdened, do something with your hands. Many people find relief in baking bread, making cakes or jam, painting, gardening, DIY and home repairs or amateur woodworking. Building or creating something obliges the mind to focus. When you are putting together a birdhouse or decorating a birthday cake, you don't have room in your brain to worry.

If you scored the most points under **TOO LOW**, you probably have a very high Stress Tolerance Point and you are operating well below it. Perhaps your stress tolerance is relatively low, but you are *still* operating below it. It could be either, since you haven't found your optimal operating level. Your peak for functioning and happiness requires more stimulation than you are currently experiencing. Perhaps your life is necessarily high in routine and you can't stand it. You long for excitement and change in any form, any at all, even if it's just moving the furniture in your living room into different positions.

Not meeting your Stress Tolerance Point can result in frustration, irritation, aggression, and depression – you aren't achieving your potential. But you can do something about it. If you are afraid to change your job, make saving a nest egg an active and systematized goal towards a financial safety net, then take the plunge. Try learning a language or joining some groups that will add social activities to your life in areas that interest you. If you feel your marriage is stagnating, for heaven's sake don't go out and have an affair – instead, go for counselling to help restore excitement and vigour to your relationship. Are you a carer tied to your home? Learn to master the Internet and you'll find a world out there waiting for you based on your personal computer. Telephone old friends, or take up painting, or write the novel that you are sure is inside you.

And stress-management techniques can help you, too. Not having enough stress to meet your Stress Tolerance Point is stressful in itself. Meet your needs with interesting, positive changes in your life, and handle your frustration, aggression or depression with stress-management techniques. Learning about stress management can be stimulating in its own right – for example, educating yourself about various meditation techniques is in itself an interesting pursuit.

If you scored **TOO HIGH**, you probably know all too well that you are operating significantly above a healthy Stress Tolerance Point. You are probably also suffering from some of the ill effects of stress, such as frequent minor illnesses, inability to concentrate, anxiety, depression or self-neglect. You may often feel as though your life is out of control or your situation is hopeless. Stay with this book! Using the stress-management techniques described in these chapters, you can improve your life and feel much better. It's never too late to start making gradual improvements in your life, so take a deep breath and keep reading.

A recent study conducted at a medical centre in Chicago, USA, suggests that a daily dosage of 300 IUs of vitamin E may significantly decrease the chance that mental functioning will decline after the age of 65.

Part II: Your Stress Trigger Analysis

Add up how many *As*, *Bs*, *Cs* and *Ds* you marked in this part. Read the sections below for each letter that you checked more than once:

Two or more As

You suffer from *environmental stress*. This is the stress that comes from the world around you. Whether you live in a polluted area, such as near a busy street or in a house with a smoker (or if you are a smoker), or are allergic to something in your surroundings, you'll be exposed to environmental stress. Environmental stress is also the stress you feel when your environment changes. Perhaps your area has changed a lot in the last few years, or you are renovating your home or moving to a new home or a new town. Changes in your household, such as the loss or gain of a family member or a pet, are included under environmental stress. So is a marriage or a separation. These are sources of personal and social stress, but are also forms of environmental stress because they change the make-up of your household.

Some people are sensitive to the weather. A blizzard, a big thunderstorm, gales or just days and days of rain are all sources of stress to some. Do you get anxious and panicky every time you hear a rumble of thunder? Do you listen to the weather forecast fearing news of storms?

Environmental stressors are largely unavoidable, but there are techniques that can help turn them from stressors into nothing more than events. Here are some stress management techniques to try if you are particularly bothered by environmental stressors:

- *Meditation* (for perspective, distance from situation): Chapter 8
- *Breathing exercises* (for calming): Chapter 6
- *Exercise/nutrition* (to strengthen physiological resources to combat environmental stress): Chapter 7
- *Vitamin/mineral therapy, herbal medicine, homeopathy* (to strengthen the immune system): Chapter 6
- *Feng shui* (to balance and promote the energy in your environment): Chapter 10

Two or more Bs

You suffer from *personal stress* – the stress that comes from your personal life. This broad category covers everything from your perception of your relationships to your self-esteem and feelings of self-worth. If you are unhappy with your appearance; have a bad body image; feel inadequate, unfulfilled, fearful, shy, lacking in willpower or self control; have an eating disorder or addiction (also sources of physiological stress); or are in any way personally unhappy, you are suffering from personal stress. Even extreme personal happiness can cause stress. If you are madly in love, have just got married, were recently promoted, came into lots of money, or just started the business of your dreams, you'll also experience personal stress. In these situations it's common to feel self-doubt, insecurity or even the kind of overconfidence that can undermine success.

In other words, personal stress happens in your own head, but this doesn't make it any less real than environmental or physiological stress. If anything, it feels even more real. The most effective techniques for dealing with personal stress are those that help you to manage your emotions and thoughts about yourself. Here are some techniques to try:

·   *Meditation:* Chapter 8
·   *Massage therapy:* Chapter 7
·   *Habit reshaping:* Chapter 6
·   *Relaxation techniques:* Chapter 6
·   *Visualization:* Chapter 8
·   *Optimism therapy:* Chapter 9
·   *Self-hypnosis:* Chapter 9
·   *Exercise (e.g. yoga, weight lifting):* Chapter 7
·   *Creativity therapy:* Chapter 9
·   *Keeping a dream diary:* Chapter 9
·   *Friend therapy:* Chapter 9

Two or more Cs

You suffer from *physiological stress* – the kind of stress that happens to your body. While all forms of stress result in a stress response in your body, some stress comes from physiological problems such as illness and pain. You catch a cold or flu and experience stress as a result. You break your wrist or sprain your ankle – that stresses your body, too. Arthritis, migraine, cancer, heart attack, stroke – all these physiological ailments, some mild, some serious, are sources of physiological stress.

Physiological stress also covers hormonal changes in the body, including PMS, pregnancy and the menopause, as well as other changes or imbalances, such as insomnia, chronic fatigue, depression, bipolar disorder, sexual dysfunction, eating disorders and addictions to substances that harm the body. Misuse of alcohol, nicotine and other legal and illegal drugs is stressful. Even prescription drugs taken as prescribed can be a source of physiological stress – while relieving one condition, they may cause stressful side effects.

You can control the stress cycle in your life. Illness and pain can cause stress, and many experts believe stress can cause illness and pain, but managing your stress can help stop the cycle. Take care of your body when you are ill; take care of your mind when you are worried or anxious. If you put a stop to one, it won't lead to the other.

While many forms of physiological stress are beyond your control, bad health habits are an important and common form of physiological stress that you can control. Sleep deprivation caused by regularly staying up too late, poor dietary habits, including overeating or undereating, too little or too much exercise and general lack of good self-care all cause direct stress on the body.

The best way to relieve physiological stress is to get to the source, and there are many stress-management techniques. Here are some to try:

· *Habit reshaping:* Chapter 6
· *Nutrition/exercise balancing:* Chapter 7
· *Massage therapy:* Chapter 7
· *Visualization:* Chapter 8
· *Relaxation techniques:* Chapter 6
· *Mindfulness meditation:* Chapter 8
· *Vitamin/herbal/homeopathic therapy:* Chapter 6
· *Ayurveda:* Chapter 9

Two or more Ds

You suffer from *social stress*. People who say they don't care what anybody thinks about them are probably not being completely honest with themselves. Human beings are social creatures, and we live in a complex, interactive society that is becoming increasingly global. Of course we care what people think. We have to care, or we wouldn't be able to live within the system. It's healthy not to care too much, but the ideal is a balance.

Social stress, therefore, is stress associated with your appearance in the world. How do people see you? How do they react to what you do and the things that happen to you? Getting engaged, married, separated or divorced, for example, while all sources of personal stress, are also sources of social stress because of society's opinions and reactions to the forming and breaking up of the marital relationship. The same goes for becoming a parent or a grandparent, being promoted, losing a job, having an extramarital affair, coming into a lot of money or losing a lot of money. Society has a lot to say about these events, which are bound to affect other people's opinion of you, rightly or wrongly, justified or not. Depending on how vulnerable you are to public (or family) opinion, you will suffer to a greater or lesser degree from social stress. If social stress is a concern in your life, some good techniques to try include the following:

- *Exercise:* Chapter 7
- *Attitude adjustment:* Chapter 9
- *Visualization:* Chapter 8
- *Creativity therapy:* Chapter 9
- *Friend therapy:* Chapter 9
- *Habit reshaping:* Chapter 6

Too much stress can result in burnout, a condition characterized by complete loss of motivation, interest, energy and engagement with work, family, or even personal hygiene. If you feel yourself heading towards burnout, seek stress management immediately. Start by taking a really long nap to catch up on your sleep.

Part III: Your Stress Vulnerability Factor Analysis

Stress vulnerabilities have to do with your personal tendencies. Just as everyone's stress triggers are different, so are everyone's personality and personal vulnerabilities to certain areas of stress. You and a friend might both have similarly stressful jobs, but you might be particularly sensitive to job stress, obsessing over work to the point where your stress is much greater than it might be. Your friend may be able to approach job stress in a much healthier way. On the other hand, you both might have two children, but your friend may be particularly vulnerable to obsessive worrying about hers, while you feel more in control of your dependant-related stress.

In this part, each answer reveals different areas in which you are particularly vulnerable to stress. Your vulnerabilities lie in the following areas if you circled these answers:

Spending too much time alone, or lack of satisfying social contact: 11.A, 13.D
An extrovert is someone who may relish time alone, but who feels drained of energy after too much time away from other people. Extroverts require plenty of social contact to keep their energy high. They work best in groups and may find working alone virtually impossible because they can't feel motivated. Personal relationships are extremely important to extroverts, who often feel incomplete without a partner. Extroverts tend to have lots of friends and to rely on their friends for energy, support and satisfaction.

Extroverts often don't know what they think until they say it. They often think things through out loud. Friend therapy, keeping a diary, group therapy, meditation classes, exercises classes and massage therapy are particularly effective for extroverts.

Spending too much time around others: 11.B, 15.D
An introvert is someone who may enjoy other people as company, but who feels drained of energy after too much social contact. Introverts require time alone to recharge after spending time socializing, and find it difficult to be productive with lots of people around. Introverts are

good at working alone from a home office or without immediate colleague contact. While introverts aren't necessarily shy, and can benefit immensely from rewarding personal relationships, they do need time alone. Introverts tend to think about what they say before they speak. Sometimes introverts can seem, and feel, distant, as if a gulf exists between the self and the outside world. This may be a sign that some time alone is needed. Your body is telling you it needs to be re-energized. In some cases, however, it may be a sign that you are spending too much time alone. Seek balance! Introspective techniques and solitary techniques, such as meditation, visualization and chakra centring, are great for introverts.

The carer conundrum: 11.D
One area that worriers tend to specialize in is anxiety about their dependants. If you are a parent or grandparent, or the carer of an ageing parent or grandparent, you have a focus for your worries right in front of you, and that focus is dependent on you for his or her health and welfare. This is quite a burden, and even if it is a position you have readily accepted, it is still stressful. Of course, as a parent you adore your children, and the burden is well worth it. But having dependants makes worry a lot easier, and worry makes the stress of being a carer a lot harder.

Dealing with the stress of being a carer means first admitting that the stress is there, then taking measures to care for yourself as well as you care for your dependants. This is not selfish. You can't be a good carer if you neglect your own physical, emotional and mental wellbeing. Self-care stress management in its many forms is exceptionally important for carers, and it includes making time for your own creativity and self-expression. Don't be afraid of admitting to the whole spectrums of feelings you have about your caring responsibilities – intense love, anger, joy, resentment, appreciation, sadness, irritation and happiness. Being a carer sounds a lot like being a human being, doesn't it? Some might say it's being human with the volume turned up.

If you are responsible for someone else's care, whether that of a child or an ageing parent, meeting your own needs is essential if you are to be an effective carer. Make time for yourself every day, even if it's only 15 minutes of quiet time spent soaking in a warm bath or reading a really good book before bed every night. Devoting all your energy to someone else will deplete your reserves, and you won't be any good to anyone.

Financial pressure: 12.A

No matter how much money some people make, it always seems to slip through their fingers – or through the proverbial hole that it's burnt in their pocket. Money is a huge source of stress for many people and a common area of stress vulnerability. Do you think that enough money really would solve all your problems? Do you spend time every single day worrying about having enough money for what you need or want? Do you obsess about where you put your money, whether your money is working for you, how you might be able to make money? Do you put a lot of importance on a person's financial status?

If money is an area of vulnerability for you, focus on stress management techniques that both help you to take responsibility for your financial situation (if that's the problem) and put finances in a whole-life perspective. Money really can't buy happiness, but freedom from financial stress can certainly help push you in that direction!

Not knowing how much money you have or where it all is can be a major source of financial stress. Face the truth, no matter how grim, and be aware of exactly how much money you have at all times. The knowledge is liberating, and you can then begin to take control over your finances.

Family dynamics: 12.B

You love 'em, you hate 'em, they see your best side and your worst side. Like it or not, you're pretty much stuck with them, even if you choose never to speak to them again. Yes, I'm talking about your family, another big area of stress for many people. Our families have an intimate knowledge of who we are or who we used to be, and that can be stressful, especially if we're trying to escape who we used to be (or who we think we used to be). Family members are notoriously adept at pushing our buttons. Who can anger you more than your brother or sister? Who can embarrass you more than your parents, even when you are an adult?

All families are stressful to some extent, but for some people family is a particular source of stress because of a dysfunctional aspect or because of painful past events. If your family is an area of stress for you, you may benefit by making amends, or by deciding to move on. You may be either estranged from your family or fully in their clutches on a daily basis. Either way, recognizing family stress is the first step to managing it, although how you manage it depends on your individual situation. You might consider techniques that bolster your people skills or techniques that strengthen the foundation of your self-esteem. Keeping a diary and other creativity techniques can be highly effective for dealing with family stress, and don't forget friend therapy. One of the great things about friends is that they aren't members of your family!

Even if family is a sacred and highly cherished part of your life, it can still be fraught with stress. This is fine – you can love your family dearly, feel fondly and intimately attached to family members, and still admit that family is a major cause of stress in your life. Recognizing the positive aspects of family, the good ways in which your family has had an impact on your life, is always an effective way to help mitigate family stress.

Obsessive worrying: 12.C, 13.B
You know perfectly well if this is you. You worry about everything, and you just can't help it. Or you have a few choice areas of life in which you are a 'worry specialist'. Perhaps it's your body shape, or the impression you make on others, or your children or grandchildren. Whatever it is, you worry. You worry about the weather. You worry about your family. You worry about your pets. You worry about school, or work, or your social circle or your friends, who probably tend to roll up their eyes and make exasperated comments like 'Will you *please* stop worrying?'

But it's not so easy to stop. Although being a worrier is really just a bad habit or, in some cases, a compulsion, it is immensely stressful. Learning how to stop worrying can be an empowering life skill that will change your daily existence more dramatically than you ever imagined. Thought control and worry stopping are excellent techniques to acquire, and exercise also provides a very good break from worry, especially when it's challenging. You can't worry if your mind is absorbed with yoga moves or a kickboxing routine. There's also nothing wrong with stopping listening to the daily news. You have enough to worry about, and if anything really important happens, you'll hear about it sooner or later. Most importantly, focus on learning how to worry effectively. Worry about things you can change, as a means to work out how to change them. If you can't change something, worrying about it is just a waste of time, and life is too short to waste time on it.

The need for constant validation by others: 12.D, 15.B, 15.C
Some people could spend their whole lives neither knowing nor caring about how 'cool' they are. Others live by the building and sustaining of their personal image. If your image is more important to you than what's behind it – or even if it just feels like it sometimes – you are probably vulnerable to image stress. It's hard not to be image-conscious these days. Appearance, charisma – the whole 'cool factor' – is hard to resist, but being too cool-conscious has a price. Going through life constantly on the lookout for how you appear to others can obliterate the real you. Do you sometimes wonder who you really are, apart from the 'you' that you choose to show to other people in the world? Image obsession is stressful, and even if a certain amount of 'cool' is important for your career or even your personal satisfaction, keeping image in perspective is as important as keeping any other aspect of your life in perspective.

Image stress is a particular problem for adolescents, but adults can fall prey to it too. Stress-management techniques that help you to get in touch with the inner you will help – the better you know the *you* inside, the more superficial and uninteresting the outer *you* will become. Know yourself and, strangely, your image will improve anyway. Maybe you've noticed that people who are unique have inner tranquillity and have found a high comfort level with who they are – and they tend to be pretty cool on all counts.

Lack of self-control, motivation, organization: 13.A, 13.B, 13.C, 13.D

You cause yourself more stress than is necessary because you haven't taken control of your personal habits, thoughts or life. No, you can't control *everything*, and if you try to, you'll just end up with the opposite problem – vulnerability to control issues. However, to a large extent, you can control what you do, how you react and even how you think and perceive the world. That's a powerful arsenal of control, and it's all the control you ever really need. Lots of us let it all go, however, making the excuse that our lives are completely subject to fate or the actions of others.

So what are some of the things in our lives that we could easily gain control over? We can control our eating habits, our exercise routines, our impulses to say unkind things, our anger, our tendency to bite our fingernails or chew the ends of pencils or never put away our things when we have finished with them. These are simply habits, and if a habit is causing you stress, why not change it? Is breaking a habit difficult? It is for a while, but living with chronic stress is much more difficult. Look for stress-management techniques that help you to gain control: be organized, be healthy, be responsible and perhaps even (oh, say it isn't true!) act like a grown-up.

In the case of addiction, self-control is probably not enough to stop indulging in certain behaviour. If you are addicted to something – whether it is nicotine, drugs, alcohol, food, gambling or sex – you are unlikely to be able to just decide to stop. The struggle is immense, and you will probably need help. Don't be afraid to ask – it isn't a sign of weakness.

Need to control: 14.A, 15.A

Where control is concerned, this is the other side of the coin. You think you know the best way to do things, and nobody had better cross you. You like to have control because you really believe you know best, and a lot of the time you probably do. The problem is that getting everyone to listen (dare I say, 'obey'?) can be stressful. How dare that person cut you up on the motorway. *You had the right of way!* How dare your colleague not take you up on your excellent suggestion for improving the efficiency of her team. *She'll be sorry!* You may also admit to requiring a certain amount of ego stroking. People should show you proper respect for your authority, shouldn't they? Is it so wrong to want reverence that is so properly due?

No, it's not. We all want to be recognized for our accomplishments, and one of your strengths is a healthy self-esteem. But as with anything else, self-esteem can be carried too far. Remember, seek balance! Knowing you are right (in a flexible way) is one thing. Demanding that everyone else admits it, too, is quite another. You can benefit from stress-management techniques that help you to (pick your metaphor) 'let go of the reins', 'coast in neutral', 'go with the flow'. You don't need to be told to 'just do it' – you 'just do it' all the time, unlike the rest of those slackers! The challenge for you is to 'just let it be', and you're always up for a challenge, aren't you? You know you can do it – just leave your ego at the door of self-awareness, and you'll have a lot less to carry. Life is more fun with a lighter load.

Your job/career: 11.C, 14.A, 14.B, 14.D

You may love your job or hate it, but one thing is certain: your job causes you stress. People who are vulnerable to job stress may indeed have particularly stressful jobs, such as those driven by deadlines, fraught with difficult people or that include high pressure to succeed. But even jobs that aren't stressful to some are stressful to others. While one person can easily say, 'I'll get it done when I get it done', another might be thrown into a frenzy of anxiety at the mere mention of an impending deadline.

If your job is an area of stress for you, concentrate on practising stress-management techniques that work in the office (even if it's a home office), specifically those that target the kind of stress you are likely to encounter on the job, such as techniques for dealing with difficult people, techniques to help relieve the strain of sitting for long periods, deep breathing and relaxation techniques for combatting ultra-high-stress moments, or whatever else is relevant to your particular job and circumstances.

According to WHO statistics, the Japanese have the longest healthy life expectancy, or years they can expect to live in 'full health' (estimated for babies born in 2001). The Japanese healthy life expectancy is 75.8 years. By comparison, the United Kingdom's figure is 70.9 years; of the 191 surveyed countries, only 27 had healthy life expectancy of over 70 years.

In addition, make a special commitment to keep sacrosanct a period of prework preparation time and postwork decompression time. Spend 15–30 minutes before and after work each day practising the stress-relieving technique of your choice to create a cushion around your workday. This will allow the rest of your life to be completely separate from work (wherever possible), and you won't feel as if your stressful work life has swallowed whole the rest of your life. Even if you work at home, set work-time boundaries – even something as simple as absolutely no work on Friday night' – then leave it behind when it's time. Again, seek balance.

Low self-esteem: 13.D, 14.D

While you may handle work stress with aplomb, you are vulnerable to attacks on your self-esteem. Perhaps a comment about your weight or age throws you into a tailspin, or perhaps you catch sight of yourself in a shop window and the negative impression you get deflates your confidence for the rest of the day.

Self-esteem isn't just about appearance. If you believe that someone is questioning your competence, do you become unreasonably defensive or suddenly insecure? Do you require constant reassurance, compliments or other self-esteem boosters from the people around you in order to feel good about yourself? Many stress-management techniques focus on bolstering self-esteem. The most important thing to remember is that self-esteem, just like your body, requires maintenance. Work on it. Take care of yourself. Keep reminding yourself how special you are, even when you don't really believe it.

Neglecting yourself may help you to ignore self-esteem issues, but it certainly won't address or solve them. Seek out sources of affirmations and positive self-talk to keep feeling good about yourself. Assertiveness training may help you to set less store by the careless comments of others. You can be your own best friend (find out more in Chapter 13). It takes practice, but believe me, no one else is better suited to the job. You are worth knowing, so get to know yourself. You are an endless source of mystery. You are fascinating. You are lovable. And no one will appreciate you until you appreciate yourself. Cliché, perhaps, but also ultimately true.

What is a perfection meditation?
Sit or lie comfortably and close your eyes. Relax and focus on your breathing. Then, every time you exhale, imagine breathing out all the negativity inside you. And every time you inhale, imagine breathing in pure, white light that fills you with positive energy. As you breathe, repeat the word *perfection* either out loud or to yourself. As you say the word, know that it describes you. No matter what your so-called faults by society's standards, or by your own standards, you are a perfect spirit inside.

Part IV: Your Stress Response Tendencies Analysis

This part reveals the ways in which you tend to respond to stress. Keep a note of how many times you marked an answer under each of the following columns:

	IGNORE	REACT	ATTACK	MANAGE
16.	A	B	C	D
17.	B	D	C	A
18.	A	C	B	D
19.	B	C	A	D
20.	D	B	C	A

The category you chose most often indicates your stress response style. Here's what each category means.

Ignore it

If you chose mostly answers in the Ignore category, you tend to ignore the stress in your life. Sometimes this can be an excellent coping strategy, but at other times, ignoring stress compounds it. Something that could have been easily corrected early on can become a source of greater and greater stress because it was never addressed. Be *aware* of your tendency to ignore stress, so that you can use this strategy consciously. Ignoring stress without realizing it can result in buried feelings that would be better acknowledged and dispatched. Learn to be fully aware of the stress in your life, then you can *choose* when to ignore it consciously and productively, and when to manage it.

React to it

If you chose mostly answers in the React category, you tend to react to stress with behaviour that can be unhelpful at best and destructive at worst. Perhaps you raid the freezer for the ice cream every time stress gets out of hand. Perhaps you get depressed, or angry, or irritable, or anxious, or panicky. Perhaps you worry obsessively. Perhaps you smoke or drink, or try to forget your stress by using other drugs. Whatever your response, reacting to stress makes you the victim and sends your psyche the message that the stress is in control and you are its hapless pawn. Don't be a pawn. Reacting to stress with occasional self-indulgence can be enjoyable in a wallowing, self-pitying kind of way. It can even be a kind of self-care, but only up to a point. Managing stress is much more effective.

Attack it

If you chose mostly answers in the Attack category, you don't just handle stress, you manhandle it, and with an aggressive jab to the solar plexus. You refuse to let stress get the best of you, but your determination can push you overboard. Sometimes the key to managing stress is letting it go, but you don't like to let things go until you've attacked them from every possible angle and pounded them into dust. This *can* be a highly effective technique – a stubborn work problem, a failing business or even a weight problem might respond well to a full-speed, vigorous, full-frontal attack. But although this kind of energy can eliminate certain sources of stress, for others an attack mode may not be ideal. Learning a variety of stress-management techniques for different types of stress can add to your coping repertoire. Put relaxation at the top of the list.

Manage it

If you chose mostly answers in the Manage category, you are pretty good at managing the stress in your life. You tend to react to stressful stimuli with a moderate rather than an extreme response. You give yourself time to size up a situation before acting, and don't worry inordinately about things you can't control. Sometimes things happen that make you feel bad, but you've learned that not everything everyone does is about you (most of the time, it probably isn't). Of course, doing a good job of managing stress doesn't preclude room for improvement. Learning more and better ways to manage stress will prepare you for future possible stressors – because everyone encounters them.

Record the results from your personal stress test in a diary – a notebook will do – set aside for stress-management work. This is your Personal Stress Profile. Date it, then try the test again in a few months, after you've worked with some of the stress-management techniques from this book. You may find that your PSP has changed quite considerably.

Your Stress Management Profile

Look at the results of your personal stress test and write a few paragraphs in your diary about your overall impression. How much stress can you take before you start to feel bad? What triggers stress for you? What are your vulnerable areas? How do you respond to stress?

This is your Stress Management Profile. Knowing your stress profile allows you to choose the stress-management techniques that will work best for you, and to organize your stress management to fit in with your life.

CHAPTER 5

Your Stress Management Portfolio

You've collected a lot of important information about the stress in your life, and you have the knowledge to create a plan that will meet your individual needs. In this chapter, you'll lay the groundwork for that plan by mapping out your Stress Management Portfolio.

The Big Picture: Building Your Personal Stress Management Portfolio

You'll write your Stress Management Portfolio yourself, and you won't do it all in one day. As you work through the rest of this book, reading about the many different approaches to stress management, write down the ones that appeal to you and, after you've tried them, describe how they worked for you.

Your Stress Management Portfolio, as you may have guessed, isn't set in stone. You write things down, try them out, adjust your approach, try something else, find something that works for part of your life, then continue to experiment in other areas. Your Stress Management Portfolio is similar to an investment portfolio. If you follow the stock market and trade your stocks and shares according to changes in the market, your portfolio doesn't stay the same. As your life changes, your Stress Management Portfolio will change, too. As you build, customize and implement it, you'll also keep a careful watch on the stress in your life. As it changes, so will your stress-management strategy.

As you work your way through this chapter, refer to your Personal Stress Profile regularly and use it to build your Stress Management Portfolio. The more personalized you make your strategy, the more effective it will be.

A recent British study showed that 20 men and women with high blood pressure took 37 minutes to complete a maths test. The same number of men and women without high blood pressure took only 10 minutes to complete the same test.

Your Stress Management Portfolio is a flexible action plan based on the details of your Personal Stress Profile and the overall knowledge gained from it. Think about the overall impression you wrote in your diary after completing your personal stress test. This impression will form the outline or silhouette of your Stress Management Portfolio, and each section of your Personal Stress Profile will help to determine your stress-management strategy.

Stress Management Diaries

One of the simplest but most potent stress-management strategies you can employ is to keep a stress diary. In such a journal you can record the results of your personal stress test, then move onto your Personal Stress Profile and Stress Management Profile, and keep track of your stress-management strategies, including what you tried and when, and how well it worked.

A stress diary is also the place for you to record sources of stress each day, and the ways you choose to manage them. You can record which stress-management strategies succeeded and failed, examine why you did or didn't deal with stress in an effective way – and you can even rant about your stress (which is a stress-management technique in itself, of course). Writing down your stressors and the way you deal with them is helpful in several ways:

· Writing down each day's sources of stress helps you to tune in to the stress in your life. You become aware of stress sources and stress patterns you might not have otherwise recognized.
· Writing about your stress and the way you actually handle it helps you to work out when your stress-management strategies are working and when they are not. You'll also discover how you really feel about the stress in your life and your stress-management efforts. Writing can be a powerful tool for discovery.
· If you are the type who tends to *ignore* stress, you'll have to acknowledge it when you write it down. If you tend to *attack* stress, attacking it with the pen is a lot healthier than saying or doing things you'll later regret. If you tend to *react* to stress, reacting on the page is a lot healthier than reacting by falling into destructive habits.

Your stress diary can take any form – an A4 pad, a beautifully bound book of blank pages, or your computer. Whichever you choose, it should be something you enjoy using. You can either simply list your stressors or write at greater length describing how you felt and what you did about them. Write in your stress diary in a way that feels right for you.

The most difficult part of keeping a stress diary is acquiring the habit of writing in it every day. Like any other habit, with a little discipline this is something you can learn to keep up – and you'll be glad you did. The discipline of writing in your stress diary every day is a kind of stress-management victory all on its own. The additional benefits gained from developing your personal stress awareness make the effort you put in easily worthwhile.

Organizing just one thing in your life can often ease stress considerably. Instead of watching television tonight, why not tackle your sock drawer, kitchen junk drawer or the coat cupboard that's been driving you mad? Don't expect to achieve anything beyond the single task you've chosen — you'll be surprised at how much better you feel with just a single drawer or cupboard put in order.

Putting Your Stress Diary to Work

Once you've decided on the form of your stress diary, you can begin to map out your stress-management plan. You have already begun by recording the details of your personal stress test under the heading Personal Stress Profile, and writing a few lines giving an overall impression of the effect of stress on your life – your Stress Management Profile. (You can check back from time to time to see if your overall impression is changing.)

Now you can begin to focus more specifically on what you've discovered about the stress in your life.

What Works

While answering the questions in the last chapter, you probably noticed patterns and trends emerging as you worked your way through the test. If you didn't, look back and try to identify some of them now. You may also have recognized, as you completed the test, that there are some areas of life you handle pretty well – some things are actually working.

If this didn't occur to you, think about it now. Recognizing what works for you will help you to see what kind of systems and attitudes you might apply to other areas of your life where things aren't going so well.

So what things in your life *are* working pretty well? What parts of your life do you generally feel good about? What are your stress-management successes? Where are your productive and efficient systems? What are your best, most supportive relationships? Which of your positive qualities are able to manifest themselves in your life? Spend some time considering what's working, and record it in your diary under 'What's Working Well in My Life'.

Oestrogen protects young women from heart disease, but stress can cause oestrogen levels to drop, allowing plaque to build up in the arteries. A 1999 autopsy study revealed that by the age of 35, most women already had substantial plaque build-up in their coronary arteries. Researchers suspect that stress is to blame.

What Doesn't Work

Now consider the areas of your life where some improvement is due. Do you need more hours in the day? More romance in your relationship? Better health habits? A more organized household? A better rapport with your children? More open communication with your friends?

List the things you would like to improve in your life – the things you'll be better able to focus and work on once you've got that excess stress under control. Put this list in your diary under 'Things I Would Like to Improve'.

Targeting Your Strategy

Return to the previous chapter and record the results of your Personal Stress Profile in your diary. The chapters in the rest of this book describe many different stress-management techniques. As you read about them, keep in mind the results of your Personal Stress Profile. Each aspect of it can be targeted with one or more stress-management techniques. As you learn about the different techniques, try applying them to the different areas of your Personal Stress Profile.

Recording Your Test Results

To record your test results in your diary and reflect on them at the same time, you might want to use a template something like the one that follows. (If you make several copies of this template, there will always be one on hand when you take the personal stress test again in the future.)

My Stress Management Profile

Date: _____

My Stress Tolerance Point is (tick one):
☐ JUST RIGHT HIGH   ☐ TOO HIGH
☐ JUST RIGHT LOW   ☐ TOO LOW

I believe I am operating (tick one):
☐ ABOVE
☐ AT   my Stress Tolerance Point.
☐ BELOW

This is how I feel about my efforts or lack of efforts to operate at or near my Stress Tolerance Point:

_____

_____

_____

My Stress Triggers are, in general:

_____

_____

_____

ENVIRONMENTAL, specifically:

PHYSIOLOGICAL, specifically:

PERSONAL, specifically:

SOCIAL, specifically:

Some of the techniques that sound interesting for dealing with my stress triggers are:

In assessing my Stress Vulnerability, I believe I am:

An (tick one):
☐ INTROVERT
☐ EXTROVERT

I want to remember to try stress techniques, such as _____ ,

_____ and _____ , that work with my

above tendency.

I am particularly likely to be subject to stress when it is related to (tick all that apply):

☐ WORK
☐ SELF-ESTEEM
☐ SELF-CONTROL
☐ MONEY
☐ IMAGE
☐ FAMILY
☐ COMPETITION/CONTROL/EGO
☐ WORRY
☐ MY DEPENDANTS

I plan to focus my stress management techniques on these areas.

These are my personal observations about my stress vulnerability:

_____

_____

_____

_____

My stress response tendency is to (tick one):

☐ IGNORE IT
☐ REACT TO IT
☐ ATTACK IT
☐ MANAGE IT

These are my thoughts on the way I tend to respond to stress:

Now you can easily refer to your test results. Use this template again when you retake the test.

The following sections will give you ideas for how to target your stress-management strategies according to your Personal Stress Profile.

Before you take a pill to help you ease into dreamland, try counting back slowly from 100 to 1. Imagine each number and visualize how it looks. In your mind, make it look beautiful, in a tranquil colour, perhaps drawn in elegant calligraphy, or formed by clouds in a fabulous blue sky. Breathe slowly, allowing long in and out breaths for each number.

Your Stress Tolerance Level Management Strategies

Whether your Stress Tolerance Level was **JUST RIGHT LOW** or **TOO HIGH**, or a combination of several levels for different areas of your life, the key to managing stress is to maintain it around a healthy Stress

Tolerance Level for you. If your level was **JUST RIGHT LOW,** you need to keep making a conscious effort to eliminate excess stress from your life so that you can continue to enjoy a low level of stress. Remember what is working – how are you already able to keep stress low? Then plan for those times when stress will surely increase. Be prepared!

If your stress level is **JUST RIGHT HIGH**, you also need to continue to make a conscious effort to keep stress at the level that works for you. While you may be able to handle more stress than some other people, you can still get overstressed. Techniques that help you to cultivate mind–body awareness will alert you to when stress is getting out of control in your life. People who can take more stress than average tend to ignore their Stress Tolerance Level, thinking they can take anything, but we all have our limits.

If your stress level is **TOO HIGH** or **TOO LOW**, you also need a plan. How can you begin to *eliminate* stress and achieve a healthy Stress Tolerance Level? Or, how can you begin to *add* stimulation to your life in healthy and productive ways and achieve a healthy Stress Tolerance Level? Remember, too much stress is hard on your body, but not enough stress (not enough for your own personal needs) makes for a pretty dull and unfulfilling life, which is in itself a source of stress in the form of frustration, irritation and depression.

Using the format opposite, record your Stress Tolerance Level in your diary. Then, as you read through the rest of this book, list possible strategies that sound interesting and, after you've tried them, describe how they worked. Finally, in the last column, record 'keeper' strategies to add to your stress-management repertoire and daily or weekly routine.

Keeping track of the effectiveness of different stress-management techniques is important. While you may remember in the short term that, say, a certain herbal remedy worked well or that a certain relaxation technique was tedious, a month later you may have forgotten – and you'll be glad you made a note of your experience.

You might like to make several copies of the blank template so that you always have one to hand when you need it.

My Stress Tolerance Level is: _____

Stress-management strategy to try	How often tried/ over what period of time? (e.g. daily for two weeks)	How effective was this technique in helping me to achieve a healthy Stress Tolerance Level? (on a scale of 1–10)	Keep (K), or not for me (N)?

Indigestion is a common reaction to stress because the body's stress response causes blood to be channelled away from the digestive system. The next time you suffer from an attack of indigestion, rather than resorting to antacids on the run, try sitting still for five minutes, breathing deeply and eating some some live natural yogurt. The 'friendly' bacteria in yogurt may help to promote healthy digestion.

Your Stress Trigger Management Strategies

Whether you get a new flatmate, flu, married, a bad exam result, pregnant or a speeding ticket, these are all stress triggers that add to the stress in your life. Managing your Stress Triggers is key to working with your Stress Tolerance Level. Remember, Stress Triggers come in four categories: Environmental, Personal, Physiological and Social. The categories in which your Stress Triggers tend to fall can give vital clues to the stress-management strategies you should try.

In your diary, record the categories into which your Stress Triggers tend to fall (see your Personal Stress Profile in the last chapter). Then you are ready to decide which stress-management techniques to try in order to manage (eliminate or ease the stress of) each of them.

As you read through the rest of this book, make a note of any techniques that you think might address the Stress Triggers in certain categories. For instance, improving your eating habits and increasing the amount of daily exercise you get might address the frequent minor illnesses in your Physiological Stress category. Social anxiety might be effectively addressed by friend therapy or regular self-esteem maintenance. Don't worry about trying to work out which stress-management techniques address which categories of Stress Triggers – I'll prompt you in each section. You just record the techniques that sound interesting.

Many Stress Triggers are best approached individually, no matter what category they happen to fall into. In your diary, make a list of your individual Stress Triggers and the way you decide to tackle each one. Keep track of what you tried, and how well it worked. You can use the template opposite as a guide. Again, you'll be glad to have this record. Not only will you be able to remember later on what worked and what didn't, but you'll be able to see in black and white how you are proactively managing your own stress, rather than letting your Stress Triggers manage you.

Look at the way you hold the phone. Many people hunch up their shoulders and bend their necks to hold phones against their ears, in an attempt to keep their hands free. This posture can contribute to significant muscle tension and misalignment in your spine. If you spend a lot of time on the phone, invest in a headset so you can be truly hands-free. Headsets work well with mobile phones, too.

My Stress Trigger	This is what I tried	Here's how it worked

Your Stress Vulnerability Adjustment Strategies

Knowing your Stress Vulnerability Factors, or the specific areas of your life in which you are particularly vulnerable to stress, means you can use specific stress-management techniques to target these areas. Whether you are vulnerable when it comes to your job, your family, or your self-esteem, you will find techniques individually suited to you; keep a note of them in your journal.

As you read through the rest of this book, also make notes of the strategies that interest you as they apply to your Stress Vulnerability Factors. If a certain strategy is particularly appropriate for a certain area of life, it will be highlighted. For example, debt-management strategies can be highly effective in managing financial stress. That's an obvious one. Not so obvious is the effectiveness of visualization for boosting self-esteem, or the power of prayer and spiritual development for boosting the immune system. Use this template to keep a record of your stress vulnerabilities in your diary:

My vulnerable area	Here's what I tried	Here's how it worked	Keep it (K) or not for me (N)

A cup of chamomile tea can help you to unwind before bedtime. Chamomile is thought to have relaxing properties, but how you drink it can be a relaxing experience, too. Focus on the taste, aroma, warmth, steam, the teacup, and how it feels to swallow the tea. This kind of meditation will calm your mind after a busy day and prepare you for sleep.

Your Stress Response Tendency Adjustment Schedule

By keeping track of the things you tend to do that work, and the things you tend to do that are less effective, or are destructive to your physical, emotional or mental health, you can monitor your natural tendencies to respond to stress.

In the previous chapter, you grouped your Stress Response Tendencies into four categories: you either react to stress, attack it, ignore it or manage it, although you probably respond to stress differently depending on what kind of stress it is. Using your diary, you can monitor your stress responses and see what progress you've made. As mentioned previously, you'll be glad you kept this record.

Use the template on the following page to check your Stress Response Tendencies every week for six weeks. During the course of each week, you'll probably respond to stress in a variety of ways – list them all and describe the kind of stress you were responding to. Staying aware of the ways in which you respond to stress is one of the best ways to keep your responses healthy and productive. In the second column, describe the ways in which you could respond more productively. (If you responded well, congratulate yourself – who says grown-ups can't get gold stars?)

My Stress Responses

	This week	**My plan for next week**

Week 1

Dates:

_____

to

_____

1._____ 1._____

2._____ 2._____

3._____ 3._____

4._____ 4._____

5._____ 5._____

Week 2

Dates:

_____

to

_____

1._____ 1._____

2._____ 2._____

3._____ 3._____

4._____ 4._____

5._____ 5._____

Week 3

Dates:

_____

to

_____

1._____ 1._____

2._____ 2._____

3._____ 3._____

4._____ 4._____

5._____ 5._____

My Stress Responses

	This week	**My plan for next week**
Week 4	1._____	1._____
Dates:	2._____	2._____
_____	3._____	3._____
to	4._____	4._____
_____	5._____	5._____
Week 5	1._____	1._____
Dates:	2._____	2._____
_____	3._____	3._____
to	4._____	4._____
_____	5._____	5._____
Week 6	1._____	1._____
Dates:	2._____	2._____
_____	3._____	3._____
to	4._____	4._____
_____	5._____	5._____

Back pain is most often experienced in the lower back. Such lower back pain can be a signal from your body that you have too much stress in your life. Listen to your body and let back pain tell you when it's time to slow down. If your back pain is at all persistent or severe, please see your doctor.

Map Out Your Stress Fault Lines

Some people just don't like writing, and if writing doesn't come easily to you or if you don't enjoy it, keeping a stress diary won't be productive. It will just become a source of more stress, one more thing lingering perpetually on your to-do list. If this sounds like you, you might be more comfortable drawing a map of your stress. Mapping stress is like writing a stress diary, but instead of words, you use pictures, symbols and signs.

Draw your stress map as if it were a map of a city. Each building is a stressor. Each district is an area of vulnerability. Each street is a link between stressors, such as the link between lack of exercise and joint pain, or the link between financial problems and lack of willpower when it comes to spending. One-way streets represent direct cause-and-effect stressors (insomnia → sleep deprivation; knee injury → chronic pain).

Don't worry if you aren't much of an artist – your map can be a simple picture of basic labelled shapes, although, if you want, it can be a work of art. The point is to find a mode of expression with which you feel comfortable, and which will help you discover or visualize the way the stress in your life is interconnected, where individual stressors originate, and how some stressors are in fact the results of other stressors. By eliminating or effectively managing a single stressor, you may find you can eliminate several other stressors, too.

Set Your Stress-Management Goals

We've spent a lot of time cultivating stress awareness because recognizing your stress is incredibly important. But it is only one step in the stress-management process – it is also important to define your goals. Do you want to be able to concentrate better? Be ill less often? Stop shouting at your children? Be more productive at work? Manage your chronic pain? Alleviate your depression? All of the above?

Think about your stress-management goals. What do you want to accomplish? Why did you choose this book in the first place? You probably had some goal in mind, even if it was just to stop feeling so stressed all the time. After giving your goals some thought, list them in your diary.

This important part of your Stress Management Portfolio will evolve just as the other parts evolve. As you achieve certain stress-management goals, you'll certainly define new ones. For now, make a list of your current goals. Don't worry about getting every one down straight away – you can record new goals as they come along and tick off old ones as they are accomplished.

When you are feeling stressed, stop for a moment and notice your expression. Is your face all scrunched up? Is your forehead wrinkled? Are your brows lowered? Is your mouth frowning? Make a conscious effort to relax your forehead, lift your chin and smile. Simply adjusting your face can make you feel a lot better (not to mention looking a lot better, too!).

Implement Your Stress Management Plan of Action

You've analyzed the sources of your stress, discovered what is working in your life and what isn't. What do you do next? Start alleviating that stress!

At first, working out exactly where to start may seem difficult. You may feel confused or frustrated by all the information and the ideas you have. You might think that you could never possibly manage all that new and extra stress.

But remember, if you don't recognize all the sources of your stress, you'll never be able to deal with them. You've accomplished an important first step and also begun to think about what to do next. As you continue to discover new stress-management techniques, add them to your lists in your diary. But for the moment, you need an orderly, achievable list as a starting point.

Put your stress-management plan into action by preparing a numbered list. Start by picking a stressor you think will be fairly easy to deal with. For example, perhaps you know you need to get more sleep. This is an excellent place to start because you'll have a hard time handling, let alone managing, any stress at all if you aren't getting enough sleep on a regular basis.

Have you heard that certain stressors, such as early childhood trauma or self-esteem issues, show up as pain or tension in certain parts of the body? While there might be some truth in these theories, the chances are that the way stress affects a body is highly individual. Your intuition is probably the most reliable source of information about where stress is 'settling' in your body. Alternatively, counselling may be called for.

Your stress-management goals should be *daily* ones for a while, as that way they will feel more manageable. It will also be easier to decide, for example, to go to bed at 10:00 PM *just for today*. The thought of going to bed that early every day for the rest of your life may sound unrealistic, even depressing – you *like* staying up late. That's fine. But if you know it's *just for today*, it will be easier. The same applies to deciding to eliminate junk food from your diet *just for today*, or to go to the gym *just for today*.

As you adopt healthier habits, you'll be able to set goals for a week, then a month at a time. As you try different approaches to stress management, you'll be able to adjust your goals so that they work for you.

Perhaps your stress-management plan of action will look something like that shown opposite.

My Stress Management Plan of Action for Today

Stressor	Action today
Sleep deprivation:	1. No TV tonight
watching television late	2. Video the shows I like
	3. Bedtime at 10:00 PM

Begin with the stressors you already have ideas about managing, and the more you learn, the more ideas you'll get about how to approach the areas of stress that seem more challenging.

Stress Management Maintenance

Learning a new system for anything is often fun, even exciting. When you first delve into the opening chapters of this book, you may have been inspired to banish every iota of unpleasant stress from your life. But after the novelty wears off, stress management must become, like anything else you want to stick to, a habit. If you don't make a commitment to stress management, and to pacing your efforts so you don't burn out with too much change all at once, you won't stick to it. You've probably already tried all kinds of new ways of living – healthier eating, step aerobics classes, throwing out half your possessions in an effort to simplify your life – and as soon as the novelty wears off, the practice appears tiresome and you give up on it.

But stress management is so important to your happiness, health and wellbeing that making it a habit and an integral part of your daily existence is worth a serious commitment. So don't try to do everything at once – make realistic goals and take gradual steps. If you change your life a little at a time, you'll find you're able to settle comfortably into the changes. Bit by bit you'll adjust your life until you are operating at a healthy Stress Tolerance Level, and when that happens you'll feel great.

After you've worked with your stress-management plan for 90 days, take the stress test in the previous chapter again and record the results in your diary. Next, fill out your Personal Stress Profile again, also recording the results in your diary. Then, you can alter your plan, adjusting your management strategies as your stress profile changes and you gradually get different areas of your life under control.

A nasty tension headache can ruin your whole day and make everything you do more stressful. As soon as you feel a tension headache coming on, try running hot water (not uncomfortably hot) over your hands for 10 minutes. This process draws blood away from your head and into your hands, which could stop a tension headache in its tracks.

CHAPTER 6

Building a
Stress-Proof Body

I t's time to start learning about stress-
management strategies. The more you
know about different techniques, the
more options you'll have when you need
them. This chapter covers some of the
most basic things you can do to start
relieving stress *today*. It describes some easy
strategies to set the groundwork for a body
and mind that can handle the inevitable
stresses of life.

Sleep Away Your Stress

One of the first and most important things for building a stress-proof body is to get enough sleep on a regular basis. According to the 2000 Omnibus Sleep in America Poll, conducted by the National Sleep Foundation *(www.sleepfoundation.org)*, 43 per cent of adults surveyed said that for a few days every month they are so sleepy during the day that it interferes with their daily activities, and one out of five (20 per cent) adults experienced this level of daytime sleepiness at least a few days or more *per week*. (No comparable surveys have been made in the UK.)

The old saying that drinking a cup of warm milk will help you get to sleep is backed up by science. Milk contains tryptophan and calcium, both of which boost serotonin levels. The release of the chemical serotonin in your body induces sleep as well as putting you in a good mood. If you have trouble digesting milk, however, this remedy could keep you awake instead of soothing you to sleep.

If you need more convincing that sleep deprivation interferes with life, consider these results from the National Sleep Foundation's survey:

· Over half of the American work force (51 per cent) reported that sleepiness on the job was interfering with the amount of work they complete.

· Forty per cent of adults admitted that the quality of their work suffered when they were tired.

· More than two-thirds of adults (68 per cent) said that tiredness interfered with their concentration, and 66 per cent said that tiredness made handling stress on the job more difficult.

· Nearly one out of five adults (19 per cent) reported making occasional or frequent work errors due to tiredness.

· Overall, employees estimated that the quality and quantity of their work was diminished by about 30 per cent when they were tired.

· More than two-thirds (68 per cent) of shift workers reported experiencing problems sleeping.

- Nearly one out of four adults (24 per cent) had difficulty getting up for work on two or more workdays per week.
- A third of adults would nap at work if it were allowed. (Only 16 per cent of employees surveyed reported that their employers allowed naps.)

Furthermore, over 30 per cent of American drivers admitted they had fallen asleep at the wheel at least once. According to the National Sleep Foundation, approximately 100,000 traffic accidents and 1,500 traffic-related fatalities were caused by a driver falling asleep at the wheel.

The numbers are even more frightening for the younger generation, or those between the ages of 18 and 29. According to the poll, over 50 per cent of young adults surveyed said they woke up feeling 'unrefreshed', and 33 per cent suffered from significant daytime tiredness – a percentage slightly higher than that of notoriously sleepy shift workers!

Herbs are a more natural, gentle method of treating occasional insomnia than prescription or over-the-counter sleep aids. A study has shown that lavender oil released through a diffuser worked as well as prescription medication for treating insomniacs.

Many young people admitted staying up too late to watch television or to use the Internet, and 53 per cent admitted to sleeping less in order to accomplish more. Young adults also suffered aggravated on-the-job stress due to sleep deprivation:

- Over 35 per cent of people aged 18–29 reported having difficulty getting up for work (compared with 20 per cent of those aged 30–64 years old and 9 per cent of those aged 65 and older).
- Nearly 25 per cent of young adults reported being occasionally or frequently late to work due to tiredness (compared to 11 per cent of people 30–64 years old and 5 per cent of workers over 65).
- Forty per cent of younger adults were tired at work at least two or more days a week (compared to 23 per cent of those 30–64 years old and 19 per cent of those over 65).
- Sixty per cent of young adults admitted to having driven while tired in the past year, and 24 per cent reported falling asleep at the wheel.

Sleep deprivation has a specific and dramatic physical effect on the body. The average adult requires eight hours of sleep per night, and teenagers require 8.5–9.25 hours. If you don't get enough sleep, you could experience the following:

· Increased irritability
· Depression
· Anxiety
· Decreased ability to concentrate and understand information
· Increased likelihood of making mistakes and having an accident
· Increased clumsiness and slower reaction times (dangerous at the wheel of a car)
· A suppressed immune system
· Undesirable weight gain.

Unfortunately, sleep disorders often disturb our sleep even if we go to bed early. Sleep disorders include insomnia, snoring (either your own or that of the person next to you who is keeping you awake), sleep apnoea (breathing disturbances during sleep), sleep walking and talking (parasomnia), and restless legs syndrome (a condition in which your legs are uncomfortable and you feel compelled to move them). Jet lag or working night shifts can also cause sleep disturbances.

So making sure you get enough sleep may require a two-pronged approach:

1. Make time for sleep.
2. Treat the sleep disorder.

However, if you do not have a sleep disorder but need to make time for sleep, or if you have plenty of time to sleep but also have a sleep disorder, you will obviously require only a single approach. Whichever is the case, too little sleep increases stress, compromises your health and probably means you are operating well below your potential. Getting enough sleep is so important that if it is one of your stressors, it should be number one on your stress-management to-do list.

Whatever your situation, the following stress-management strategies will soon have you sleeping peacefully.

Restless legs syndrome is a disorder than can affect sleep. According to medical experts, its symptoms are an urge to move the legs, often accompanied by uncomfortable sensations such as a creeping or crawling feeling, tingling, cramping, burning, or pain. Symptoms worsen when the person tries to lie or sit still. Some patients only experience the need to move. There are various treatments available, from relaxation techniques to medication.

Stress-Management Strategies: Sleep

If you commit to getting a good night's sleep, you'll find you have more energy for other areas of stress management. Here are some tips to help you get eight hours of quality sleep each night:

- Work out why you can't get to bed earlier, and commit to changing your routine accordingly. Where are you wasting time during the day? How could you rearrange your timetable so that some things are done earlier, allowing for an earlier bedtime? Could you organize things so that you can get up later? If you are staying up late to watch TV or surf the Internet, try giving these media a miss for a few nights to see how the extra sleep changes your mood and energy levels.
- Create a bedtime ritual for yourself. Parents are often advised to give their sleep-resistant children a routine, and it works for grown-ups, too. Your ritual should include a series of steps that are conducive to relaxation – for example, a bath or shower, then perhaps a few minutes of deep breathing or some other relaxation technique; a cup of herbal tea; a good book instead of the television or computer; swapping back rubs, neck rubs or foot rubs with a partner; writing in your diary. Then lights out.
- Try not to get into the habit of falling asleep in front of the TV. If you have got into the habit, falling asleep without the TV will probably take longer, and you may not sleep as well. If this happens, try some relaxation techniques.

- If you feel you are wasting precious time by sleeping when you should be getting things done, remind yourself that sleep *is* getting things done. While you sleep, your body is busy healing, recharging by conserving energy, growing and regenerating cells, and consolidating memory and discharging emotions through dreams. You're actually being very productive when you sleep, and you'll be even more productive after you've had enough sleep.

- Don't get stressed about not being able to get to sleep. An occasional night of too little sleep won't hurt you as long as you usually get enough. Rather than lying in the dark, tossing and turning in frustration, turn on the light and find something to read. Make sure you are comfortable. Sip some warm milk or chamomile tea. Meditate. Steer your mind away from worries and think about pleasant things – not sleep, just pleasant things. Breathe. Even if you don't get to sleep, you'll relax – and you'll probably feel drowsy.

One technique for treating insomnia is recommended in *The Breathing Book,* by Donna Farhi. Lightly wind a soft cotton bandage around the forehead, eyes and temples just before sleep. The pressure against the muscles in the face quickly induces a relaxed state.

If you are having trouble sleeping, try these suggestions:

- Don't drink or eat anything that has caffeine in it after lunch: this includes coffee, tea, cola and many other fizzy drinks (check the label); certain over-the-counter pain medications and cold medications (check the label); stimulants designed to keep you awake; and even cocoa and chocolate.

- Eat a healthy, light, low-fat, low-carbohydrate supper. Fresh fruits and vegetables, whole grains instead of refined grains, and low-fat protein such as fish, chicken, beans and tofu will help your body to be in a calmer, more balanced state at bedtime. Avoid high-fat, overprocessed foods in the evening. They will make you more likely to suffer digestive problems that can keep you from sleeping.

· Eat a light supper – late, large meals are upsetting for your digestive system. For a peaceful night's sleep, make supper your lightest meal.

· If you have an evening snack, eat foods high in tryptophan. This is an amino acid that encourages the body to produce serotonin, a chemical that helps you to sleep. Serotonin also regulates your moods, helping you to feel good. Foods high in tryptophan include milk, turkey, peanut butter, rice, tuna, dates, figs and yogurt. A light snack that includes any of these foods about 30–60 minutes before bedtime can help promote restful sleep.

· Don't drink alcohol in the evening. While many people have a drink thinking it will help them to sleep, alcohol actually disrupts sleep patterns, making your sleep less restful. Alcohol may also increase snoring and sleep apnoea.

· Get enough exercise during the day. A well-exercised body will fall asleep faster, sleep longer, and sleep more productively.

· If you are still having problems sleeping, talk to your doctor about this. Studies show that most people have never been asked by their doctors how well they sleep, but as much as 80 per cent have never brought up the subject with their doctors, either. Tell your doctor you are concerned about your sleep problems. He or she may have a simple solution.

If you are too stressed to sleep, a cup of herbal tea may help. Herbal tea helps you to relax in three ways. Herbs such as lemon balm, chamomile and blends designed to promote relaxation and sleep can help to calm the body. The slow process of boiling the water and steeping the tea in the steamy cup slows you down and helps you to relax and focus. Then the process of drinking the tea requires sitting still and slowly sipping. Let yourself relax and enjoy the process as a restful night-time ritual.

Stress-Management Strategies: Hydration

Sometimes one of the most helpful things you can do for your body when you're feeling anxious is to drink some water. Human bodies are made up of about two-thirds water, but many people are mildly dehydrated (3–5 per cent below their body weight due to fluid loss) and don't know it.

While severe dehydration (10 per cent or more fluid loss) has dramatic symptoms and can even result in death, mild dehydration may go unnoticed. It is more likely to occur after intense exercise, in extreme heat, while dieting, and after vomiting or diarrhoea, either because of illness, such as food poisoning, or drinking too much alcohol.

When you don't have enough water in your body, your body will experience stress, and you'll be far less equipped to handle stress from other sources.

Symptoms of dehydration include the following:

· Dry mouth
· Dizziness
· Light-headedness
· Dark urine (should be pale yellow)
· Inability to concentrate
· Confusion.

Dehydration is very dangerous for infants and small children, and is a real danger during periods of gastrointestinal illness. If your child has a dry mouth, sunken eyes, dark urine, seems listless or has a sunken fontanelle (the opening between the plates of the skull in infants), seek medical treatment immediately. Dehydration can also be dangerous for older people, who may not recognize the symptoms and may not be inclined to drink much water.

One reason why dehydration is so common is because caffeinated beverages are so popular and widely available. You may feel as though your thirst is being quenched when you drink a can of cola, but the caffeine actually acts as a diuretic to flush water out of your system.

The other reason for dehydration is simple: people don't drink much water any more. While water used to be the main and often only practical drink of choice for most people, today it's much easier and, many feel, more pleasant to choose a can or bottle of something fizzy, a sugary fruit drink or a cup of coffee or tea. While bottled water is widely available (and often safer than tap water in many areas), some people rarely if ever drink water in its plain, original form.

Yet water can offer your body many benefits, not least of which is a better defence against stress. If you are dehydrated – and according to the statistics, you very well may be – your body can't rally its energy in the cause of stress management because it is too busy trying to compensate for its lack of water.

Drinking more water is one of the easiest changes you can make to help manage your stress. With a well-hydrated body you'll feel better, your skin will look better and you'll have more energy.

Make drinking water a habit. If you don't make it a habit, you'll drink water for a few days then go back to your five-cans-of-fizzy-drink-a-day habit. Here are some tips on how to establish this healthy habit:

- If you really don't like the taste of plain water, try adding a wedge of lemon, lime or orange to it. If you just have to have bubbles, try plain soda water instead of other fizzy drinks. Still not convinced? Dilute real fruit juice (not the sugar-added stuff) with half water or half soda water. You can also get sparkling natural water with a hint of flavour.
- Ideally, you should drink two litres of water each day. That may sound like a lot, but if you spread it out over the day, it's not so much. Have half a litre first thing in the morning, half a litre with lunch, half a litre with supper, and a final half a litre in the evening. Add another half litre or more if you've been sweating or taking a lot of exercise.
- We have become so removed from our natural sensations of hunger that we often mistake thirst for hunger and eat when all we really need is a tall cool glass of water. A glass of water before each meal, and whenever hunger pangs strike between meals, should satisfy your body's need for water and help to curb excessive eating.

Take Control of Bad Habits

What makes a habit bad? A bad habit is a habit that makes you less healthy or less happy. Even if you feel good while *indulging* your habit, you probably know it's just a temporary high, for example when you go shopping and spend £250 on things you don't really need. You get a rush of pleasure, but as soon as you get home and put the things away, you begin to feel guilt, regret or even anger at yourself. The habit was controlling you, rather than the other way around.

Bad habits can be irritating, to ourselves and others, and they can also be stressful. Many bad habits undermine physical health, emotional wellbeing and mental acuity. To begin building a body capable of coping with the stresses that life necessarily entails, take control of your bad habits – they are unnecessary stresses.

Habits are stressful in three ways:

1. **Direct.** Many habits have a direct, negative effect on the body. Smoking, drinking too much alcohol and taking certain drugs (legal or illegal) can introduce toxic or harmful substances into the body. These can compromise the body's ability to function properly, lead to addiction and even encourage disease. Habits can also have a direct effect on our emotional or mental wellbeing. Becoming intoxicated, over-distracted or otherwise impaired can make us more prone to accidents, rages and mistakes. When your body and/or mind are directly affected in a negative way by a habit, your stress level will increase.

2. **Indirect.** Habits also have an indirect effect on your stress levels. Knowing you drank too much, stayed up too late and ate too much the night before can reduce your self-esteem and make you feel frustrated the next day at work. Your stress will be higher than it would have been had you not spent the previous evening being controlled by a bad habit. Perhaps someone will comment on your unwashed hair and make you feel embarrassed and angry at yourself. Later you might snap at a friend because you feel bad about your lack of self-control. Habits can make us feel helpless when they control us. We worry about our lack of self-control, the effect our habit may have

on others, and the consequences to our health of the habit, and this all contributes to our stress.

3. **Combination.** Some habits can have both direct and indirect negative effects. Most bad habits probably fall into this category. After all, anything that affects us negatively, and that we could have controlled but didn't, will tend to undermine our emotional state and sense of self-esteem, leading to related stress. Compulsive overeating, for example, is dangerous to the body because the body isn't designed to take in large amounts of food all at once. It can also create negative emotional states – frustration, depression and anxiety.

   Even less dramatic bad habits, such as habitual untidiness, can have a combination effect. If you can never keep things in order, for example, you might suffer frustration because you can never find anything, financial loss because of your disorganization, and low self-esteem because everyone but you seems to be able to keep things neat and tidy (which, of course, is not true).

Attitudes and personality determine behaviour, but behaviour can also determine attitude and personality. Rather than succumbing to the notion that you'll always smoke, overeat or interrupt people because 'that's just the way you are', pretend for a single day that you aren't 'like that'. Pretend you don't have that bad habit. It may be easier than you think, and soon you may find that you can be that person all the time – that that person was you all along!

Some habits, of course, are good. If you always tidy up after yourself, are polite, or are devoted to your daily helping of fresh salad, you probably already know that these habits are a bonus.

Some habits are neutral, such as always eating a favourite cereal, preferring a certain petrol station or humming while you do the washing-ups. If these habits don't bother anybody, they are no problem.

You may feel helpless in the throes of your nail-biting, hair-twirling, crisp-munching, TV-watching or procrastinating habit. But as helpless as you feel, rest assured that it's just a habit, and habits can be broken.

How do you break a bad habit? First, decide if the habit really is bad. If, for example, you drink a cup of coffee every morning because you really enjoy it, that's probably fine, but if you gulp down fresh coffee by the litre all day long and feel panicky or nonfunctional without it, you've got a bad habit, which is controlling you.

Once you've decided that you have a bad habit (most of us have several), the next step is to identify it and make sure you understand, logically, why it is, indeed, a bad habit. Once you've recognized and admitted to your habit, you can work on taking control of it. Let's look at some common bad habits and the ways they can cause stress. See where you recognize yourself.

When your bad habit is also an addiction, typical habit-control methods may not work. Addictions such as those to cigarettes, drugs, alcohol, gambling or even sex are more complex than simple habits and can be life-threatening or life-destroying. When your body chemistry or a complex psychological process is involved, you may need additional help, whether it be a nicotine patch, counselling, or a stint in rehab. Talk to your doctor or a specialist counsellor about the best way for you to handle your addiction.

Personal Habits

Personal habits are the things you do that probably drive somebody else mad, or that you never do in front of other people because you know it *would* drive them mad. Personal habits include nail-biting, hair-twirling, knuckle-cracking, fidgeting, whining, habitual coughing or throat-clearing, newspaper-rattling and tea-slurping. You can probably think of plenty of others. A personal habit is worth getting rid of if it annoys you, annoys people around you (at least those that you'd rather not annoy), makes you feel bad about yourself or is bad for you.

Drugs: The Legal Ones and the Other Ones

Drugs can be an important means of maintaining or regaining good health. When used for purposes other than correcting a health problem, however, they can cause imbalances in the body that actually contribute to health problems. There are people who use legal drugs, which include alcohol, nicotine, caffeine and prescription drugs. And there are other people who use illegal ones. Both types of people use drugs to make them feel good, increase their energy or have a calming effect.

Some substances used occasionally in moderation (such as alcohol or caffeine) probably aren't harmful for most people, but other drugs – especially 'hard' drugs such as cocaine and heroin – can be very damaging to the body. A glass of wine with dinner is fine for someone who isn't addicted to alcohol, isn't prone to alcohol addiction, and who enjoys wine. One marijuana cigarette could be dangerous to somebody with asthma and has immediate short-term stressful physical effects on everyone (even if you think it makes you feel relaxed). Illegal drugs pose multiple risks, not the least of which is the potential for getting into trouble with the police. If you want to talk stressful, consider a gaol term.

Any substance that artificially alters your mental state, when taken too often or in large amounts, will, at best, keep you from dealing with stress and, at worst, add significantly to your stress. Legal though it is, few would dispute the dangers of overconsumption of alcohol. Of course, it's easier, when you're feeling stressed or don't like your life the way it is, to use a drug to distract you or help you to forget about how things are. But working to improve things – to manage your stress rather than lose it in a temporary euphoria – is a lot more productive in the long term. If you use mind-altering substances to avoid issues in your life, it's time to rethink this destructive habit.

Overeating

Eating too much weighs down your body and makes you feel sluggish. Overeating at night keeps your digestive system working overtime and can disturb your quality of sleep. Eating too many simple sugars can raise your insulin levels and promote bingeing, which perpetuates the cycle of overeating. Eating too much can also lead to being overweight, and unfortunately, it has already done so in nearly half the men and a third of the women of the United Kingdom.

In many cases, eating disorders are the cause. Well-known disorders such as bulimia and anorexia nervosa, as well as lesser-known but quite common ones such as binge eating disorder, often have complex psychological as well as physical causes. Please seek help from your doctor or a counsellor if you think you or someone you care for has an eating disorder. Left untreated, both bulimia and anorexia can be fatal.

In some cases, overeating is simply a habit, encouraged by a society that is obsessed with food (and also with being thin, ironically). Eating a lot of food that tastes good can be enjoyable. Food is everywhere and often doesn't cost much. Watch television for an hour and you'll see many commercials for apparently mouth-watering food. Plus, when life is stressful, it's easy to convince yourself that you deserve that bar of chocolate or that double pepperoni pizza at midnight.

In the next chapter, you'll learn more about how to eat to maximize your stress-management potential. But for now, if overeating is one of your bad habits, you can learn to retrain yourself using the stress-management strategies for breaking bad habits at the end of this section.

Overworking

Working hard may often seem to be a necessity rather than a habit, and for some people, that's certainly the case. For others, however, overworking really is a habit. Perhaps you work to forget that you don't have a social life. Perhaps you work because you are obsessed with being promoted. Perhaps your colleagues and working life have become a surrogate family that you depend on for your sense of wellbeing – which may be OK up to a point, so long as you don't expect them to provide something that isn't going to be forthcoming.

Whatever the case, if you are in the habit of overworking and work is intruding into your life – that is, you feel you have no time to yourself, no time to just relax without thinking about work, no privacy because people from work call you at home at all hours – then overworking has become a habit. It is one, however, that you can gradually reshape.

Too Much Media

Digital cable, satellite dishes, premium movie channels, video and DVD rental shops on every high street, radio on the Internet, CD players in cars, high-speed Internet connections – ours is a technological world, and it can be pretty seductive. Some people can't resist the pleasure of watching a film on DVD on their laptop while curled in bed, or having the highest of high-end stereo equipment, or exploring the world through the Internet for hours at a time.

If you do have a media habit, you certainly aren't alone. According to statistics compiled by a group called TV Free America, 98 per cent of American households have at least one television, and 40 per cent have three or more TVs. The television is turned on in the average American home for 7 hours and 12 minutes every day, and 66 per cent of Americans eat supper while watching TV. Eighty-four per cent have at least one VCR, and 6 million videos are hired every day, compared to 3 million books from libraries. And the UK is coming up fast...

Like most things, technology and media are fine – in moderation. But also, like most things, too much of a good thing soon becomes a bad thing. If your media habit is taking up more than its fair share of your time and you are sacrificing other, equally important or more important parts of your life because of your media fixation, then it's a *bad* habit.

Consider the daily news. People rely on the news in order to be informed about world events, to hear the next day's weather forecast and to keep up with what's happening locally. But obsessive news-watching can result in a preoccupation with events far removed from your own life, anxiety about the state of the world (justified in many cases if you can actually do something about it, but not worth lying awake at night for, otherwise), even depression as a result of focusing so much on all the bad things that can happen. Unfortunately, news often focuses on tragedy. Seek balance in your media habits. Set boundaries. Don't let surfing the Internet or channel-hopping keep you from sleeping enough, eating properly or getting out of your chair and taking some exercise.

According to the UK 2000 Time Use Survey, by the Office for National Statistics, the average Briton spends 2 hours and 43 minutes watching television every day, which comes to a total of more than 42.5 days of nonstop TV each year.

The Noise Habit

The noise habit is related to the media habit. If you always have to have the television or the radio on, whether you are watching it or not, if you can't make it to work or do your homework without music or television in the background (or foreground), if you've tried to meditate but absolutely can't stand the silence, if you always fall asleep to the TV or radio or to music, then you've probably got a noise habit.

Silence can be not only therapeutic, but also remarkably energizing. Time each day for silence and stillness allows the body to recharge. There is nothing wrong with noise, but constant noise keeps your mind from focusing completely on anything and encourages your concentration to fragment. You may be able to work or do your homework in front of the television, but it will probably take you longer, and you probably won't do as good a job.

Feeling overwhelmed?
Take a vow of silence, choosing not to speak for an entire day, or just an hour. The experience can be constraining in some ways but liberating in others. Let yourself appreciate the beauty of silence, and teach yourself how to listen well. Taking a vow of silence can be a spiritual discipline, but it also happens to be an excellent technique for slowing down the thought process and focusing on the sounds of the world that aren't being made by you.

People who live alone often like to have noise in the background. Noise can temporarily mask your loneliness or nervousness. It can calm an anxious mind or distract a troubled one. Constant noise can provide a welcome relief from oneself, but if it is compromising your ability to think and perform well, if it is keeping you from confronting your stress and yourself, then it's time to make some space for silence in your life.

Too much noise is stressful for the body and the mind. Take a break and let yourself experience silence at least once a day for a minimum of 10 minutes. Don't be afraid of silence – it's a good thing.

Shopping

Some people get a fantastic high from shopping, and shopping can, indeed, become a bad habit – and even an addiction. If you head for the shops whenever you are feeling frustrated, depressed, anxious or worried about something – even not having enough money to pay the bills – and if the feeling you get from spending money really makes you feel better, you can be assured you are shopping for the wrong reasons.

We live in a consumer society, and are encouraged from many different directions to buy things. But we should only buy things for good reasons, such as because we need or really want them. Just wanting to buy 'anything at all', no matter what it is, is not a good reason to go shopping. You work hard for the money you earn. Is the effort you put in at work worth the bags of shopping you bring home, full of things that you probably won't ever wear, use, eat or look at again?

The shopping habit can be redirected, just as the overeating habit can be redirected. If you think you shop for the wrong reasons (it's a very common habit), work on finding something else that is fun to do whenever you feel the shopping impulse. How about something that doesn't cost any money? It may not feel as good at first, but once you get *out of the habit*, you'll wonder how you could possibly have spent so much money on so much rubbish. To quote a car sticker I saw the other day: 'The best things in life aren't things'.

Procrastinating

Who doesn't procrastinate once in a while? But if you can never get anything done on time or by a deadline, no matter how much preparation time you have, no matter how easy the task, then you probably have a procrastination habit. Some procrastination stems from a basic lack of organization – in the home, personal life, office or wherever – but it can equally be a habit all on its own. It doesn't matter how organized you are, you still have a mental block about getting anywhere or doing anything on time.

Procrastination is all in your head – but that means it has a lot of power! When the thought of doing something is so overwhelming that it keeps you from taking action, one way to overcome the paralysis is to meditate on the *thought itself*. Sit quietly, make yourself comfortable and focus on your dread. Whatever it is, focus on it. Immerse yourself in the dread. Then imagine enclosing the dread in a bubble. There it is, just a thought, made of nothing. Watch it float away. What's left? A thing that simply needs doing. So do it!

Chronic procrastinators sometimes despair that procrastination is an ingrained part of their personality and impossible to change. Not true! Procrastination is a habit, and it can be reshaped, just like any other habit. It will certainly take some doing – breaking any bad habit is challenging, but certainly not impossible. Just remember, you don't have to stop procrastinating all at once. Choose areas to tackle first, such as getting to work on time. How can you reorganize your morning and inspire yourself to get up in the first place? Perhaps paying bills on time will be your first target, or retraining yourself to tidy up or do the washing up before bedtime. You can do it!

The Top Bad Habits

According to *The Complete Idiot's Guide to Breaking Bad Habits*, by Suzanne LeVert and Gary McClain, PhD, the following are the top ten bad habits.

1. Lying
2. Being late
3. 'Forgetting' and other acts of carelessness
4. Knuckle-cracking
5. Belching and passing wind
6. Obsessing over tidiness
7. Being unable to make a commitment
8. Being mean with money
9. Procrastinating
10. Cigarette-smoking

How many are you guilty of? The fact that a bad habit is common doesn't mean it's OK. Let's look at some tips for curing the first three: lying, being late and 'forgetting', as well as other acts of carelessness.

1. Lying is a habit, not necessarily a character flaw. Some people find themselves bending the truth habitually, even if they don't have a good reason to do so. Do you exaggerate situations or pad out the facts so that they are just a little more dramatic? Do you say what you think people want to hear instead of what is really so? Truth-telling is a habit, too, and the best way to start is to always pause and think before you say something. Ask yourself, 'What am I about to say?' And if your answer is something other than what you know to be the truth, ask yourself, 'Is there really a good reason for bending the truth? What would happen if I simply said what is the case?' The more you become aware of your habit as you do it, the more you will be able to slowly alter it.

2. Why are you always late? Are you perpetually disorganized? Do you like the power that comes from making people wait for you? Being late is inconsiderate, even rude. It makes you look bad, and it sets a bad example for anyone who looks up to you (for example, your children). The best way to handle disorganization is to tackle problems one at a time. Let your tardiness be your first goal. Planning is the key. Start getting ready for anything you have to do about an hour early, and make sure you have everything you need well in advance. If you are late because you like to make others late, keep reading.

3. 'Forgetting' and other acts of carelessness, including being late all the time, show a blatant disregard for other people. You may have plenty of excuses: you were 'running late', you have 'too much on your plate', you 'didn't think'. But these are only excuses. The way you treat other human beings is a direct reflection on your character, but it is also something over which you have control. Take control of your behaviour and work on doing something thoughtful for someone else every day. Try to imagine yourself as the recipient of your 'careless' actions. How would you feel if a friend said that, or did this, or forgot you or failed to turn up? As with any habit, once again, awareness is the key.

Stress-Management Strategies: Reshaping Bad Habits

Knowing you need to change things can feel overwhelming, but having a variety of specific strategies helps you to set goals and work on things one step at a time. Use the following list as a guideline to help you set your goals. Try one strategy each week, and don't get frustrated. You've had that habit for a long time, and it may take a while to retrain yourself, but you can do it!

· Practise the *pause*. Know your habit, and when you are about to fall into your habitual behaviour, learn to pause, just for a moment, and think. Ask yourself these questions: will this nourish my body? Will this nourish my spirit? Is this good for me? Will I feel good about doing this later? Or will I feel guilty about it later? Is it worth the momentary pleasure? Is it *really* worth the momentary pleasure?

· Don't have habit triggers in your house. If sugar sets you off on a binge, don't keep sugary snacks around. If you can't resist shopping, don't take your credit card in your purse or wallet when you know you have to go to the shops – leave it at home, and bring as much cash as you need to make your purchase, and no more. Don't keep alcohol in the house if that's your weakness. If watching night-time television is your bad habit, remove that TV from your bedroom. Put it in the kitchen to make cleaning more interesting, or even... pack it away.

· If you use your bad habit to soothe stress, replace this habit (food, cigarettes, excessive Internet surfing) with another kind of 'treat' that is just as good or better. Make that 'treat' easily accessible in situations where you know you'll be tempted to lapse into the bad habit. For example, if you automatically turn on the television as soon as you get home from work, allow yourself 20 minutes of quiet time instead. Don't let anyone disturb you! Put on relaxing music and breathe, meditate, have some tea, read a book, peruse a magazine or just take a catnap. That 20 minutes will recharge you far more effectively than an hour of soap operas or the news could have done.

· Turn your habit into your speciality by becoming a connoisseur! Let food become a genuine pleasure. Focus on quality, not quantity. If you want food, eat a small amount of something really good. Savour every bite. Never waste your time, energy or health on large amounts of substandard food. The same goes for alcohol. Rather than drinking as much as you can of whatever is available, settle for only small amounts of the very best. Likewise shopping. Don't just buy whatever you see, collect something valuable and learn all about it. For example, make a study of old postcards, early train sets, Victorian hat pins or a particular type of porcelain – whatever strikes you as interesting.

If you love to watch television, watch only quality television. Become an expert on classic movies or independent films. Watch and learn from nature or science programmes, or ones about art or cooking – whatever appeals to you. You might even learn how to make your own films. If you can't do without music, discover more about classical music or jazz or classic rock – whatever your preference. Life's too short *not* to live it well.

Becoming a connoisseur doesn't work for every habit, of course. One can't really become a connoisseur of procrastination, for example. But a little creativity can still transform any habit into a hobby or even a speciality. If procrastination is your bad habit, become an expert on simplicity. This means that you'll have less to do (less to do late) and fewer places to go (fewer places to arrive late).

Or you can throw yourself into the reverse of your habit. A nail-biter? Learn how to do manicures and pedicures. A slob? Become an expert at organizing your household and its routines in a way that minimizes cleaning. Many self-professed slobs have reformed and created successful careers for themselves as professional organizers.

Habit Attack Chart:
Your Bad Habit Summary

It's time to pull out your stress management diary again. Copy this chart into your diary and use it to list your habits, describing what you think triggers them, and then how each habit causes you stress. For example, you might write 'nail-biting' in the first column, 'feeling nervous or bored' in the second column and 'social embarrassment, feeling unattractive, annoyance at myself' in the third column.

Even if you aren't quite ready to give up a habit – perhaps you know you are addicted to television but you aren't ready to stop watching your 12 favourite shows just yet – record the habit in the chart anyway. You can deal with it when you are ready, even if you won't be ready in the foreseeable future. At least this way you'll have all your bad habits officially identified in one place.

When you've filled out the chart with the bad habits you think are causing you the most stress, read on to find out how to manage your habits, one at a time.

HABIT	TRIGGERS	STRESS EFFECTS

HABIT	TRIGGERS	STRESS EFFECTS

Vitamins, Minerals and More

One way to help build a healthy body that is best able to combat excessive stress is to make sure you aren't suffering from any basic deficiencies in vitamins, minerals and phytochemicals (substances in plants thought to improve health and strengthen the immune system). While not everyone agrees that supplements are important, most of us don't have the opportunity to eat a completely balanced, well-rounded diet every single day. So think of supplements as an insurance policy.

FOR YOUR BEST NUTRITIONAL DEFENCE AGAINST STRESS, FOLLOW THESE GUIDELINES

- Eat a balanced diet.
- Take a multivitamin/multimineral tablet every day to strengthen your reserves and cover all your nutritional bases.
- Vitamins C, E, beta carotene (a form of vitamin A), selenium and zinc are antioxidants. Studies suggest that extra antioxidants in the diet can reduce the risk of heart attack, stroke and cataracts, and can slow the ageing process. (Note: Antioxidant supplements have been shown to increase the risk of cancer in smokers.) Antioxidants from citrus fruits, broccoli, tomatoes, leafy greens, dark orange, yellow and red vegetables, nuts, seeds and vegetable oils are always good for you.
- The B vitamins are beneficial in lots of ways. Many of them are thought to boost immunity, improve skin quality, protect against cancer, help arthritis symptoms, help the body to metabolize food and produce energy, and even help to reduce the effects of stress in the body.

· Calcium is a mineral that is essential for maintaining bone mass, preventing cancer and heart disease, reducing blood pressure, treating arthritis, promoting sleep, metabolizing iron and reducing PMS symptoms.

· Many other trace minerals keep the body healthy and working correctly, including copper, chromium, iron, iodine, selenium, vanadium and zinc.

· Amino acids and essential fatty acids are also necessary for a healthy, functioning body.

· Much is made of other so-called 'miracle' substances. There may be something to some of these claims; others may later prove false. Read about supplements if they interest you, but remember that the most important thing is to eat a healthy, balanced, varied diet.

Don't become obsessed about supplementation – if it complicates your life or stresses you to have to swallow a handful of vitamins every morning, just eat well and stick to a single multivitamin/multimineral supplement – you'll be fine.

Preventative Vitamin Regimen

Some studies indicate that an increase in certain vitamins and minerals is helpful in boosting the body's ability to heal certain maladies. An extra dose of vitamin C (500–1,000 milligrams per day) and a few zinc lozenges may help to shorten the length and lessen the severity of a cold, and many people swear by these remedies. Extra calcium has been shown to lessen the severity of PMS symptoms in women. Some studies suggest that vitamins C and E, as well as other antioxidants, can protect against certain cancers and heart disease.

The chart overleaf shows which vitamins are found in abundance in which foods. It will help you to target your stress with a nutrient attack.

Vitamin/Mineral	What It Does	Where to Find It
A	Promotes good vision Aids bone growth Aids proper cell division May help prevent certain cancers	Liver, eggs, milk Orange- and green- coloured vegetables Vitamin-enriched cereal
B_1	Maintains nervous system May protect against heart disease Helps combat anaemia	Pork Milk Eggs Whole grains
B_2	Aids metabolism Aids vision Protects against stress Promotes healthy skin	Milk, eggs Vitamin-enriched bread and cereal Leafy vegetables
B_3	Promotes a healthy nervous system May lower cholesterol Reduces blood pressure	Meat Fish Eggs Wholegrain cereals
B_5	Aids energy production Promotes healing Protects against stress Governs metabolism of fat	Eggs, yeast Brown rice Wholegrain cereals Organ meats (liver etc)

B_6	Boosts immune system
	May protect against
	  certain cancers
	Relieves PMS and
	  menopausal symptoms
		Fish
		Meat
		Milk
		Wholegrain cereals
		Vegetables

B_9 (folic acid)	Prevents certain birth defects
	May protect against
	  heart disease
	May protect against
	  certain cancers
		Leafy greens
		Wheatgerm
		Eggs
		Bananas, oranges
		Nuts

B_{12}	Maintains nervous system Boosts memory Increases energy and healthy growth May protect against certain cancers	Pork, beef Liver Fish Eggs, milk

Vitamin/Mineral	What It Does	Where to Find It

C	Boosts immune system
	May protect against
	   certain cancers
	Speeds wound healing
		Citrus fruits
		Leafy greens, broccoli
		Most fresh fruits and
		   vegetables

D	Aids in calcium absorption
	May help prevent
	   certain cancers and
	   osteoporosis
		Vitamin-enriched milk
		Oily fish
		Sunlight

E	Protects against cell
	   damage from free radicals
	May help protect against
	   certain cancers and
	   cardiovascular disease
		Vegetable oils
		Nuts
		Leafy greens
		Wheatgerm
		Mangoes

Calcium	Strengthens and
	   maintains bones
	Helps prevent osteoporosis
	   and arthritis
	Helps prevent muscle
	   cramps
		Milk
		Cheese
		Leafy greens
		Tofu
		Salmon
		Eggs

Iron	Increases energy Boosts the immune system Prevents iron deficiency anaemia	Shellfish Wheat bran Brewer's yeast
Selenium	Keeps skin and hair healthy Boosts immune system Keeps eyes healthy Improves liver May protect against certain cancers	Tuna fish Wheatgerm Bran Onions Tomatoes Broccoli

Zinc	Boosts the immune system
	May protect against
	   certain cancers
	Helps prevent and treat
	   the common cold
		Mushrooms
		Oysters
		Meat
		Whole grains
		Eggs

Herbal Remedies

Herbalism is an ancient and time-tested art that remains alive and well today. Many people take herbal remedies, from the popular echinacea for colds to more complex preparations for every imaginable ailment. A good herbalist can help you treat your health problems naturally and can offer an excellent complement to conventional medicine.

Herbal remedies come in many forms: they can be infused into water for teas, decoctions and infusions; taken as a syrup, to make herbs more palatable; prepared in alcohol for tinctures; as an oil, to rub into skin; mixed with cream, for external application; formed into tablets or put inside capsules for easy swallowing, or added to the bath.

Although many herbal remedies can be bought at a chemist or health-food shop, it is probably best to go to a qualified herbalist with a good reputation. Herbalists know about the side effects of different herbs and how they interact with other types of medication. The Complementary Healthcare Information website (see Appendix B) gives details of professional bodies for herbalists.

While many prescription medications are made from or derived from herbs, herbalists use herbal preparations to treat the whole person, not just an isolated condition. Herbalists believe in a holistic approach to medical treatment, involving the least possible intervention and trying to strengthen the body's own healing powers.

At time of writing, the market in herbal supplements is unregulated, so you can never be completely sure that the herbs you are buying are consistent in their ingredients or quality. It is best to stick to 'tried and tested' remedies if choosing them yourself, and rely on a trained herbalist for additional ones. Always check with your doctor before taking herbal supplements if you are taking or begin taking other medications, or if you have a health condition. Many herbs have side effects, and some could interact with other medications and even certain foods.

Homeopathy

Like herbalism, homeopathy is holistic, but the remedies, which can be bought in many chemists and healthfood shops, are so diluted that they are safe for anybody to use. Homeopathy is a healing therapy that works on the principle that like cures like. Herbs and other natural substances that cause certain symptoms in a healthy person are made into an extremely dilute remedy that supports and encourages the body's own healing efforts. Homeopathy is based on several basic principles: that symptoms of disease are a sign that the body is healing itself, so symptoms shouldn't be suppressed; that a substance that causes the same symptoms as those of a particular disease will, in minute amounts, negate the effects of the disease; and that symptoms will clear up in the opposite order from which they appeared.

Because the remedies are so safe, you don't have to understand the whole philosophy behind homeopathy to try it. In fact, homeopathy is an exceptionally safe way to deal with health imbalances, although it typically works more slowly than conventional medicine. Many people prefer it because it is less invasive and has fewer side effects than conventional medicine, and because it is holistic. Homeopathic remedies are effective for physical ailments such as colds, chronic problems such as arthritis or allergies, and emotional problems such as anxiety or depression. Also, homeopathic remedies, which can be made with anything from herbs and berries to roots, to minerals such as gold, to oyster shells to whole honeybees dissolved in alcohol and diluted, are typically far less expensive than prescription medications because they contain such minute amounts of the substance on which the remedy is based. Note, however, that homeopathy should not be seen as a substitute for conventional medicine.

Balancing Your Stress With Relaxation

Fortifying your body with sleep, water, nutritional supplements and holistic health care will help to put you in good condition for managing stress. But what about that active mind, those tense muscles, that parade of worries that keeps running through your head like a looped videotape?

When your body begins to experience the effects of stress, knowing how to react to combat those effects before they do too much damage is a powerful skill.

Have you heard the saying that for every action, there is an equal and opposite reaction? When stressed, the body responds by releasing stress hormones that have certain effects. When relaxed, the body experiences something very different:

- Decreased oxygen consumption
- Muscle relaxation
- Decreased metabolism
- Change in brain waves.

In his influential book *The Relaxation Response*, Herbert Benson, an American doctor, described how his research reveals that, no matter what your relaxation technique, to consciously and purposefully invoke the relaxation response through meditation, the following four basic steps are involved:

1. A quiet environment
2. Something to focus on (a sound, an object, a thought)
3. A comfortable position
4. A passive attitude.

It seems that the most important of the four for inducing a relaxed state is the passive attitude, which means not judging oneself and one's relaxation efforts or becoming too distracted. A passive attitude can be helpful in many areas of life and can be effectively invoked when you sense stress mounting. People get very stressed when they are feeling decidedly *un*-passive about something. It could be a client's condescending comment, disrespectful words from your child, finding the toothpaste cap behind the toilet *again*, doing something clumsy like spilling your coffee on your computer keyboard, breaking your grandmother's crystal glass, or backing out carelessly and denting someone's car.

At times like these, especially when they seem like the last straw after a stressful day, you can feel like exploding. You experience a surge of cortisol. Your muscles tense. Your breathing increases. A recent study suggested that these sudden cortisol surges can actually cause tiny nicks and tears in your blood vessels.

If you know you have a stressful day ahead, what can you do? Have a bowl of porridge for breakfast. Oats help to maintain a healthy nervous system, and a bowl of porridge for breakfast can help to promote a feeling of calm throughout the day. It has been demonstrated that porridge, more so than other breakfast food, including cold cereal made with oat flour, can raise an athlete's endurance level. And studies show that it can lower your cholesterol as well.

When you feel a rage, a surge of irritation, a flood of despair, a panic or a fit of yelling coming on, one way to circumvent the surge is to consciously adopt a passive attitude. You may not be able to stop and meditate – find a quiet place, focus on a mantra (a word or sound you repeat while meditating that helps clear and centre your mind, bringing a feeling of peace) – or even get comfortable, but you can adopt a passive attitude. How? Two words: *Oh well.*

These two little words are extremely powerful. Someone criticizes you? You spilled coffee on your keyboard? Oh well. Something is broken, wrecked, ruined? Oh well. Your child is insolent? Oh well.

This response may seem all wrong at first. Oh well? Won't that keep you from learning from your mistakes? Won't that encourage people to walk all over you? Certainly not. If your child is disrespectful, that doesn't mean that he or she shouldn't have to suffer the consequences, but neither does it mean you have to get all worked up about it. Besides, a serene parent issuing consequences is much more in control than a flustered parent.

If you make a mistake, do learn from it – you'll be more careful next time. But 'Oh well' means you recognize that attaching negative emotions to a mistake will cloud your thinking. If you aren't filled with rage, you'll be better able to behave and react appropriately. You'll respond calmly and politely to the client. You'll patiently clean your keyboard rather than throwing the whole computer against the wall. You'll write a sincere and heartfelt letter of apology to your grandmother – one that isn't stained with tears. You'll buy your own tube of toothpaste rather than getting irritated with your partner for leaving off the cap.

'Oh well' can become a mantra of its own, reminding you at the onset of your stress reaction to let go of the stress part of the experience. It doesn't mean you ignore the entire experience. It means you stop your body from damaging itself with a surge of unnecessary stress hormones. Unless you need to fight or flee, you're better off without that cortisol surge.

So relax and say 'Oh well'. You're balancing your stress response with the relaxation response, which is good.

Relaxation Techniques

When you do have time to work on relaxation techniques, you can choose from many. Throughout the ages, different cultures all over the world have developed their own relaxation techniques. Some involve meditation, some breathing, some specific kinds of movement. Some work quickly, others are meant to take time. Some involve more physical effort but relax the mind. Others involve mental effort but relax the body. If you learn about a variety of them, you'll be able to pick the one that suits you in any given situation. A few of these techniques are described in more detail in the following sections, and you'll find out about more in later chapters throughout this book. Many of these techniques aren't designed specifically for relaxation, but relaxation is a side effect (as is the case with yoga and certain types of meditation).

Body Scan

The body scan is a popular relaxation technique. It involves a mental scanning of the entire body in search of tension and the conscious release of that tension. You can do a body scan on your own, or you can be directed by someone speaking out loud and naming the parts of the body, in order, so that you know when to relax what. You can also record your own body scan cues onto a tape and play it back for yourself.

The body scan is an excellent way to wind down after work or to calm down before a stressful event. Practised every day, it can become a way to maintain a tension-free body and a body-aware mind.

Different people do the body scan in different ways. Some people like to tense each area of the body in turn, then fully relax it. Others prefer to visualize the release of tension, without actually contracting the muscles first. Or you can imagine breathing into and out of each body part, exhaling the tension one area at a time. You might like to try several ways to find out which one you prefer, but whichever you choose is fine.

If you would like to make your own body scan tape, you can use the following script. Record this passage out loud onto tape, or ask someone with a relaxing voice do it for you. Don't forget to pause after mentioning each body part to give yourself time to focus on relaxing and releasing tension. When the script tells you to pause, don't repeat the word *pause*, but actually pause in your reading for 5–10 seconds or more.

Lie down comfortably on your back on a firm surface. Feel your shoulders, middle back, lower back and hips settling into the floor. Relax your upper arms, lower arms, hands, thighs, calves and feet. Let your feet fall open, away from each other. Relax your neck and let your head feel heavy against the floor. Breathe deeply. [PAUSE]

Become aware of your feet. Are they relaxed? Search for tension in your feet and let it go. Release all tension and strain from your feet. Don't forget to breathe. [PAUSE]

Feel your lower legs and calf muscles, from your ankles to your knees. Are your lower legs relaxed? Search for tension in your ankle. Let it go. Search for tension in your calf muscle. Let it go. Search for tension in your shin. Let it go. Search for tension in your knee. Let it go. Release all tension and strain from your foot. Keep breathing. [PAUSE]

Now, bring your attention to your upper legs – the muscles on the fronts of your thighs, the muscles on the backs of your thighs, and your hip joints. Search for tension. Let go of the tension in the fronts of your thighs. Let go of the tension in the backs of your thighs. Breathe it away. Let your hips go, relaxing them even further into the floor. Let all the tension out of your hip joints. Breathe deeply. [PAUSE]

Feel the muscles of your lower abdomen and your buttocks. Feel how these muscles hold tension, then let that tension go. Let the muscles relax completely, releasing all strain and tightness. Breathe. [PAUSE]

Now, bring your attention to the muscles over your stomach. You probably hold these muscles in all day. Let them go. Fully relax and release your abdominal muscles. Breathe deeply, and exhale all the tension. [PAUSE]

Feel the muscles that radiate around the sides of your body and extend into your upper back. Feel your shoulder blades, ribs, chest, and upper spine relaxing. Let the tension go. Breathe out the tension. [PAUSE]

Bring your attention to your shoulders and neck. Feel all the stress and tension lingering there, making your neck and shoulder muscles tight and tense. Slowly let it all go, taking several long deep breaths. Completely relax your shoulders and your neck. [PAUSE]

Feel the muscles in your upper arms – your deltoid muscles at the top, and your biceps and triceps around your upper arms. Search out any hidden pockets of stress and tension in your upper arms and let it go. Relax your upper arms and breathe. [PAUSE]

Feel your elbow joints, the muscles of your lower arms, your wrists, your hands and each one of your fingers. Imagine a radiating circle of warmth moving down each arm and dissolving all tension from your elbows, lower arms, wrists, hands and each finger and thumb. [PAUSE]

Now, feel the muscles in your head, feel your scalp, your facial muscles, your chin, your jaw. Release the tension in your scalp, along your temples, around your ears, in your forehead, around your eyes, your cheeks, your jaw, your mouth, your chin. Let it all go. Relax. Breathe. [PAUSE]

Now, imagine a warm radiant circle of light moving slowly up your body, starting around your toes, moving to the crown of your head, then slowly moving back down again. As it moves over you, it scans for any remaining areas of stress or tension and immediately dissolves them. You feel warm, deeply relaxed and infused with a sense of wellbeing. [LONG PAUSE]

Lie still for a few more minutes, savouring the feeling of total relaxation. Then, when you are ready, very slowly roll over to one side and carefully sit up. [PAUSE]

Focusing on your peripheral vision can be deeply relaxing. The Kauna shamans of ancient Hawaii called this technique 'hakalau', which means 'to focus in and spread awareness'. To use this technique, sit comfortably and relax. Pick a spot in front of you and relax your eyes, blurring your vision just slightly. Then, without moving your eyes, focus for a few minutes on what you can see in your peripheral vision. Instant relaxation.

Breathe Away the Stress Response

One of the easiest relaxation methods is as simple as breathing in and out. In fact, it *is* breathing in and out. Many people are in the habit of shallow breathing, or chest breathing. While this allows quicker respiration and is handy for emergencies, shallow breathing doesn't reach the depths of the lungs the way deep breathing does. A few slow, purposeful, truly deep breaths can stop stress in its tracks. Deep breathing also helps to expel more air from your lungs, which is important for efficient lung functioning.

When told to breathe deeply, the tendency for many people is often to gulp in a huge amount of air with a dramatic uprising of the chest. Actually, deep breathing takes place much deeper, and it is the stomach and abdomen that should rise and fall, not the chest – and especially not the shoulders.

In addition, in deep breathing, the *exhalation is the focus*. With a truly deep exhalation, the inhalation will take care of itself.

Breathing from deep in your torso is hard to do if you aren't used to it. You used to do it naturally as an infant, but as an adult in a high-stress world, you may have forgotten how.

The easiest way to retrain yourself to breathe deeply is to begin by lying down. Lie comfortably on your back and put one hand on your abdomen and the other on your chest. Then do the steps shown on the following page.

1. Begin by breathing normally. Be conscious of your breathing, but don't try to manipulate it. Which hand is moving more, the hand on your chest or the hand on your abdomen?
2. Now, try to exhale every last bit of breath slowly, making a 'sss' sound. When you think you've exhaled every bit of breath, give your lungs one more push and let out a final 'sss' of air. As you exhale, feel the hand on your abdomen sinking in, lower and lower, as the breath empties out of the body.
3. After this deep exhalation, you'll naturally take in a deep breath, but don't try to suck in air. Just let your body take it in on its own. Don't try to suck air into your chest. Just let your body refill. As it refills, try to keep your chest and shoulders still. Be conscious of how the hand on your abdomen rises up again as breath enters the body.
4. Exhale again, slowly, as fully as possible, feeling the hand on your abdomen sinking in.
5. Repeat for 10 deep breaths.

Once you've mastered the feeling of deep breathing, you can try it sitting up. Again, focus on the exhalation. A good calming breathing exercise is to measure your breathing by silent counting, making the exhalation twice as long as the inhalation. Try this exercise when you are feeling tense (before you say or do something you'll later regret!):

1. Slowly breathe in through your nose to a slow count of five, filling your torso, from the bottom up, with air. Keep your shoulders and chest still. Instead, feel your body expanding from the abdomen and lower back.
2. Slowly breathe out through your mouth, lips pursed, making an airy, whispering 'whhhhhh' sound, to a slow count of ten. Keep your shoulders and chest still. Feel your body deflating from the abdomen and lower back.
3. Repeat several times, or until you feel calm.

You'll read more about breathing as a meditation in Chapter 8. In the meantime, let your breath work for you as the ultimate no-frills, any-time, any-place relaxation tool.

Imagery Power

For instant relaxation, imagery can also work well. Imagery is simple and fun. If you feeling stressed, anxious or hopeless, go on holiday. Don't leave your desk and head for the airport, but simply close your eyes, relax, breathe and use your imagination to visualize the place you would most like to be.

Do you remember your imagination? When you were a child, it was that thing that allowed you to fly like a bird, stamp like an elephant, bark like a dog, save the world from disaster, go on safari, jump from an aeroplane with a parachute and visit a land made entirely from chocolate, all in one day.

Your imagination is still there, even if it's now a little rusty from disuse. Now is the time to use it in the service of stress management. You might not decide to imagine that you are a superhero (then again, you might, and why not?), but why not imagine wandering down a secluded beach at sunset, the balmy tropical winds rippling the turquoise sea? Perhaps you would prefer to be cuddling up in front of the fire with someone special (even if you haven't met him or her yet) in a cosy cottage in the country? Perhaps images of the Far East, the rainforest, or hiking up a glacier in the Alps create a sense of peace for you. Perhaps you like the desert... or would prefer a really extravagant dessert! (There's nothing wrong with visualizing a land made entirely out of chocolate, after all.)

Let yourself daydream a little. Consider it personal time – time to recharge. It's fun, it's legal and it's also an excellent way to manage stress. After all, that's what holidays are for!

CHAPTER 7

Get Strong, Get Healthy

I f you've ever tried to lose weight, you will have heard the mantra, 'Eat less, exercise more'. The same prescription can help to decrease the effects of stress in your life. You should eat moderate amounts of food high in vitamins, minerals, complex carbo-hydrates, low-fat proteins and fibre, and decrease your intake of highly processed food and food that is high in sugar and fat. Exercise builds muscle, increases lung capacity, improves cardiovascular function and triggers the release of chemicals that counteract the effects of stress.

Don't set yourself up for an energy crash by breakfasting on sugary things such as Danish pastries, or sugar-loaded breakfast cereal. Complex carbohydrates and a little protein will keep your blood glucose levels steady and your energy steady, too. Wholemeal toast with low-fat spread, a bowl of porridge with a sprinkling of nuts or dried fruit, scrambled eggs on wholemeal toast, and good-quality muesli with no added sugar are all good choices.

Move It or Lose It!

Exercise may be one of the best stress-management tools we have, yet it's often the first thing to suffer when we get too busy. Because there is no sense of urgency associated with daily exercise, it's easy to put it at the bottom of the priority list.

Or should there be a sense of urgency? According to studies, despite the growth in the number of gyms and fitness centres in the last 20 years, still far too many adults do not get even a moderate amount of exercise – enough to achieve health benefits. Many researchers believe that poor health habits – most essentially, lack of exercise, poor diet and smoking – are responsible for a significant proportion of deaths from heart disease and cancer. Are we in fact fast approaching a 'deadline' because we have not established good health habits? Perhaps it would be wise to move the deadline forward so that we *don't* lose it.

But this book is primarily about stress, and only peripherally about disease prevention. Moderate exercise, according to an increasing number of experts, may be the single most effective way to get stress under control. Are we sabotaging our stress-management efforts because we think we're too busy to get up and go for a walk? We certainly do not help our bodies deal with the effects of stress if we persist in leading a sedentary life. Why?

We know that stress evokes the 'fight or flight' reaction by releasing into the body stress hormones designed to give us sudden, quick reactions, extra strength, and endurance. When we don't act on the stress response by moving quickly, using our strength or taking advantage of the added endurance, we have a body that is ready for action, but with no outlet for its energy. Muscles stay tense, blood pressure stays high, breathing stays shallow and cortisol and adrenaline course through the body, causing all kinds of problems.

To boost your energy when you just can't seem to get up and exercise, take a shower. A shower can be an in-home hydrotherapy centre. Start with body-temperature water for three minutes, focusing the shower stream on your major muscle groups. Then increase the cold water and stand for 30 seconds under the cooler stream. Jump out and get going! The stimulation of the water on your skin and the cool temperature at the end will kickstart your mind and improve your circulation, helping you to feel awake, alert and ready to move.

Exercise changes the picture, accomplishing two important things in the wake of the stress response:

1. Exercise allows the body to expend energy. Although your brisk walk around the block may not actually be 'fight or flight', to the body, the message is the same. The extra energy available to your body is being used, telling it that after exercise, it can return to its original state of equilibrium.
2. Exercise also releases chemicals such as beta endorphins, which specifically counteract the effects of stress hormones. They let the body know that the danger has passed and the relaxation response can begin.

In other words, exercise allows the 'fight or flight' stress response to run its natural course. It lets your body respond in the way it needs to respond. Rather than sitting and fuming (what caveperson ever did that in the face of a charging predator?), you get up and move. 'Ahh...' the body responds, 'ahh, this is what I want to do!'

But you do actually have to get up and take the exercise. While not meaning to demean them, our prehistoric ancestors didn't have much choice – it was a case of move or die – but we have plenty of choice. We can manage very well most of the time without moving very much at all. We might move from room to room in the house, or from house to car to office to car to house, but that's relatively insignificant compared to the kind of hardworking, on-the-move everyday kind of existence humans once knew.

Getting enough exercise is certainly possible, however, in modern life. Resources are widely available, making exercise easy to accomplish for those who really want to accomplish it. For some people, exercise is already a good habit, or a priority to keep energy high and weight under control. For others, exercising is akin to having root canal work: they don't like it, they don't want to do it, and they see absolutely no reason to break into a sweat.

Most of us are probably somewhere in between. We know exercise is good for us, and perhaps we do it occasionally – when we're in the mood or time permits. The trouble with this is that exercising in fits and starts isn't enough to achieve long-term stress management or decrease the risk of developing chronic illness.

How do you make exercising a regular habit? The secret is to find an exercise plan you can stick to. Since you aren't compelled, you need to be motivated. When life is busy and full, forcing yourself to spend 30 minutes a day doing something you hate when nobody is *making* you do it... well, it's not going to happen.

However, even if you are a die-hard exercise-hater, there will still be something that suits you. Perhaps your concept of exercise is an aerobics class and you can't bear the idea of standing in the middle of all those young, fit, barely-20-year-olds. Perhaps you are one of those 20-year-olds, but you can't seem to master the aerobic footwork. Or perhaps you think exercise is jogging, or team sports, or calisthenics, and you'd rather eat worms than become involved.

Whatever your preconception, fear not. Exercise is a broad term, and anyone can find some kind of activity they actually enjoy. Perhaps joining a gym is the answer for you – all the classes, all the equipment, the sauna and spa to relax you afterwards, and in some cases child care! Perhaps you need something more tranquil than high-impact aerobics, and you'll find inspiration in a yoga class. Perhaps you just need to get out for a walk in the fresh air. What could be easier?

Even if you find something you can only, at best, tolerate, try it for a while. At the same time, expand your fitness horizons and keep an open mind. Try one form of exercise, then another, then another. You'll accumulate a lot more hours' exercise than if you just reject the prospect altogether. Once you begin to experience the stress-relieving benefits of regular exercise, the trip to the gym or the yoga class may seem a lot more attractive, even an essential part of your day. You may even learn to actually enjoy it.

In recent years, there has been an increasing interest in strengthening the core muscles through targeted weight machines, yoga and Pilates exercises (I'll discuss the benefits of yoga and Pilates a little later in this chapter). Strengthening the core muscles means building the abdomen, lower back and the other supporting muscles in the body's 'core'. These exercises do more than help hold in your tummy. Core muscles, when strong and supple, lend grace, lightness and control to the entire body. Ask any ballet dancer about the importance of a super-strong torso.

Quiz: Your Exercise Profile

Are you exercising enough? Are you exercising too much? Are you doing the right kind of exercise to relieve your stress? The following quiz will show you what the best exercise routine is for you:

1. Which of the following best describes your opinion of exercise?

    A. Love it, love it, love it! Couldn't do without it!
    B. Sometimes it's fun, and sometimes it's just tolerable, depending on my mood.
    C. It's a necessary evil.
    D. It's something other people do.

2. After exercise, how do you typically feel?

   A. Exhausted but satisfied
   B. Grumpy and irritable
   C. Euphoric
   D. Relieved that it's over

3. How often do you exercise each week?

   A. Once or less per week
   B. Two or three times a week for 15–30 minutes
   C. Daily for an hour or more
   D. On most days for 30–60 minutes

4. If you miss your regular exercise routine, how do you feel?

   A. Panic-stricken
   B. As if I've been let off the hook
   C. Inconvenienced, but I'll make up for it later
   D. What regular exercise routine?

5. Which of the following is most likely to keep you from exercising?

   A. Nothing
   B. Boredom with the exercise routine
   C. Stress
   D. Lack of energy and motivation

You may be addicted to exercise if you identify with the following:

- You absolutely *have* to exercise every day, even if you are ill or injured.
- You often exercise for longer than two hours.
- You have given up other activities you enjoy for exercise.
- You work out twice as long the day after a missed workout.
- You feel intense guilt and anxiety if you miss a workout.
- You suffer from a lot of exercise-related injuries.

Give yourself points as follows:

1. A: 1, B: 2, C: 3, D: 4
2. A: 2, B: 4, C: 1, D: 3
3. A: 4, B: 3, C: 1, D: 2
4. A: 1, B: 3, C: 2, D: 4
5. A: 1, B: 3, C: 2, D: 4

If you scored between **5** and **8** points, you are super-motivated to exercise, and that's great... unless you have become so dependent on it that you get stressed if you miss an occasional workout, or unless you have become addicted to exercise. If you are exercising too much, or if your exercise routine is controlling you rather than the other way around, it's time to ease off a bit and seek balance by developing other areas of your life that promote health. For example, perhaps you could concentrate more on eating a nutritious diet, drinking plenty of water, getting sufficient sleep and enjoying spiritual renewal through meditation and relaxation. Make sure you find time to spend with the people you care for, too, and every now and then, see if you can relax and do absolutely nothing at all.

If you scored between **9** and **12** points, you have probably established exercise as an integral part of your routine and are already reaping the benefits. Remember to stay flexible, vary your routine and maintain balance in the other areas of your life, too. Congratulate yourself for having been able to master this most effective stress-relieving technique. If stress does interfere with your regular routine, simply substitute something easier and more relaxing, such as taking a slower walk or following an easy yoga routine.

If you scored between **13** and **16** points, you know exercise is good for you and manage most of the time, but you aren't always happy about it. You may need to try a different form of exercise to keep yourself motivated. Consider your likes and dislikes and try to match them with something that will inspire you, such as a state-of-the-art new exercise machine at the gym or a trek in the wilds.

If you scored between **17** and **20** points, you either simply don't like exercise, or you just can't find the time to fit it in. Whether you are worried that you don't know how to go about exercise , or exhausted from too much stress and a too-hectic lifestyle, you are letting the most effective stress-relieving technique there is pass you by. Try starting slowly and building up your exercise routine at a comfortable pace – exercise shouldn't be painful or unpleasant. The more regular your exercise becomes, the more you'll be able to see it working its magic in your life.

The Whole-Body Effects of Exercise

You know that exercise is good for you – you feel better after you do it, so it has to be good. But exactly what effect does it have, and how does it help to relieve stress? Exercise benefits the body in very specific ways. Here are some of the benefits of moderate exercise:

- Stronger muscles
- Better flexibility
- Increased heart and lung efficiency
- Decreased risk of developing heart disease
- Decreased risk of developing lung disease
- Improved overall circulation
- Reduced cholesterol levels
- Reduced blood pressure
- Strengthened immune system
- Decrease in excess body fat
- Increased energy
- Decreased symptoms of depression
- Decreased symptoms of arthritis
- Decreased risk of diabetes and decreased risk of complications from diabetes
- Decreased risk of osteoporosis and decreased risk of complications from osteoporosis
- Improved quality of sleep and decrease in insomnia
- Increased mental acuity
- Improved posture
- Improved self-image
- Decreased frequency of injuries in daily life

- Decreased effects of stress
- Improved ability to manage stress.

Not only does exercise help the body to deal with the physical effects of stress, it also helps the mind feel more in control and able to manage stress. Add to that the positive effect exercise has on so many other disorders, and its ability to help prevent so many physical problems, and you've got a stress-management tool that is both preventative and proactive.

If you need variety in your exercise routine, vary your workouts (sometimes called cross training) to keep yourself interested and motivated. Walk one day, go to the gym the next, play tennis the day after that. At the weekend, drive somewhere interesting and take a long walk in uncharted territory. You might even forget to call it exercise!

Finding a Movement Plan You Can Live With

So many types of exercise, so little time! Not every type of exercise in the following sections will appeal to you, but perhaps you will be inspired by some new ideas. Below are brief descriptions of some of the more common forms of exercise. Don't be afraid to try something new, especially if you feel you are in an exercise rut or need inspiration to get started in the first pace.

If you are very overweight, have a specific health problem or haven't exercised in the last six months, please consult a GP before beginning any exercise programme.

Walking

Walking is fantastic. It's easy, costs nothing, gets you out in the fresh air, and can provide an opportunity for socializing with friends while you all get fit together. Walk at a brisk pace for 30–60 minutes at least three times a week, and preferably five or six times a week.

According to research in the USA, between 1975 and 1995 walking declined among American adults by 42 per cent. Some blame urban sprawl or suburbs in which walking is unsafe and/or impractical, and the connection between urban sprawl and the 60 per cent increase in obesity in adult Americans in the past decade is currently being studied.

Swimming

Swimming is ideal for people who love the water, those with joint or orthopaedic problems, and anyone who has a lot of weight to lose. The water buoys the body so that joints, bones and muscles don't feel any impact, making injuries less likely for people who are vulnerable to the impact. Work up gradually to 30–60 minutes of steady swimming. Varying your strokes – crawl, breaststroke, backstroke, sidestroke – will help work all your muscles.

Water aerobics is very popular, lots of fun, and can be tailored to any fitness level. Check with your local pool or health club for water aerobics classes. Water yoga classes are available at some pools.

Join a Gym

For some people, joining a gym is the inspiration they need. A gym provides fellowship, a wide range of fitness possibilities from aerobics classes (step aerobics, kickboxing, and many other types of aerobics are offered these days) to yoga to squash or badminton to swimming to weightlifting to the latest in exercise machines, from high-tech treadmills to no-impact elliptical trainers. In many clubs, you will also find personal trainers, nutritionists, sports leagues and creches, as well as other amenities such as massage therapists, saunas, steam rooms and snack bars filled with healthy fare.

Also, having paid for membership, you might be more inspired to get your money's worth. Going to the gym can be a mini-break, a special treat, something you look forward to every day.

A recent study showed that 30 minutes of brisk exercise three times per week was just as effective as drug therapy in relieving the symptoms of major depression. A follow-up study revealed that only 8 per cent of the study's exercise group experienced a depression relapse, while 38 per cent of the drug-only group and 31 per cent of the exercise-plus-drugs group experienced a depression relapse.

Yoga

Yoga originated in India and is designed to 'yoke' body and mind. It involves specific postures, breathing exercises and meditation. Hatha yoga, one of the most popular types in the West, consists primarily of the postures and breathing exercises.

Yoga is an excellent fitness activity on its own, and because it increases strength, flexibility, circulation, posture, and overall body condition, it is the perfect complement to other fitness activities. Yoga is great both for people who have difficulty in slowing down (you'll discover how good it feels, and how important it is, to move your body with slow control) and for people who may find it particularly difficult to participate in high-impact or fast-paced exercise (yoga is adaptable to all fitness levels and is decidedly low-impact).

Yoga is one of the best forms of stress-management exercise. Its original purpose was to gain control over the body and bring it into a state of balance so that the mind was free for spiritual contemplation. Yoga can help you to master your body rather than it mastering you.

Pilates

Pilates is an increasingly popular and very effective core-strengthening routine that uses either special machinery or a simple mat. Pilates concentrates on strengthening and gaining control over the body's core muscles, or the torso, especially the abdominal and back muscles. Many fitness centres and private individuals offer Pilates classes. The exercises are based partly on yoga, partly on gymnastics and partly on ballet.

Because Pilates is so popular, instruction is widely available, and there are books on the subject as well, but the best place to start is with a qualified Pilates instructor, to make sure you get the exercises right. Many Pilates exercises are advanced, and doing them incorrectly could cause injury, so be wary of trying to teach them to yourself in the first instance. Once learned from an expert, however, Pilates can easily be practised at home on your own.

Tai Chi/Qigong

Tai chi and its precursor, Qigong, are ancient Chinese Taoist martial arts forms that have evolved to fit into the 21st century. Rarely used today as a method of defence, tai chi consists of a series of slow, graceful movements in concert with breathing. This is designed to free internal energy and keep it flowing through the body, uniting body and mind, and promoting good health and relaxation. Tai chi is sometimes called a moving meditation. Qigong involves specific movements and postures as well as other health-maintenance procedures such as massage and meditation to maintain and improve overall health and balance the body's internal energy, or 'chi'.

While today's average life expectancy is in the mid- to upper 70s, the longest a human has ever lived, according to authentic documentation, is over 120 years. In 1997, Jeanne Calment of Arles in France died of natural causes at the age of 122, leading some scientists who study longevity to speculate that under the right conditions, many more humans could feasibly live to 120 or beyond.

The Great Outdoors

If you feel particularly inspired by wonderful views, fresh air and the lovely and varied smells of the natural world, choosing an outdoor form of exercise can inspire you to keep up the habit. Whether you walk, jog, run, cycle, rollerblade, cross-country ski, go hill-walking or climb mountains, exercising outdoors is good for your body and soul. Even rain and snow don't have to stop you. Exercising outside, even for just a short while each day, helps to keep you in touch with the natural world, which helps to put things in perspective – and that all on its own can relieve a lot of stress!

Dance

Whether you take an organized class – ballet, jazz, tap, ballroom dancing, swing dancing, country dancing, square dancing, Irish dancing, to name but a few – or go out dancing with your friends at the weekend, dancing is great cardiovascular exercise and also a lot of fun. Something about music makes exercise seem less like exercise, and dancing, especially for fun, even alone in your house with the music turned up, is about as 'unexercise-like' as you can get, but with all the benefits. Vigorous dancing is an excellent way to relieve tension and anxiety, so get up and hit the dancefloor!

Team Sports

For people who like to play on a team and are motivated and energized by the energy of others, team sports can be an excellent way to get exercise and a social life at the same time. Weekend rugby or football games, tennis, squash or badminton tournaments, organized or impromptu basketball games, volleyball on the beach or whatever else is available in your area and interests you can be so much fun that you'll forget you're exercising!

Variety Is the Spice of Exercise

No matter what type or types of exercise you choose, you'll work a wider range of muscles and reap a wider range of benefits if you have variety. Perhaps try a different kind of exercise once a week.

Varying your pace can also add up to increased health benefits. Author and exercise physiologist Greg Landry, MSc, suggests interval training, a simple way to vary any exercise you're already doing. Interval training involves warming up for five minutes, exercising at your regular pace for four minutes, then stepping up the pace for one minute. Then, for the rest of the workout, work four minutes at a regular pace, then one minute at a fast pace, and so on. Interval training can help you to break past a weight loss plateau, help you to get fit faster, increase your energy and your body's rate of calorie burning by raising your base metabolism rate, and keep your workout more interesting. Changing pace every five minutes may also help to keep you more focused on your workout, too, which is a welcome break for your busy brain.

Weightlifting

Weightlifting isn't exactly aerobic activity, but it's an important part of any fitness routine. Lifting weights is beneficial for any adult. It builds bone mass and can reverse osteoporosis. It increases muscle tone and helps your body to burn more calories – this is because the more muscle you have, the more calories you burn during the aerobic portion of your workout. Stronger muscles mean that everyday activities, from carrying shopping bags and small children to taking a box of office supplies into the stationery store, are easier. Apart from feeling better, your posture will improve and your body will look firmer and shapelier.

When your day has been more stressful than usual, don't exercise beyond your limit. Take a long walk in the fresh air, practise yoga or tai chi, or go on a leisurely bike ride. Let your workout be gentle and meditative. Even if you know you need to get in shape, don't worry about it. When your severe stress is under control, you can step up the pace.

Lift weights either no more often than every other day, or every day, but alternating which muscles you work. To establish a routine that meets your needs, talk to a health club trainer, consult a good book on weight-lifting that addresses your personal goals (toning or building), or subscribe to one of the specialist magazine that keeps up with the latest news and research on weightlifting and includes different routines with detailed explanations of technique and benefits.

At about the age of 35, people start to lose bone mass, and with that loss of bone mass comes a greater susceptibility to fractures. Weightlifting can counteract bone loss. It's never too late to start – as soon as you begin a regular programme of weightlifting, your bones start getting stronger. What an easy way to ward off a broken bone!

Massage Therapy

When you are starting to get into the exercise habit, your muscles might feel a bit sore. While you shouldn't push yourself to the point of pain, movement and effort often result in sore muscles, aching joints and injuries such as strained ligaments and pulled tendons.

Massage therapists are trained to knead and manipulate the muscles and connective tissue in the body to help it find its equilibrium after exercise. Regular massage is beneficial, even for non-exercisers. It stimulates muscles and skin, improving circulation and organ function.

Massage is an excellent stress-management tool. It helps your body and mind to relax as it encourages the body to heal itself. Massage can give you a feeling of control and mastery over your body as it responds to the effects of targeted massage. Pain may disappear completely. Posture may improve. Muscles and joints may begin to work better and more easily.

Massage also feels great and shouldn't be regarded as an occasional indulgence. Consider regular massage as a serious stress-management tool – it can equal mental and physical maintenance.

Your GP may be able to refer you to a professional massage therapist, and in some cases therapies such as massage and even acupuncture are available on the NHS. If you are interested in less mainstream types of massage therapy such as reflexology, acupressure or Reiki, talk to anyone you know who has had such treatment, a yoga teacher or perhaps the employees at your local healthfood shop for recommendations. Some areas have directories of natural health-care providers.

Overleaf are some of the common types of massage.

Swedish Massage

This common form of massage involves the practitioner applying oil to the body and using certain types of massage strokes – namely, *effleurage* (gliding), *petrissage* (kneading), *friction* (rubbing) and *tapotement* (tapping) – to increase circulation in the muscles and connective tissue, help the body to flush out waste products, and heal injuries. Swedish massage induces a feeling of deep relaxation and increases the body's range of motion. Some Swedish massage practitioners also use hydrotherapy, or massage through soaking, steaming, or applying jets of water to the body.

Shiatsu and Acupressure

Shiatsu is the Japanese word for 'finger pressure' and is sometimes known as acupressure. It is an ancient form of massage, still widely practised, that involves the application of pressure through fingers, palms, elbows or knees to certain pressure points in the body. These pressure points are found along the energy meridians defined within the body by Japanese and other Asian cultures. Pressure on these points is thought to release energy blockages that cause pain and disease, resulting in balance, equilibrium and greater physical health. Acupuncture is based on the same principle, but uses very fine needles inserted painlessly into the pressure points. Although the idea may sound strange to a Westerner, research supports the effectiveness of both acupuncture and acupressure in the relief of pain and the treatment of certain disorders.

Reflexology

Reflexology is a little like acupressure, but here all the pressure points are in the hands and feet. According to the theory, the entire body, including all the parts, organs and glands, is represented in a 'map' on the hands and feet, and pressure applied to the right area of the map will help to balance the problem in the associated area of the body. Once you know the map, you can work on yourself by massaging your own hands or feet in the appropriate area.

You can perform reflexology on yourself — try this to start. To stimulate your brain when you really need to think clearly, hold up one thumb, then squeeze the tip with the thumb and index finger of your opposite hand. Squeeze in the middle of your thumb's tip, then make little squeezes in seven slow circles around the tip of your thumb, never fully releasing pressure. Repeat on your other thumb.

Reiki

Reiki (pronounced RAY-KEY) is an energy healing technique based in ancient Tibetan practices. Practitioners of Reiki put their hands on, or just above, the body in order to balance energy by acting as a sort of conduit for life force energy. Reiki is used to treat physical problems as well as emotional and psychological ones, and is, more positively, also used as a tool for supporting and facilitating positive changes. Becoming a Reiki practitioner is a complex and also somewhat mysterious process. Advanced Reiki practitioners are even thought to be able to perform long-distance healing.

Rolfing

Rolfing is a type of deep massage designed to restructure the body's muscles and connective tissue to promote better alignment. If you like your massages hard, this is for you. Some people claim that the deep tissue massage actually releases deeply buried emotions, and that emotional outbursts are common during the course of a 10-session treatment.

Alexander Technique

The Alexander technique is less massage than movement instruction. Clients are taught to hold and move their bodies with full consciousness and in a way that releases tension and uses the body to its best advantage. People say that practising the Alexander technique makes them feel lighter, easier and more in control of their bodies. The Alexander technique is popular with actors, musicians and other performing artists.

Applied Kinesiology

This is a muscle-testing technique that helps people to determine where they are experiencing an imbalance or problem in the body. Following the diagnosis, massage, in addition to movement of certain joints, acupressure, and advice on diet, vitamins and herbs is then offered as treatment. Applied kinesiology is practised by some health care professionals such as doctors, osteopaths, chiropractors or dentists who are trained and licensed to diagnose illness.

Most complementary health practitioners are well-qualified, experienced, competent and trustworthy. Because the industry is still largely unregulated, however, do be careful when choosing a practitioner of an alternative or complementary therapy. Try to get recommendations from friends, and do ask about qualifications and experience.

Polarity Therapy

Polarity therapy is a little like Reiki, in that it is designed to free and balance the body's internal energy, but it is more of a combination of Eastern and Western approaches. It includes massage, dietary advice, certain yoga exercises and psychological counselling for a full mind–body approach to energy balancing.

Self-Massage

If you learn about acupressure, Swedish massage, reflexology or some of the many other techniques, you can perform massage on yourself. You can massage your own neck, scalp, face, hands, feet, legs, arms and torso. Many yoga positions also result in internal and external massage – by bending the body in certain ways against itself, or by using the pressure of the floor against certain parts of the body, massage takes place.

Fuelling Up: The Stress Connection

If you're going to exercise (or even if you aren't), you have to eat. But what will you choose to eat? Many Westerners are notorious for making less than ideal dietary choices, and statistics reveal that nearly half the men and a third of the women in the UK are overweight. But whether or not you are cursed with a sweet tooth or a penchant for pepperoni pizza with extra cheese, stress can make you less likely to keep compulsive eating under control.

What's worse, stress-related eating may be particularly dangerous to your health. Recent research has revealed that there is a difference between 'regular fat' and 'stress fat'. Stress fat is not the lumpy, wobbly stuff that jiggles about on your thighs, belly and upper arms, it is the fat that accumulates deep inside the body, specifically around the internal organs of your torso, and is the only fat that is known to contribute to heart disease, cancer and diabetes.

This dangerous fat is called stress fat because research shows that compulsive eating related to stress is more likely to result in fat accumulation around the internal organs.

Other studies suggest that cortisol, a powerful appetite stimulant that can trigger excessive eating in the more stressed among us, actually *encourages* the body to accumulate fat in the abdominal region, especially in 'apple-shaped' people – those who tend to gain weight around the middle rather than in the buttocks and legs.

Stress-related eating is the beginning of a vicious cycle. You feel stressed, so you eat foods that are likely to increase your susceptibility to stress. Consequently, you feel more stressed and eat more of those same stress-promoting foods. How do you stop the madness and regain the equilibrium that your body deserves?

Knowledge is power, and although knowledge may not equal *will*power, it is the first step. Certain foods are known to have a disruptive effect on the body's equilibrium, while other foods are known to have a more balancing effect. Many cultures have discovered this food/body connection. Ayurveda, an ancient system of health maintenance and improvement from India that is still popular today, focuses on balancing the body through food as well as other practices.

(I'll tell you more about Ayurveda in Chapter 9.) Much contemporary research also emphasizes the importance of the link between good health, balance, energy and the food we eat.

If you can't see stress fat, how do you know you have it?
Lie on your back on the floor and look at your abdomen. If it protrudes above your hip bones while you are lying down — that is, stays inflated, in the shape of a pregnant belly or a beer belly even when you're on your back — that protrusion is caused by stress fat. The fat deep in your belly is pushing up the outer, visible fat. This fat can seriously damage your health. Isn't it time to start doing something about it?

Diet of the Week

It's easy to find fad diets that promise miraculous results, and it's equally easy to find people to proclaim how this or that diet was the only thing that worked for them. Many of these diets are controversial. Some people swear by the diet that suggests that those with specific blood types should focus on specific foods. Others are devoted to the low-carbohydrate diets, such as the Zone Diet, the Atkins Diet, the Protein Power diet and the Carbohydrate Addict's diet. Some people choose a vegetarian or vegan (no animal products at all including dairy and eggs) diet. There are countless others.

Perhaps one of these diets will work for you. They all make interesting points and include healthy eating plans (not everybody agrees they are all healthy, but then again, not everybody agrees on anything).

The blood-type diet is low in calories and high in natural, minimally processed foods. The low-carb diets make a good point: refined carbohydrates tend to cause surges in insulin, and in some people, insulin fluctuations seem to cause food binges and unusual weight gain. For the last few decades, the common wisdom has been 'carbs, carbs and more carbs'. Now the low-carb diets suggest that we need to get more protein back into our lives, and for some people this is the answer to carbohydrate binges and can put a stop to unusual weight gain.

Vegetarian and vegan diets have merit, too. Animal products have been associated with an increased risk of certain diseases, and many available animal products, from rich cheeses to fat-marbled meats to processed meat products such as hamburgers and cured meats, are high in saturated fat, calories and, particularly in the case of cured meats, salt and preservatives, some of which are known carcinogens. Vegetarians eat more vegetables, fruit, whole grains, beans, nuts and seeds, and other healthy, unprocessed foods. That's certainly an improvement over lunch at a fast-food outlet (although more fast-food restaurants are serving healthier fare, by popular demand).

But if all the diets out there baffle you, you can feel comforted. They all boil down to a few simple rules which, when applied, will help just about anybody to reach and maintain a healthy weight, feel energized and manage stress from a dietary perspective:

· Whenever possible, eat food as close to its natural state as you can. Eat an orange instead of drinking orange juice, but drink orange juice instead of orange squash. Eat a grilled free-range organic chicken breast instead of a minced, shaped, breaded, fried chicken nugget. Choose brown rice over white, traditional porridge over instant flavoured oatmeal, but instant oatmeal over a sugary breakfast cereal. Eat wholemeal bread or, better, sprouted wheat bread instead of plain white bread, and spread it with a natural, organic topping.

· Choose nutrient-dense foods instead of foods that are mostly empty calories. For example, dried fruit is more nutrient-dense than chocolate, pieces of raw broccoli and carrot with yogurt dip are more nutrient-dense than crisps or salty snacks, and freshly squeezed fruit or vegetable juice is more nutrient-dense than a fizzy drink. Less nutrient-dense food can be useful to help fill you up if it is low in calories and you are trying to lose weight (popcorn, for example, can help stave off hunger pangs, if it isn't covered in butter).

· Start and end the day with protein and complex carbohydrates rather than simple carbohydrates such as sugar.

· Eat a hearty breakfast, a moderate lunch and a light supper, or if you aren't a breakfast person, a light breakfast, a hearty lunch and a light supper.

Foods that exacerbate the negative effects of stress on the body are those that are high in the following:

Sugar	Fat, especially saturated fat
Caffeine	Calories
Salt	

Foods that help to ease the negative effects of stress on the body include the following:

- Vegetables, especially organic
- Fruit, especially organic
- Low-fat, organic or free-range protein sources such as fish, chicken, turkey, lean red meat, soya products such as tofu and soya milk, low-fat dairy products and legumes
- Monounsaturated sources of fat such as olive oil and sunflower oil
- Complex carbohydrates such as whole grain breads, pastas and cereals

· Stop before you feel full, and don't eat more calories than you need.
· Don't let more than about 30 per cent of your calories come from fat, and try to eat fat mostly from sources that contain a high proportion of monounsaturated fat (olive oil, sunflower oil, avocados, walnuts and walnut oil) and omega-3 fatty acids (in fatty fish like salmon and tuna), rather than saturated fat (meat and dairy products), trans-fatty acids (in margarine, lard, butter and partially hydrogenated oils), and polyunsaturated fats (prevalent in many vegetable oils).

Rethinking the 'Treat'

Some people eat sensibly most of the time, but can't get around the notion that on special occasions or when they've had a hard day (and lately, most of them have seemed pretty hard), they deserve a treat. If you are one of those people, you can rethink the 'treat' concept.

It is so easy to eat in response to stress – many people do it. After all, don't you deserve a treat?

Of course you do, but a treat doesn't have to be in the form of food. A treat could be a film, a day out, a full hour of doing nothing, a visit to the hairdresser, a game of golf in the middle of the afternoon on a Wednesday, allowing yourself to go to bed at 9:00 PM. There is plenty that is wonderful, fun and rewarding in life that has nothing to do with food, so get into the habit of thinking creatively about how to reward yourself.

Bingeing on any food, no matter how wholesome the food itself, contributes to physical stress because the body isn't designed to process large amounts of food all at once.

If you positively *have* to reward yourself with food, make it absolutely worth the indulgence. A small amount of something superb is a far more rewarding and sensual experience than a whole, huge excessive amount of low-quality anything. A single piece of the highest-quality imported chocolate, a sliver of cake and a tiny cup of espresso from the best patisserie or coffee shop in town, a small but perfect filet mignon wrapped in the best bacon, or whatever your indulgence – savour every single bite you take, and don't do anything else while enjoying it.

If the television is off, the answering machine is on, no one is talking to you, you aren't reading the newspaper – you are simply experiencing your treat – then that tiny bit will be plenty. You'll feel supremely satisfied, and so elegant, too!

Your Personal Eating Plan

If you need to change your ways, how will you go about it? Like anything else, do it one step at a time. It may sound tedious, but if you get into the habit of keeping a food diary in which you write down every single thing you eat each day, and how you were feeling when you ate it, you'll be surprised at how obvious your bad habits are. You might notice that when you are feeling stressed or insecure, you eat sugar, and that when you are feeling calm or confident, you eat really well. Keep at it until you feel in control of your eating habits. If you start to slip again, simply go back to keeping your diary.

Opposite is a sample food diary. Notice that food choices seem directly connected with mood. Yours may not be this obvious to start with, but you'll probably see patterns after keeping the diary for a while.

DATE: *October 23rd*

TIME	WHAT I ATE	HOW I FELT	COMMENTS
7:00 a.m.	Two slices of wheat toast with butter 1 glass orange juice 1 apple	Tired but in a good mood	This was a good breakfast.
10:15 a.m.	Four handfuls of M&Ms	Insecure and vulnerable	Jenny just told me I made a mess of that report.
12:00 noon	Large plate of pasta with meat sauce and cheese Large salad with blue cheese dressing Three bread rolls	Anxious and stressed out	I can't get over my mistake. How could I have done that? I hope everyone doesn't think I'm incompetent!
3:35 p.m.	Four more handfuls of M&Ms	Depressed	I'm thinking of leaving.
6:45 p.m.	Stir-fry with prawns and lots of vegetables Brown rice	Happy and energized	Jenny told me not to worry about the mistake and said I'm doing a great job.

Below is a sample food template for you to copy and use. Eat well and keep moving! You'll be feeling strong and stress-proof soon.

DATE: _____

TIME	WHAT I ATE	HOW I FELT	COMMENTS

CHAPTER 8

Stress Relief
for Your Mind
and Spirit

Stress-management techniques that strengthen and reinforce the body will also help to strengthen the mind's ability to resist the negative effects of stress. But some stress-management techniques deal directly with the mind – the thought processes, emotions, intellect and, extending beyond the mind, the quest for spiritual meaning. In this chapter, we look at meditation techniques, which are the most effective techniques for targeting your mind and spirit.

The Negative Mental Effects of Stress

- An inability to concentrate
- Excessive, uncontrollable worrying
- Feelings of anxiety and panic
- Forgetfulness
- Sadness, depression
- Nervousness
- Fatigue, low energy
- Irritability
- Restlessness
- Negativity
- Fearfulness
- Unrealistic expectations
- Despair

Some of these symptoms of stress can be directly connected to the body, but they are often a product of the mind and its interpretation of, and obsession with or attachment to, stressful events. How do you stress-proof your mind? With mental stress management, of course.

Stress management for the mind and the spirit is specifically intended to help still, calm, and quiet an overactive mind, which is so common in people who are experiencing stress beyond their stress tolerance levels. These techniques help you to recognize the thought processes that increase your stress, the attitudes that can trigger a stress response, and the way you tend to cling to certain ideas as if they were life preservers. They can also help to fulfill the desire for higher meaning, which, when thwarted by a life that isn't what we wanted it to be, can slowly erode our happiness and self-esteem.

Some of these techniques are related to physical stress-management techniques (specifically, relaxation techniques) because, again, mind and body are inextricably connected. But if you are experiencing even a few of the negative mental effects of stress, or feel that your spirit is sorely in need of reinforcement and want to go straight to the source, try these stress-management techniques for mind and spirit.

Meditation for Peace of Mind

Meditation is one of the most widely practised stress-management techniques worldwide. It is an excellent way to cultivate control of your mental processes, but in many cultures (including ours), meditation is often practised primarily for spiritual reasons – stress management is merely a fringe benefit.

Westerners are more likely to practise meditation either solely for stress management, or out of a combined desire for stress management and a more spiritual life. Whatever your reason for meditating, the effects are the same. Meditation has a profound effect on both the body and the mind, helping to still the constant chatter in our heads so that we can think more clearly. It cuts through all our expectations and attitudes. It cultivates mental discipline and, in addition, is exceptionally relaxing for both mind and body.

Meditation teaches us, most significantly, to live in the now. Rather than letting our restless minds, worried thoughts and anxious feelings carry us away into what might happen next, or what we could have done before, meditation teaches us to still that mental turmoil. What's left? The perfection of the present moment, in which you are only and exactly what you are, with no need for improvement. And that doesn't leave much room for stress.

Some people hesitate to meditate because they think it might be against their religion. Meditation, however, is a technique that crosses the boundaries of all religions, and is just as effective without being part of any religious practice. It is mental discipline, not religious ritual.

Why Meditation Really Works

Meditation is effective in relieving stress. Studies show that people who are meditating have lower blood pressure, slower breathing and heart rates, and brain waves that signal a state of alert but, at the same time, deep relaxation. Meditation also works to train the mind to avoid negative thought patterns and processes, vicious cycles of feelings of failure and low self-esteem, and even the perception of chronic pain as an intensely negative experience.

The brain is a complex and amazing organ, and meditation can teach you to harness its power, integrate your mind and body, and feed your hungry spirit. Meditation comes in many forms, including sitting meditation, walking meditation, mindfulness meditation, yoga meditation, mantra meditation, mandala meditation, visualization and even prayer. Whether or not you are affiliated to any specific religious tradition, you can pray to God, Goddess or whatever makes sense for you – the universe, the spirit of love, positive energy.

As many types of meditation as there are, it all boils down to one thing: the honing of focus. Modern life promotes an unfocused mind. We are constantly bombarded with stimuli – from the media, from our environment, from people, from our computers. Television changes shots every few seconds and many programmes are broken up with commercial after commercial. Films move fast and often don't demand too much concentration any more. At work there is so much to do that it isn't easy or even possible to spend enough time on any one task, even if more time would result in higher quality. It tends to be a get-it-done-fast-and-move-on-to-the-next-thing-quick kind of life for many of us, and so the mind gets used to multiple points of focus and constantly moving focus. The ability to concentrate becomes less relevant and consequently begins to disappear.

If your concentration seems really poor, you can boost it with herbs in addition to meditation. Much research points to ginkgo biloba as an effective brain booster that improves circulation to the brain and, consequently, improves concentration, memory and mental clarity. Because of possible drug interactions or side effects, you should always check with your GP before taking any herbal remedy, especially if you are on any other medication or have a specific health condition.

Imagine your life as an all-you-can-eat buffet. You've got 30 minutes for lunch, and there you stand with your plate, faced with a fantastic array of options: three kinds of lettuce, two kinds of tomatoes, carrots, cucumbers, cheese, hard-boiled eggs, peppers, olives, broccoli, cauliflower, eight kinds of dressing, cottage cheese, potato salad, macaroni salad, three different marinated salads, a pasta bar, four soups, three breads, spare ribs, chicken wings, ham, beef, crab sticks, drumsticks, turkey, pork, corn on the cob, mashed potatoes, strawberries, cantaloupe, honeydew melon, watermelon, peaches, pears, pineapples, three trifles and four different flavours of some kind of creamy whipped dessert (are you hungry yet?).

It doesn't take most people long to dive in and start loading their plates with the things they like. You may start out with good intentions – 'I'll just have a small salad and a little of one main course' – but with so many tempting options, most people end up taking just a little of this, and that, and this, and that, and this...

What often results is a plate filled with so many different things that it's hard to focus on or fully enjoy any one of them. There is such an overwhelming variety piled on the plate that the pleasure comes from a feeling of indulgent excess, the 'Look at all this food!' response – never mind the food's quality.

This is why all-you-can-eat buffets can get away with food of lesser quality than a restaurant that serves just a little of a few select dishes. If you're impressed with the array of choices, you won't notice so much that everything isn't exquisite in taste. You might be impressed by the price: 'Well, as long as it's all I can eat...' Or perhaps you are seduced by the possibilities of sampling lots of things you don't normally get to eat: 'Wow. Five kinds of potato salad? I'll have to try them all!' The experience of the all-you-can-eat buffet can even become addictive, and you can lose sight of the pleasure of the food itself because you have become so enamoured with the vast quantities on offer and the impressive arrangement.

Now, let's carry over the analogy. Life is full of things to think about. What you have to do today, what you didn't finish yesterday, what to wear, where to go, who to go with, how to do things, not to mention what to eat. We have timetables, lists, projects, deadlines and responsibilities. We have dependants, friends and pets. We have houses or flats and cars or vans to maintain. Some of us have more than one house, more than one car or van, even a boat. We have to worry about looking good, behaving correctly, making a good impression. What do others think of you? How well did you complete that task? How much money do you have, and what should you spend it on? Or should you save it?

The list of things the average person thinks about in one day far exceeds the list of items on any all-you-can-eat buffet, so just imagine how much more deluded, and seduced into accepting the unacceptable our minds (like our buffet-abused palates) become. They are pulled in different directions, at a pace that can be described, pretty accurately, as frantic. When the amount of information coming in and the thoughts being generated as a result of this become overwhelming, we start to forget things, lose things, fail to pay attention, make more mistakes, have more accidents and feel more frustrated and less in control of our lives than ever.

But it's hard to stop. Thinking and taking in information can be even more addictive than the indulgent prospect of five kinds of potato salad. Have you ever turned on the television while working on your laptop, even though you have a lot to get done and know that watching the TV will slow you down and distract you? Have you ever turned up the stereo while reading or called one person after another on your mobile phone while on a bus or parked in a lay-by? We can't stop generating input! We feel comforted, dulled perhaps, or at least lulled, by the incessant flow of media, noise, distraction.

But the price is high. Going through life without ever really being fully alert means going through life as a watered-down, lukewarm version of yourself. Perhaps spending your days distracted and only partially aware feels safe because you don't have to confront big questions or strong emotions. Or perhaps you would like to cut down on all the distraction but don't have the first idea where to start or, for that matter, have time to work it out. But to go through life with your mind going in so many directions all at once isn't really living, and it certainly isn't living up to your potential.

Meditation puts a slow, painless end to this life-numbing process. It hangs a 'closed' sign on the buffet restaurant's door for just a few minutes each day. And those few minutes give your mind the opportunity to slow down, wake up, come out of its stupor and pay attention. To what? To you. To who you are, how you feel, what you are right now – regardless of all the incoming information, regardless of all the internal worries, anxieties, thoughts and emotions. Meditation also helps you to pay attention to the world around you while at the same time managing to remain unengaged and not caught up in that world. You can step back and look, an uninvolved observer, and that can be very enlightening.

If you are ill or in pain, meditation can help to support the healing efforts of your body. Meditate on your illness or pain with an open mind and without judgment, as an observer, separate from the negative feelings attached to your condition. As you become comfortable with this process, pose the question, What can I do to help you heal? Don't grasp for an answer, just stay open. This technique taps into your intuition. Eventually, very specific thoughts may arise about what you can do to support your body's healing efforts.

How to Meditate

If you are interested in taking up meditation, read the following sections first. Many different meditation techniques are described, so you should be able to find one that appeals to you. Then set aside a time each day – first thing in the morning, just before supper, or just before bed are all popular choices – and practise. Practise, practise, practise. At first, meditation can be difficult – you'll probably find it hard to keep your mind focused. Soon, though, you'll learn to recognize your mind's wanderings as natural, and as you gently redirect your mind to its point of focus, you'll stop judging yourself and learn simply to be. And learning simply to be is a crucial and significant step towards a lifetime of successful stress management.

Meditation Techniques

Meditation comes in many forms. The following are a few of the most popular techniques; one is sure to be right for you.

Zazen

Zazen is the sitting meditation of Zen Buddhism, but many people who don't practise Buddhism practise zazen. Zazen can be accurately defined as 'just sitting' and is exactly that – just sitting. It doesn't require any religious or philosophical beliefs. All it requires is the ability to apply the seat of the pants to the floor and stay there for a while. Does it sounds easy? It isn't. For those of us accustomed to achieving something at every moment of the day, just sitting is quite a challenge.

But just sitting accomplishes something amazing if it is practised every single day for an extended period of time. The mind becomes calmer. The muscles stay more relaxed. Stress fails to get the rise out of your body and your mind that it once did. Suddenly, you hold the reins, not your stress. Suddenly priorities seem clearer, truths about life, people and yourself seem more obvious, and things that used to stress you seem hardly worth consideration.

> The Rinzai sect of Zen Buddhism is most known for a meditation technique called koan contemplation. The Zen master gives the students a koan, or an enigmatic question or statement such as, *What is the sound of one hand clapping?* During meditation, students must contemplate the koan until they exhaust all rational understanding and their minds shift into a more enlightened state.

Just sitting doesn't remove you from the world, however. Choosing not to dwell on, worry and obsess about things means you can concentrate on the real business of living. Just sitting teaches you how to be, right now, in the moment. As your mind opens up, the world opens up, too. All your anxieties suddenly seem like ropes that were tying you down. Just sitting can dissolve the ropes and set you free to really be who you are and live the life you want.

This may sound like pretty powerful stuff, especially as a result of just sitting there. Can just sitting really do all this? Believe it or not, it really can, but you will only begin to perceive its power if you try it and persist with it. The power of zazen isn't really so mysterious. Just as exercise trains the body, and just as regular, targeted exercise can train the body to do truly amazing things (think about gymnasts, acrobats, Jonny Wilkinson...), zazen trains and exercises the mind.

All those worries and anxieties – the panic, the nervousness, the restlessness, the inner noise – they are all holding you back from your true potential in the same way that being unfit and undisciplined holds you back from athletic potential. Just sitting is the way to train your mind to let those things go.

From the Buddhist perspective, zazen is thought to be the path to enlightenment because, thousands of years ago, the Buddha attained enlightenment while 'just sitting' under a bodhi tree in India. He sat and sat and sat and continued to sit, and legend has it that he proclaimed (I'm paraphrasing), 'I'm going to sit here until I perceive ultimate truth, and that's final.' Supposedly it took about one night, then he understood the meaning of all existence. This was, of course, after six years of intensive searching for truth.

Enlightenment may or may not be your goal. But whatever the case, learning to sit, cultivate stillness and inner silence, and become fully and totally aware of the present moment makes for powerful stress management.

If enlightenment sounds foreign, strange or even a little scary, don't worry. Enlightenment isn't weird. It just means you become fully aware of who and what you are. You are still you – you just know more. Also, there is nothing wrong with you if you never 'attain' it. Some people don't even believe such a thing exists.

How to Practise Zazen

You can learn zazen at a zendo, a place where Zennists or Zen Buddhists gather to meditate together. The rules for meditation will depend on the individual zendo and whether or not the zendo is based in Soto or Rinzai Zen (differences include things like whether you will sit facing the centre of the room or the wall).

Or you can learn zazen on your own. While, eventually, you should be able to practise zazen under any circumstances, you can help yourself along, especially in the initial stages, by practising it in a quiet place where you're not likely to be distracted. Set aside about five minutes for the first time, then gradually work up to 15–30 minutes once or twice each day. Increase the length of your meditation session by about two minutes each week.

To begin zazen, sit cross-legged or on folded legs (sitting on your feet) with a firm pillow under your hips so that you aren't sitting directly on your legs. Make sure you are wearing enough clothes to stay warm, or wrap yourself in a blanket. Sit up straight, feeling a lift from the crown of the head towards the ceiling and an openness in your spine. (In other words, don't hunch over.) Keep your shoulders back and your chest open, and place your tongue on the roof of your mouth. Look down, but don't hang your head. Your focus points should be slightly downwards with your eyes relaxed. Now, unfocus your eyes just a little so that you don't really see what's in front of you. This will help you to focus inwardly.

Rest your hands in your lap in either of these two positions: rest your left hand, palm up, in the open palm of your right hand, bring your thumbs together so the tips touch just slightly; or make your left hand into a loose fist and rest it inside the open palm of your right hand, rest your hands against your body about 5cm (2in) below your navel.

Keep your mouth closed and breathe through your nose. At first practise concentrating by counting each breath. In your mind, count from one to ten, with each full breath (inhalation and exhalation) constituting one number. Or simply follow your breath, keeping your awareness focused on the sound and feel of your breath moving in and out of your body. Don't try to control your breath – just notice it.

Soon you'll probably notice that you aren't paying attention to your breath, or even counting – your mind has wandered. Notice it, then bring your attention back to your breath. Keep going for five minutes. Once you become really adept at focusing, you won't even have to count. You'll just sit, breathe and be.

And that's it. If it sounds too simple to be true that's because zazen is simple. But it isn't easy, for several reasons. Let's be frank:

· It's boring, especially at first.
· It's really hard to sit still.
· It's difficult to 'just sit' when you know how much you have to do.
· It's hard to justify the time when you don't see immediate results (we are so impatient).
· Your mind will try to talk you out of it. Discipline is hard work, and your mind will resist the effort.
· At first, you'll probably think you are hopeless and could never do it.
· It's frustrating when you can't concentrate on anything.
· It's frightening to confront some of the emotions that arise unexpectedly.
· The dropout rate is high. Most people don't keep it up long enough to see the benefits.

But what happens if you don't drop out? What happens if you sit through the boredom, keep sitting despite the other things you think you should be doing, sit out the frustration and the fear, keep sitting until you've learned how to really sit still, physically and mentally? The answer is simple: clarity, peace, acceptance, satisfaction and, yes, a lot less stress.

You can practise zazen without any props, but if you become a devotee and want to spend the money, you can buy several props to make your meditation more comfortable. A zafu is a firm, small, round cushion to sit on during Zen meditation. A zabuton is a larger mat on which to place the zafu. You can also buy a small wooden bench designed so that you don't actually put weight on your legs. Look for these and other meditation tools in specialist shops and mail-order catalogues. You can also look and enquire in a local healthfood shop, New Age bookshop or meditation centre.

Walking Meditation

In Zen, walking meditation (kinhin) is the counterpart to sitting meditation (zazen), but walking meditation doesn't necessarily have anything to do with Zen. It is as it sounds: meditation on the move. Walking meditation is different from sitting meditation in that you have to be aware of what you're doing so that you don't wander into traffic or bump into a tree. On the other hand, it is also quite similar, because in sitting meditation, you become acutely aware of your surroundings – they just don't change as they do when you walk.

Walking meditation is an excellent alternative to sitting meditation. Some people like to sit for most of their meditation session and then spend the last few minutes in walking meditation. For others, who practise sitting meditation for longer periods of time, walking meditation gets the body moving without breaking or distracting from the meditative flow.

Walking meditation is more challenging than sitting meditation for the same reason that it is more interesting to many people – you have more to look at. With more to look at comes more temptation to let the mind become frantic again. For this reason, walking meditation is often best practised as a counterpart to sitting meditation.

But for most people reading this book, walking meditation could be a really good way to enjoy walking and reap the benefits of meditation at the same time. It's also ideal for people who simply refuse to sit still. Walking meditation can be a good way to ease into the meditation concept without the commitment of sitting (and sitting for even five minutes is a fairly serious commitment for some people). It's an enjoyable form of meditation in its own right, which can serve as the basis for a meditation practice, or be used as an occasional alternative to any other form of meditation.

How to Practise Walking Meditation

To practise walking meditation, first decide where you will walk. You can do walking meditation outside, or around a room. You should have a prepared path in mind so you don't spend time thinking about where to go during the meditation. Know exactly where you are going: around the block, to the end of the path, around the periphery of the living room.

Begin by spending a moment focusing and breathing, to centre yourself and prepare for the meditation. Then, taking slow, deliberate steps, walk. As you walk, notice how your breath feels as it comes in and out of your body. Notice how your limbs move, how your feet feel, how your hands and arms hang, the position of your torso, your neck, your head. Don't judge yourself as you walk – just notice.

Once you feel you've observed yourself well, begin to observe the environment around you as you walk. Don't let it engage you. If something you see sets you off on a long, involved train of thought that has nothing to do with how you feel walking your chosen path – as soon as you catch your mind so wandering (and it will so wander), gently bring your thoughts back to your breathing.

While new to walking meditation, stay with your breath for a good long while. Before you can start noticing and focusing on the rest of your body and your environment, you need to be able to focus on your breath, otherwise your mind will be all over the place.

Start with five minutes and add two minutes every week until you are up to 15–30 minutes of daily walking meditation. Or alternate walking meditation with another form of meditation every other day. Or once you are up to 15–30 minutes of another type of meditation, spend the first or last 5–10 minutes of each session in walking meditation.

Yoga Meditation

Yoga, practised in India for thousands of years, preceding even Hinduism, may be the oldest of all meditation traditions. While Hatha yoga, the yoga most known to people in the West, focuses on physical postures and exercises, these are in fact designed to get a troublesomely twitchy and unfocused body under control, so that the all-important meditation can be more easily practised.

While yoga has many different sects, each with slightly different beliefs and each orienting its meditation and other techniques in slightly different directions, many forms of yoga have certain things in common:

- The belief that throughout the body channels of energy run up and down. Along these energy channels are chakras (wheels of light), or spinning energy centres (see 'Chakra Meditation' a little later in this chapter). Chakras are focal points for energy in the body and represent different organs, different colours and different aspects of the personality and life force.
- The belief that deep at the base of the spine is the seat of kundalini energy, sometimes called 'serpent energy' or 'serpent power' and likened to a coiled serpent waiting to be awakened. Kundalini energy is thought to be a powerful force that, through the proper practice of postures, breathing and meditation, can be activated or awakened. As kundalini energy awakes, it rises through the body, activating each of the chakras in turn until it reaches the seventh chakra at the crown of the head, resulting in an intense physical experience that actually, it is said, physically restructures the body.

Most of the yoga practised today is profoundly influenced by a text called the *Yoga Sutras*, which describes and explains yoga via a long list of aphorisms that were written thousands of years ago by a man named Patanjali. Many of these aphorisms can be seen as ancient and interesting approaches to stress management, which, in a sense, they are, for isn't stress one of the things that keeps us from enlightenment, and isn't seeking enlightenment about ridding ourselves of obstacles such as stress so that we can perceive the truth and finally be wholly happy?

In the *Yoga Sutras*, Patanjali describes what he calls the Eightfold Path to enlightenment. The steps aren't necessarily to be followed in order, although in a sense, they are, progressive. (Note the placement of meditation.)

1. **Yamas**, or lifestyle guidance. If you want to make your path to enlightenment (and your path away from stress) easier, these are the things you should not do: you should not lie, steal, be greedy, commit violence or let yourself be carried away by lust or disrespect for other humans. Very good advice.

2. **Niyamas**, or more lifestyle guidance. These take the form of healthy places to focus your attention and energy, including purity (keeping both mind and body clean), contentment, discipline, studying oneself and being devoted to something. Also good advice.

3. **Asanas**, or yoga postures. These are designed to help you gain mastery over the body.

4. **Pranayama**, or breathing exercises. These are specifically designed to infuse the body with life-force energy (called *prana* in yoga).

5. **Pratyahara**, or learning to become detached. Now we're coming into more familiar meditation territory. This step is about learning to step back from the world and your own thoughts, feelings, emotions and sense impressions, to view them with an unengaged, unbiased eye.

6. **Dharana**, or learning concentration. This is also familiar meditation territory. It involves concentrating on something – a sound, an object, a thought – until the boundaries between you and the object dissolve and you are one.

7. **Dhyana**, or meditation. In this step, all the previous steps come into play. The lifestyle guidance sets the stage, the asanas and pranayama prime the body, and the detachment and concentration discipline the mind. The goal of yoga meditation is to recognize your ultimate oneness with the universe, which can result in a state of pure, joyful bliss called samadhi.

8. **Nirvana**, or ultimate bliss. This is the final step and the final goal of the Eightfold Path. It is what happens when we finally recognize truth and our oneness with the universe. It is enlightenment.

If the yoga path interests you, you should certainly go out and learn everything you can about it. If not, don't be put off by all the steps – this is just background information. You can still practise yoga meditation without committing yourself to a complete yoga lifestyle.

How to Practise Yoga Meditation

To practise yoga meditation, first choose a quiet, comfortable, warm place where you are unlikely to be distracted. If possible, turn off any sources of noise and anything that emits electricity (TV, stereo, computer – but leave the fridge plugged in so as not to spoil the food). Take off all jewellery, especially anything metal. Electrical currents, metal and anything encircling a body part can disrupt the flow of energy.

Wear something comfortable. Take off your shoes, but keep your socks on if you think your feet will get cold. Wrap yourself in a blanket to keep warm if necessary.

Sit cross-legged, or in the half lotus position (one foot placed, sole facing up, on the opposite thigh). If you are very flexible in the hips or experienced with yoga asanas, sit in the full lotus position (legs crossed and each foot placed, sole facing up, on the opposite thigh). To create additional stability, sit on a small, firm pillow so that your knees point towards the ground, forming a tripod.

The full lotus position isn't for beginners because it requires quite a lot of hip flexibility. However, once mastered – through the practice of other yoga exercises that work up to it and then the practice of the position itself – it is the most stable of sitting positions. It can be held for long periods of time, and some people claim to have fallen asleep in this position without toppling over.

Next, put your right hand, palm up, on your right knee and your left hand, palm up, on your left knee. You can leave your fingers open or make a circle with each index finger and thumb or middle finger and thumb. Making these circles with your fingers is meant to keep energy concentrated in the body rather than allowing it to escape from the fingertips during meditation.

Rock back and forth and side to side on your sitting bones to find a nice, stable, centre position. Imagine the crown of your head being lifted up as the tip of your coccyx sinks down, lengthening the spine and straightening the posture.

Next, simply begin to notice your breath as it flows in and out. Inhale and exhale through your nose, or inhale through your nose and exhale through your mouth. Once you feel relaxed, think of or say a syllable, word or phrase – this is called a mantra. The traditional mantra of yoga meditation is the sound/word 'Om'. Say it slowly on the exhale of the breath. Let the 'm' resonate through your body.

'Om' is meant to imitate the sound of the universe, from which everything originated and of which everything is a part. Some people think of it as the sound of God. By saying/making this sound, you are supposed to be able to feel a connection with the universe, and that is the philosophical basis of yoga (and Hinduism) – we are all one with the universe. All matter, all energy, everything is connected – everything ultimately merges together. Beneath the surface of reality, which we experience with our senses, all is really just one. Some people who practise meditation like to use the mantra 'One' instead of 'Om' because it more directly evokes this idea.

Repeat your chosen sound with each exhalation for five minutes the first time, then slowly increase the time spent in meditation. Yoga meditation feels good. It feels spiritual. It can be a complement to any religion or can be practised by itself. It can be an energizing spiritual reinforcement, which is important for getting stress under control. If you are feeding your spiritual side, you tend to be less stressed by the less important things in life.

Many who practise yoga meditation and other forms of mantra meditation (described later in this chapter) believe that the sound vibrations produced within and from the body, by the chanting of a mantra, actually have a physical effect on the body, helping it to align and reinforce its life-force energy.

Savasana

Savasana, or the corpse pose, is also a yoga asana, or exercise – one of those postures designed to help keep the body under control so that it doesn't interfere with the pursuit of meditation. And savasana does just that – it helps to rein in the body and gets it working in the way it is meant to work. For that very reason, savasana is an excellent stress-management technique.

Many yoga teachers consider savasana to be the most important of all the yoga asanas. It is both easy and challenging because all you do is lie on your back and relax, but... you actually have to lie on your back and relax!

How to Practise Savasana

To practise savasana, find a comfortable spot on the floor. A bed usually isn't supportive enough, but you can lie on a mat. Lie on your back with your legs about 60cm (2ft) apart at the ankles and flat on the floor, your arms flat and away from your body, your palms facing up. Let your feet fall to the side.

Now, begin to relax as you breathe in and out through your nose. As you breathe, concentrate on fully relaxing your body: bones, joints, muscles, everything. Let it all sink comfortably down towards the floor. Don't worry about how you look or what you should be doing. Just let it all go. Relax deeply. Stay in this position for five minutes to start with, and work up to 15–20 minutes.

One problem with savasana is that if you are tired, lying on your back with your eyes closed and relaxing is likely to result in a catnap. Don't be angry with yourself if you fall asleep in savasana – you probably need the rest. Just try again when you are better rested. (And get to bed early tonight – your body is sending you a message.)

This pose is ideal after a yoga routine or any other kind of workout. It's also an energizing way to start the day and a relaxing way to end it. Doing savasana is like pushing the RESET button on your personal computer. It lets your body reset itself, realign itself, re-energize itself and reverse that insidious stress response.

Breathing Meditation

Breathing meditation is part zazen and part pranayama, the breathing techniques associated with yoga. Breathing meditation takes qualities from both. In zazen, you watch your breath without judging, following it in and out. In pranayama, you control the length and character of the inhalation and exhalation.

Breathing is, obviously, a vital function. We do it throughout our lives. It constantly infuses our body with oxygen and, according to some traditions, life-force energy. Our breathing rate is also directly affected by our stress level. When stress chemicals pump through the body, the breathing rate increases. What happens when we consciously slow our breathing rate? We send a message to our bodies to relax. We defuse the stress reaction. And it's so easy to do!

How to Practise Breathing Meditation

First, practise breathing deeply (see Chapter 6). Then, when you feel you can breathe from the lower part of your body rather than from your upper chest, sit comfortably (don't lie down for this one), either on the floor, in one of the positions described in previous meditations or in a chair. Sit up straight so that you aren't scrunching up your body's breathing space. Imagine you are being suspended from above so that the effort of sitting up straight feels effortless.

Now take a long, slow, deep breath through your nose, and in your mind count slowly to five. When you've inhaled fully at five, hold the breath for five more counts. Then slowly release the breath through your nose to the count of 10.

As you breathe and count, your mind will need to concentrate on the counting. This will help you to stay focused. Eventually, when you get used to the rhythm, your mind won't have to stay so occupied. Now it's time to focus on the sound and feel of the breath, as in zazen meditation. Focus completely on the breath as it enters, waits and leaves the body. When your mind wanders, guide it gently back to the breath.

Keep breathing in this way for several minutes. Increase your breathing meditation time by two minutes per week until you've reached

15–30 minutes once or twice every day. After a session of breathing meditation, you will feel directly and immediately energized. Try it in the middle of a stressful day, at the end of the day, at the beginning of the day when you need a boost... any time you need a shot of energy. In addition to infusing your body with energy, you also are filling it with the oxygen it needs to function properly.

Breathing meditation can be practised anywhere, anytime, even for only a few breaths. Even in small amounts, it is instant stress relief.

While most meditation techniques suggest breathing through the nose, mouth breathing is fine if you have nasal congestion or if you feel more comfortable doing it like that. Better to do your breathing exercises through your mouth than not at all.

Mantra Meditation

Yoga meditation is a mantra meditation, but there are many other kinds of mantra meditation. Any concentrated focusing while repeating a sound can be called a mantra meditation, whether it's Sufi chanting or the recitation of the rosary prayer. Some people believe that the sounds of a mantra actually contain certain powers; others believe that the key to mantra meditation is not the sound but the repetition itself. In either case, if you choose a word that has significance for you, your meditation may seem to have a more personalized meaning and feeling. Your mantra can even be an affirmation, such as 'I am happy'.

Any word or phrase will do. Perhaps you already have something in mind. If not, here are a few you might wish to try (the possibilities, of course, are endless):

- Om
- One
- Peace
- Love
- Joy
- God

- Sky
- Mind, body, spirit
- I am happy (or good, perfect, special, loving)
- Hallelujah
- Shalom

· Goddess   · Amen

· Earth

Mantra meditation is an ancient tradition practised by many different cultures in many ways. If time is the ultimate test, then mantra meditation may be the ultimate form of meditation. It disciplines the mind, hones the focus and even improves the depth of the breath and the capacity of the lungs. It's also supremely relaxing.

Another stress-management benefit of practising mantra meditation is that, like Pavlov's dog, you learn to associate a sound with something positive. After practising your mantra many times during meditation and experiencing the benefits of relaxation, calm and inner peace, the mere mention of the word can immediately invoke some of these feelings. For example, if your mantra is 'One', then in a stressful situation just say 'One' the way you would during your meditation periods. Notice the immediate feeling of calm.

How to Practise Mantra Meditation

To practise mantra meditation, find a quiet place to sit. Take up the position described for yoga meditation or Zen meditation, or sit in a chair. Make sure you are stable, centred and in a comfortable position. Take a few relaxed breaths, than slowly begin to repeat your mantra with every exhalation of your breath. Repeat for five minutes at first, then build up by two minutes each week until you've reached a comfortable period between 15 and 30 minutes once or, if possible, twice each day.

Mandala Meditation

In mandala meditation, which is a significant kind of meditation in Tibetan culture, the focus of meditation isn't placed on a sound but on a beautiful object: a mandala. Mandalas are circular pictures, sometimes very plain, sometimes highly ornate. Their round form and, often, the inner lines of the picture (whether painting, drawing, mosaic, sculpture or something else), draw the eye to the centre of the mandala, helping the mind to focus on that centre point.

In Tibet, where the making of mandalas is an art form, fantastically complex and beautiful, brilliantly coloured and intricately designed ones, large and small, are made with coloured sand, and are then brushed away. Mandalas are thought to be a symbolic representation of the universe, making them the perfect point of focus. Again, the concept of oneness with the universe recurs. But you don't have to believe that concept to practise mandala (or any other kind of) meditation. You can learn all about the philosophy behind it if you choose, or you can just practise it to help train, discipline and teach your mind to be still and clear.

How to Practise Mandala Meditation

First you need a mandala. You can find mandalas in books, in shops that sell imported items from Tibet and in New Age shops that stock meditation supplies. Or you can make one yourself, as simple as a circle with a centre point or as complex and ornate as you want to make it.

Hang or place the mandala at just below eye level from a sitting position, and sit 1.2–2.4m (4–8ft) away from it, depending on how comfortable you feel (and how well you see). Sit comfortably cross-legged, in a kneeling position, or on a small bench or chair. If you are sitting on the floor, use a cushion to make yourself more comfortable. Take a few relaxed breaths.

Then look at the mandala. Instead of following your breath or a sound, use the mandala as your point of concentration. Examine it in detail. Notice everything about it. Notice how your eyes move towards and away from the circle. Let the mandala become the entire focus of your concentration.

The labyrinth at Chartres Cathedral in Paris is a medieval version of a mandala. Walking along the path of the maze-like pattern is a concentrated form of walking meditation designed to mimic the journey into the soul and back out again.

When your mind starts to wander (which it will), and you realize it has wandered – 'Hang on, what am I doing thinking about what we're having for supper tonight?' – gently guide it back to the mandala.

The more you practise mandala meditation, the easier it becomes. However, it also becomes more challenging, because after many sessions you are still looking at the same mandala and your mind must learn to continue to find it a point of complete focus. It's great mental exercise.

Start with five minutes, then add two minutes every week until you are up to around 15–30 minutes of mandala meditation once or twice every day.

Chakra Meditation

According to yoga and other traditions, chakras are centres or 'wheels' of energy at key points along the energy channels in the body. Each chakra has a colour and is thought to represent different parts of the body, both physically and emotionally. Meditating on the chakra that represents an area in your life that needs reinforcement can be a powerful, even life-changing form of meditation. Meditating to open and energize all the chakras is also an effective technique for freeing the body to extinguish the negative effects of stress.

While the body is filled with minor chakras, the seven major ones exist on a line from the base of the spine to the crown of the head. Different people put them in slightly different places and attribute slightly different meanings to each one, but the following is basically in accordance with standard interpretations of the chakras:

·   *The First Chakra* is located deep at the base of the spine. Its colour is red. This is the seat of instinct, including appetite, the instinctive sexual urge, aggression, violence, fear and that instinctive, non-intellectual joyful response to the satisfaction of the basic urges and needs. Meditate on this chakra if you are having trouble controlling your primal urges.
·   *The Second Chakra* is located behind the navel or just slightly below. Its colour is orange. This is the seat of creativity, including both procreation and the deep-seated urge to create art. This is also the

seat of passion. Meditate on this chakra if you are having trouble with blocked creativity, including reproductive problems.

- *The Third Chakra* is located just behind the solar plexus in that indentation beneath your rib cage where both sides of your ribs meet. Its colour is yellow. This is the seat of action and consumption. Your digestive fire lies here, turning food into energy. Meditate on this chakra if you are having trouble with your appetite, for food or for life. If you have difficulty taking things in, work on this chakra.
- *The Fourth Chakra* is located just behind the heart. Its colour is green. This is the middle chakra of the seven and the centre of compassion, emotion and love. This is the chakra of giving away, in contrast to the third chakra, which takes and consumes. Meditate on this chakra if you are having trouble giving of yourself, being compassionate or loving or feeling emotions.

Some people believe that chakras can be energized or unblocked by placing crystals corresponding to that chakra's colour over the area of the body in which that chakra lies. Crystal healers place crystals on the body to balance the energy of the chakras and promote the flow of life-force energy through all the chakras.

- *The Fifth Chakra* is located in the throat. Its colour is sky blue. This is the seat of communication energy. Meditate on this chakra if you are having trouble communicating your feelings or expressing yourself, or if you have writer's block.
- *The Sixth Chakra* is located between and just above the eyebrows. It is sometimes called the Third Eye chakra. Its colour is deep, dark blue or indigo – like the night sky, as opposed to the bright blue sky colour of the fifth chakra. This is the centre of intuition, unclouded perception and psychic abilities. Meditate on this area if you want to develop your intuition or if you feel your intuition is blocked.
- *The Seventh Chakra* is located at the crown of the head. This is the highest chakra, sometimes called the Thousand Petalled Lotus chakra. Its colour is violet. This is the source of enlightenment and knowing your true self.

If enlightenment is your goal, meditate on all the chakras and the energy that flows between them, culminating in the seventh chakra.

How to Practise Chakra Meditation

To practise chakra meditation, choose a quiet spot where you are unlikely to be disturbed, and sit comfortably. The yoga meditation positions are most common for chakra meditation, but you can also sit in a chair or even lie on the floor (but don't fall asleep!).

Rock yourself, as for yoga meditation, into a straight position. The primary energy channels in your body run along your spine and into your head. If you keep your spine straight, energy can flow more easily through the chakras. Close your eyes and breathe easily.

If you plan to move through all the chakras, focus on the first one; otherwise, the chakra on which you want to focus. Imagine the chakra's colour and feel it pulsing in the area of that chakra. Think about what that chakra represents. Reflect on those qualities in your own life. Don't judge yourself – observe, and let thoughts come and go.

For example, if you are meditating on the fifth chakra, because you are feeling creatively blocked, imagine a bright blue colour, like the colour of the sky on a breezy, sunny spring day. Feel the blue colour cooling and opening your throat, letting your thoughts and ideas come pouring forth. Think about your creativity. Do you wish to be a writer but have difficulty getting yourself to try? Do you love to write but have trouble getting started? If you find you are lecturing or berating yourself ('Why can't I just sit down and write?'), notice what you are doing and let it go. Concentrate on your throat, the bright blue colour, and the creativity in your life, as an observer would.

This kind of meditation often brings up surprising solutions. If you let go of the worry and the blame in the area you are concentrating on, simply letting yourself see and reflect, ideas arise like bubbles, breaking loose from the side of a glass and floating to the top. Pop! The answers become clear.

If you don't get any answers or feel renewed after one try, keep at it. Sometimes it takes a while to get used to this kind of concentration and reflection, but with persistence you can open and energize your chakras.

Your body will help you to let go of unnecessary stressors and heal the negative effects of stress. You will find your consciousness breaking into new territory.

To meditate on all the chakras, as a kind of whole-self-maintenance, start with the first chakra, its colour, its function, and concentrate on it for two to five minutes. Then imagine the energy rising into the second chakra, and concentrate on that for two to five minutes (don't worry about watching a clock – try to feel when it's right to move up). Keep going until you reach the seventh chakra. If you feel particularly blocked in any one area, spend a little more time there.

Chakra meditation is superb for stress management. You feel you are really doing something to take care of yourself, and it's a lot cheaper than therapy, although it's also an excellent complement to it.

In addition to colours and aspects of the self, the seven primary chakras also have associated planets, vibrational syllables and glands:

- First chakra: Saturn, sound is LAM, glands are sex glands
- Second chakra: Jupiter, sound is VAM, glands are adrenals
- Third chakra: Mars, sound is RAM, glands are digestive
- Fourth chakra: Venus, sound is YAM, gland is thymus
- Fifth chakra: Mercury, sound is HAM, gland is thyroid
- Sixth chakra: Sun, sound is OM, gland is pineal
- Seventh chakra: the universe, sound is also OM, glands are pituitary and hypothalamus

Mindfulness Meditation

Mindfulness meditation is different from other meditations because it can be practised anywhere at any time, and no matter what you are doing. It simply means focusing on total awareness of the present moment. Mindfulness meditation is inherent in many other forms of meditation but can also be practised while walking, running, playing football, driving, studying, writing, reading or eating. Anything you are doing, you can do with mindfulness. Your entire day can be one long mindfulness meditation – although it's pretty hard to sustain.

Mindfulness meditation has been popularized both by those from the East, such as Thich Nhat Hanh, the Vietnamese Buddhist monk, and Westerners such as Jon Kabat-Zinn, PhD, the founder and director of the Stress Reduction Clinic at the University of Massachusetts Medical Centre. It is easy to do for short periods, but harder over an extended time because our minds resist staying in the present moment. But it is a rewarding mental discipline that teaches us to cherish and relish the miracle of the present moment, no matter how ordinary. It is also supremely relaxing and satisfying.

How to Practise Mindfulness Meditation

Wherever you are, whatever you are doing, you can practise mindfulness meditation by consciously making the decision to be fully and completely aware of everything around you. Notice the impressions from all your senses – see, hear, feel, smell, taste. When your mind begins to think about something else, gently bring it back to the present moment. Don't judge the impressions of your senses. Just observe. You may be amazed at what you notice about yourself and the world around you.

A famous Buddhist saying, paraphrased here, asks, 'If you hear a dog barking, do you think of your own dog, or do you think only "bark"?' Thinking 'bark' means you are practising mindfulness. Thinking of your own dog means that you are making an association and that your mind is somewhere else.

If practising mindfulness just anywhere sounds overwhelming, you can start by practising it while doing something very specific, like eating. Pick a single thing to eat – not a complicated dish with lots of ingredients, but a vegetable, a piece of fruit, some simple soup or a piece of bread. Eat it slowly, slowly, and notice everything about the process. How do you bring the food to your mouth? How do you put it in? How does it feel in your mouth? What does it taste and smell like? How does the food look? What spurs you to take another bite? How does your body react to the food?

Practising mindfulness meditation while eating is a good way to hone your mindfulness skills. It is also a way to help overcome mindless eating – a common problem, especially among those of us who are stressed.

Prayer

Several studies that continue to baffle the mainstream medical establishment suggest that when hospitalized patients are prayed for, *even when they don't know they are being prayed for*, they recover more quickly than those who aren't prayed for. These studies suggest that people can experience stress relief if others pray for them.

If you're stuck for words when trying to pray and aren't really associated with any religious tradition, borrow a prayer from any of the world's religions. The Lord's Prayer, the Rosary Prayer, the Hail Mary prayer, a Gregorian chant, one of the Kabbalah's 25 names for God, the Jesus prayer of the desert fathers, a Sufi chant, a Buddhist chant, a Hindu chant. Go to the library and do some research. It's a place to start, and once you get comfortable you can generate your own words.

What is prayer? Prayer is a focused, concentrated communication, statement of intention or opening of the channel between you and divinity, whatever divinity means to you. A prayer can be a request, thanks, worship or praise to God. It can be an expression of gratitude directed to the universe. It can be used to invoke divine power or to attempt to experience divine or universal energy directly. Many different traditions have many different modes and types of prayer. Prayer can mean whatever you want it to mean.

The practice of any centred, reverential concentration is a form of at least a cousin of meditation, and they all work to relieve stress. The meditation traditions of all cultures have common themes and techniques. The Eastern mantra meditation in which 'Om' is chanted is similar to the Western practice of saying prayers.

How to Practise Prayer

To practise prayer, first decide what you want your prayer to be. To whom, to what, or towards whom or what is your prayer addressed? What is the substance of your prayer? Are you praying for healing for yourself or someone else? Are you praying for something you want or need? Are you praying to say thank you for everything you already have? Are you praying to praise, to express your inner joy, to release your inner sadness?

Once you have a specific intention in mind, sit or lie quietly in a place where you are unlikely to be disturbed. Focus your thoughts on your prayer and say it, out loud or in your mind. Stay focused on your prayer and the energy of your prayer. Imagine where it is going. Let your prayer continue to radiate from your heart towards its intended destination. As you open this channel from your heart to the outside, also allow a space for a return message. You might be filled with a warm, joyful feeling. Or you might receive a message. Or you might not.

Whatever happens, continue to focus on your prayer as it flows from you, and don't judge the results. Just let it happen and let this outpouring of positive energy from your heart fortify and strengthen you. Because, as we all know, the more you give, the more you receive!

Imagery Meditation and Visualization

Imagery meditation and visualization are meditations that use your imagination to make positive changes in your thinking and even in what happens to you. The purpose of imagery meditation is to imagine yourself in a different place (the beach, the mountains, Paris) or circumstances to effect instant relaxation. Visualization is a technique for imagining something you want (a different job, the love of your life), or a change you would like to see in yourself (to be less reactive to stress, more self-confident, perfectly organized). Both imagining and visualizing have two separate effects.

1. Instant stress relief because of the positive feeling you associate with what you are imagining.
2. Life changes because continually visualizing something can help to bring about those changes in your life.

Even if your imagination is a bit rusty, you can practise imagery meditation and visualization. Perhaps you will use imagery meditation to take a five-minute holiday at the seaside in the middle of your working day. Perhaps you will use visualization to help you change your eating and exercise habits to finally achieve a healthy body and a healthy weight. Whatever you use them for, these imagination generators are powerful stress-management techniques, both in the short and the long term.

How to Practise Imagery Meditation

Get comfortable, either sitting or lying down. Close your eyes. Take a few deep, relaxed breaths, then form a picture in your mind. Perhaps it is the place you wish you could be right now, a place you visited in the past and loved, or a place you invent. What does it look like? What do you see around you? What colours, what textures? Notice every detail about the place you are visualizing.

Then, imagine touching things around you – sand, water, grass, trees, great art or architecture, your favourite person. Listen. What do you hear in this place? Wind, waves, rustling leaves, traffic, talking? Next, think about what you smell. Freshly cut grass? Salt? A storm? Cooking food? Perfume? Focus on each of your senses and explore the place you've created or remembered in your mind. Stay here as long as you like, but for at least five minutes. Then, slowly, let the images fade away and open your eyes. Instant relaxation!

How to Practise Visualization

Get comfortable, either sitting or lying down. Close your eyes. Take a few deep, relaxed breaths, then form a picture in your mind of a positive life change. Perhaps it's a career goal, a change in health or appearance, a situation, confidence, or anything else. Keep it simple and stick to one thing, as you can always tackle other areas in a separate session.

Imagine yourself in your new situation. How do you look, act and feel? How do you like being like this, looking like this, having this job?

Explore yourself in your new situation. If you like it, if it feels right, then stick with your visualization every day and imagine it with fervent and confident intention.

As your life changes, your visualizations may change and grow. This is good. You may realize, for example, that as your life becomes less stressful and more rewarding, you don't really need to be financially wealthy – you have gained emotional and spiritual wealth instead. The trick is to keep it up. The more you use your imagination, the stronger it becomes, just like a muscle.

With a strong imagination, you become a more creative problem-solver, and your brain works better. You'll be better able to manage the stress in your life as you work on eliminating it.

To add power to your visualization, use an affirmation as a mantra for your meditation. It must be worded as if the change has already taken place, and worded positively – for example, 'I will be well' rather than 'I won't be ill'.

Examples of positive affirmations:

- 'I am healthy, strong and well.'
- 'My body is healing quickly and growing stronger.'
- 'I am confident and self-assured.'
- 'I am relaxed, calm and tranquil.'
- 'I have found the perfect life partner for me.'
- 'I am rich in many areas of my life.'

Meditation Tips for Sticking With It

Once you've started to meditate, you may find that the attraction wears off after a few sessions. How do you stick with it so that you can reap all the benefits of regular, long-term meditation?

Here are some tips:

· Stay with one kind of meditation most of the time so that you feel focused on and familiar with your chosen technique.

· If you absolutely can't stand the thought of meditating on a given day, choose a different type of meditation, just for a change of pace.

· Put meditation into your timetable just like any other appointment. It's an appointment with yourself, and you should be the most important person in your life!

· Meditate at the same time or times each day, to get into a routine and embed your meditation into your timetable.

· If possible, meditate on an empty stomach, either before a meal or two hours after (one hour after a light meal). Your body will be able to focus more easily if it isn't busy digesting.

· Meditate at a high-energy time of day rather than a low-energy one. If you are a morning person, meditate in the morning. If you get going at night, meditate at night. You'll lessen your chances of nodding off, and you'll have better focus and concentration.

· Throughout the day, make a point of remembering the feeling of meditation. Recalling the relaxing feeling of meditation can actually re-create that feeling, helping to extend meditation's stress-relieving effects all day long.

· Start meditating with a friend. Whether you meditate together, at the same time and/or in the same place, or maintain your separate meditation practices, you can call each other on those days when you don't feel like meditating and give each other encouragement and motivation.

Your stress management diary can be part meditation diary. After meditating each day, make an entry that includes the date, time, how long you meditated for and how it felt. Your entries can be as long or short as you wish, but a diary will help you to keep a record of your practice and progress. You might also detect patterns in your mood and energy levels that affect your practice.

Above all, just keep practising. Practise, practise, practise. Practice may not make perfect (because nobody's perfect), but practice is what will eventually make dramatic changes in your life, your health and your stress-management mastery.

CHAPTER 9

More Stress-
Management Tools

We've already covered a number of highly effective stress-management techniques, but the world is a wide and interesting place, and many more tools for managing stress exist. In this chapter are listed some techniques that don't fall into the categories already covered. Browse through this list in the spirit of adventure and enquiry, in search of stress-management tools that you can use. Perhaps one or more of these will be just what you are looking for.

Attitude Adjustment

There is a Country and Western song about giving people an attitude adjustment on the top of the head. The attitude adjustment here has nothing to do with violence. It's about subtly changing your attitude.

Negativity is a huge drain on your energy and exaggerates any stress already in your life, magnifying it until it seems huge and uncontrollable. Many people have the negativity habit. Are you one of them?

What is your attitude? Are you a glass half-full or a glass half-empty type? Do you see the upside or the downside first?

Being negative is simply a habit. It may be a habit caused by lots of past suffering, and that's perfectly understandable, but it can stop right now. Even in suffering, you don't have to be negative. Some people remain positive through tragedy; others despair. What's the difference? Attitude.

How do you change your negative attitude? First, become aware of when you tend to be negative by keeping a negativity diary. Whenever you feel like being negative, don't express it out loud, write it down in your diary instead. Get it out of your system and onto the page, and look at it more objectively later. Eventually (as with any kind of diary work), you'll start to see patterns.

Has stress sapped your sense of humour? Try to keep your sense of humour when life gets stressful. A light-hearted approach is much less stressful, and sometimes a funny face or a well-timed joke can put an immediate and happy end to an escalating situation.

Once you know what kinds of things trigger your negativity (it may be triggered by many things), you can begin to catch yourself in the act. When something unexpected happens, do the first words out of your mouth tend to be a frantic 'Oh NO!'? If so, stop yourself after that first 'Oh...' Notice what you are doing. Tell yourself, 'I don't have to respond like this. I can wait and see if a full-blown, all-out "Oh NO" is really warranted.' This stopping of your thought process and negative reaction can help you to be more objective and, eventually, more positive about any situation. Even if, after stopping, you realize that an 'Oh NO' really *is* warranted, at least you won't be crying wolf at every little mishap. You'll save your 'Oh NOs' for when you really need them.

As with any habit, the more you get used to halting your negative reactions and replacing them with neutral or positive ones, the less you'll find yourself reacting negatively. Instead of 'Oh NO', react with silence, taking a wait-and-see attitude. Or react with an affirmation: 'Oh... I can learn something positive from this!'

You might encounter obstacles along the way, and that's to be expected. Perhaps in your negativity diary you'll discover that you are comforted by or even *enjoy* being negative. Perhaps it makes you feel safe: if you always expect the worst, you'll never be disappointed. But obstacles are meant to be overcome. Even if a negative attitude is comforting in some ways, is it worth the drain on your energy and happiness? Keep working through it and being honest with yourself. You may discover that your negative reactions are all about protection and that you can find much better ways to protect yourself. What about good friends, a really fulfilling hobby or regular meditation?

If you are serious about kicking your negativity habit, you *can* adjust your attitude; it just takes some concentration. (For a related technique, see 'Optimism Therapy' later in this chapter.)

You can oppose your tendencies to think irrationally by evaluating your feelings. Ask yourself these questions:

1. Is the situation, or just my perception of it, causing me stress?
2. Am I expecting things to be other than they are?
3. Am I stressed because of someone else's mistake?
4. Conflict requires two people. Am I contributing?
5. Am I wasting time looking for the cause of this situation instead of changing my behaviour now?

Autogenic Training

Autogenic training, or autogenics, was designed to allow the benefits of hypnosis to be reaped without the need for a hypnotist or the time typically involved in a hypnosis session. Autogenics uses a relaxed position and the verbal suggestion of warmth and heaviness in the limbs to induce a state of deep relaxation and stress relief. Autogenics has been used to treat muscle tension, asthma, gastrointestinal problems, irregular heartbeat, high blood pressure, headaches, thyroid problems, anxiety, irritability and fatigue. It can also increase your stress resistance.

The verbal suggestions of autogenics are designed specifically to reverse the body's stress response. The suggestions have six themes:

1. Heaviness, which promotes relaxation of the voluntary muscles of the limbs, reversing the tension in the limbs typical of the stress response.
2. Warmth, which opens the blood vessels in your arms and legs, reversing the flow of blood to the centre of the body typical of the stress response.
3. Regular heartbeat, which helps to normalize the heart rate, reversing the quickened heart rate characteristic of the stress response.
4. Regular breathing, which helps to normalize breath rate, reversing the quickened breath rate characteristic of the stress response.
5. Relaxation and warming of the abdomen, which reverses the flow of blood away from the digestive system typical of the stress response.
6. Cooling of the head, which reverses the flow of blood to the brain typical of the stress response.

In other words, all the major symptoms of stress in the body caused by the release of stress hormones are systematically targeted and reversed through the suggestions in autogenic training.

If you feel stress or discomfort during autogenic training, skip to the next area. If you suffer from ulcers or other gastrointestinal problems, skip the step that warms the abdomen and stomach.

You can do autogenic training on your own, but visiting a professional autogenic training instructor to learn how to do it correctly may be a good idea. Check with psychotherapists in your area who practise hypnotherapy, or check with qualified complementary health practitioners such as chiropractors, herbalists or massage therapists who might be able to refer you to someone nearby.

If you can't find an instructor, look for books on the subject and follow their directions. Or simply find a quiet place to relax where you are unlikely to be bothered, get comfortable and warm, turn down the lights, sit or lie easily, then focus on each of the six areas in the following manner, repeating the verbal suggestions listed and concentrating on what you are saying to yourself and on the named area. Don't force yourself to concentrate – keep your attitude passive and accepting. However it happens is fine. You can't do it wrong.

You can put these suggestions onto tape, or you can memorize them. Repeat each phrase slowly four times before moving on to the next one:

1. My right arm is heavy.
2. My left arm is heavy.
3. My right leg is heavy.
4. My left leg is heavy.
5. My right arm is warm.
6. My left arm is warm.
7. My right leg is warm.
8. My left leg is warm.
9. My arms are heavy and warm.
10. My legs are heavy and warm.
11. My heartbeat is slow and easy.
12. My heart feels calm.
13. My breathing is slow and easy.
14. My breathing feels calm.
15. My stomach is warm.
16. My stomach is relaxed.
17. My forehead is cool.
18. My scalp is relaxed.
19. My whole body is calm.
20. My whole body is relaxed.
21. I am calm and relaxed.

Goodbye stress response.

Ayurveda

Ayurveda (pronounced I-YOUR-VAY-DA) is an ancient science of living a long and healthy life, defying disease and ageing, and promoting wellbeing and good health through a variety of practices. Ayurveda may be the oldest known health care system, probably over 5,000 years old, and it is still widely practised today. In fact, thanks to the efforts of Dr Deepak Chopra, doctor and author, the science of Ayurveda has enjoyed a new surge in popularity in the last decade.

In Ayurveda, stress equals imbalance. When the body isn't balanced, pain, illness, injury, disease and psychological and emotional problems result. The theory of Ayurveda is complex, but to simplify, it uses certain foods, herbs, oils, colours, sounds, yoga exercises, cleansing rituals, chants, lifestyle changes and counselling to put the body and mind into the ultimate state of health. It also has at its heart a very specific philosophy suggesting that disease and even the ageing process can be halted, even reversed, through certain practices.

While Ayurveda treats imbalances in the different doshas, or types, in many ways, here are some generalizations:

- **Vatas** benefit from warm, moist, comforting foods (porridge, soup) and holding to a regular daily routine. They feel aggravated by the cold.
- **Pittas** benefit from cold food, anger management and long walks. Heat and spicy foods aggravate them.
- **Kaphas** benefit from warm, dry foods, stimulating events and exercise. Too much sugar and fat aggravate them.

The Ayurvedic system divides people (and everything else – weather, tastes, seasons, temperatures and so on) into three main dosha types. Many people are a combination of two, or even a balance of the three doshas, but most people lean towards one dominant dosha. One's dosha determines what kinds of foods, herbs, oils, colours, sounds, yoga exercises, cleansing rituals, chants, lifestyle changes and counselling will be most beneficial.

VATA	PITTA	KAPHA
Thin build; if overweight, irregularly so, with spongy rather than solid tissue	Muscular or average build; easily builds muscle	Heavyset, or large-boned; when overweight (common for Kapha), body is solid
Curly, thin, brown hair; can be frizzy	Reddish hair, either dark or strawberry blonde; redhead complexion, freckles, rosy skin	Dark, thick, glossy or oily hair, smooth skin, full lips, creamy or olive complexion
Small, darting eyes	Sharp, piercing, somewhat bloodshot eyes	Large, wide eyes
Dry, cracking joints	Loose, soft joints	Large, thick, sturdy joints
Can't keep to a schedule; erratic eater, sleeper	Good appetite, eats quickly	Low, constant appetite, eats slowly
Low or variable endurance	Moderate endurance but heat intolerant	Strong, steady endurance
Prone to pain, arthritis, and disorders of the nervous and immune system	Prone to infections, fever, and inflammatory diseases	Prone to respiratory diseases, swelling and obesity
Fast, unsteady, erratic lifestyle	Purposeful, goal-oriented, assertive lifestyle	Slow, steady, elegant lifestyle
Sensitive to noise	Sensitive to bright lights	Sensitive to strong odours
Adaptable but sometimes indecisive	Intelligent but sometimes critical	Steady but sometimes dull

Most people have one dominant dosha, although some are a combination of two, but every person has all three in them and can experience imbalances in any one. Vata goes out of balance first, then pitta, then kapha. Ayurveda treats dosha imbalances in many ways.

An Ayurvedic physician can sometimes determine your dosha from nothing more than feeling your pulse. Typically, a rigorous and detailed analysis is made of a patient who seeks Ayurvedic therapy, including detailed questions covering everything from physical make-up to habits, likes and dislikes and profession. Many do-it-yourself quizzes are available in books and on websites to help you determine your own dosha. Some people visit Ayurvedic centres or receive in-patient ayurvedic treatment. Others take dietary and lifestyle advice only.

Ayurveda is a fascinating and complex system, and this book can only scratch the surface. But just to get you started, the table on page 197 shows some qualities commonly associated with each of the dosha types. This list is by no means exhaustive, and is only meant to give you a very general idea of what the three doshas mean.

If Ayurveda interests you, do some research. Books and other sources of information on this ancient science of life and longevity are plentiful. Here are a few I like.

BOOKS

- *Ageless Body, Timeless Mind,* by Deepak Chopra, MD (Rider Books)
- *Creating Health: How to Wake up the Body's Intelligence,* by Deepak Chopra, MD (Rider Books)
- *Perfect Health: The Complete Mind-Body Guide,* by Deepak Chopra, MD (Bantam Books)
- *The Ayurveda Encyclopedia,* by Tirtha, Swami Sada Shiva (Ayurveda Holistic Center Press)

WEB SITES

Ayurveda Holistic Centre: *www.ayurvedahc.com*
The Complementary Healthcare Information Service:
 www.chisuk.com
Everyday Ayurveda: *www.everydayayurveda.org*

Biofeedback: Know Thyself

This high-tech relaxation technique, designed to teach the body how to directly and immediately reverse the stress response, puts you in control of bodily functions once considered to be involuntary. Biofeedback was developed in the 1960s and was popular in the 1970s and 1980s. A biofeedback session involves being hooked up to equipment that measures certain functions such as your skin temperature, heart rate, breathing rate and muscle tension. A trained biofeedback practitioner then guides the subject through relaxation techniques while the subject watches the machine monitors. When heart rate or breathing rate decreases, for example, you can see it on the monitor. You learn how your body feels when your heart and breathing rates decrease. Eventually, after a number of sessions, you learn to lower your heart rate, breathing rate, muscle tension, temperature and so on, on your own.

The first time some people try biofeedback, they actually experience a heightened stress response. This is normal and natural. Once the subject becomes comfortable with the process of monitoring physical reactions, body functions normalize.

Because biofeedback requires special equipment and a trained practitioner, it isn't something you can work out on your own at home, but once you've learned the technique, your vital functions are in your own hands – or head!

To find a qualified biofeedback practitioner near you, start by looking on the Complementary Healthcare Information Service's website at *www.chisuk.com*.

Creativity Therapy

Creativity therapy is the use of drawing, painting, writing, sculpture or playing music as a form of stress relief and also as a way of dealing with emotional or psychological problems. Art therapy has a long history of helping patients work through problems and unblock creativity by using certain techniques, and it requires a trained art therapist. Creativity therapy is a more general term to describe using creativity on your own to help relieve stress. Art therapy is a kind of creativity therapy, but it is not the only kind. In creativity therapy, you can write poetry, play the piano, even model home-made salt dough to help relieve your stress and express your creativity.

Creativity therapy is an excellent way to relieve stress. When you become immersed in creation, you can achieve a kind of intense, all-consuming focus similar to the intense focus and concentration you can achieve through meditation. Allowing yourself to become one with your creation – your painting, drawing, poem, short story, diary entry, sculpture, music – helps you to let go, even if only for a little while, of the stresses in your life. Your body responds by relaxing, counteracting the effects of too much stress.

As with meditation, creativity therapy teaches your mind to concentrate for a long period of time on a single thing – it's excellent practice and a great way to hone your mental powers. Creativity therapy can also help you to feel good about who you are. Rather than spending your entire day doing what you're supposed to do, or what other people want you to do, creativity therapy gives you a space solely for yourself. During this time you can express your innermost thoughts, feelings, problems, anxieties, joys and the imagery that sits deep within your subconscious waiting to be released.

How do you do it? Set aside 30–60 minutes each day. Choose your creative outlet. Perhaps you will write in your diary, or practise a musical instrument, or paint with watercolours, or draw the flowers in your garden or dance to music in your room. Whatever you choose, commit to this time as you would to meditation time. Make it an unbreakable appointment. Then find a quiet place where you are unlikely to be disturbed, and start creating – or dancing or playing or whatever you have chosen to do.

Try not to look at your creations or analyze your performance, at least not closely, until you've practised creative therapy for one month. When the month is over, look carefully at what you've accomplished. Do you see patterns? Motifs? Themes? Words and images that recur in writing or painting or drawing are your personal themes. Movements or sounds can also have meaning for you, personally, if you are dancing or playing music. Spend some time meditating on what they could mean for you. What is your subconscious trying to tell you?

Let your creativity therapy be a private event. Whether you are painting, drawing, writing, sculpting or playing music, the important thing is not to try to create a 'masterpiece'. This is private creation – this is just for you. Promise yourself you won't show it to anyone – at least not for a month, and then you can decide. For now, just let whatever is inside you flow out through the medium.

It doesn't matter if you don't know how to draw, paint, write poetry or whatever you have chosen to do. This is not work to be judged, analyzed or displayed. This is work that comes directly from your subconscious and is a process of releasing what you are holding onto, mentally, deep inside. And that is a good process.

Here are some tips to remember when engaged in any kind of creativity therapy:

· As you work, don't stop. Write or draw continuously. If you stop, you'll be more likely to judge your work.
· Don't judge your work!

- Try creating when you are very tired. Sometimes fatigue dulls your conscious, organized, critical mind, allowing more images from the subconscious to flow through.
- Promise yourself you won't read what you've written or survey what you've drawn until the session is over, or you're likely to start judging.
- Don't be critical of or disappointed by what you come up with. There is no wrong way to do this, unless you are judging yourself.
- Stuck? Faced with a blank page? Just start writing or drawing without any thought or plan, even if you end up writing 'I don't know what to write' for three pages or drawing a page full of stick figures. Eventually you'll get tired of that and something else will come out.
- Commit to the process. Even if it seems as if it isn't working at first, 30 minutes (or just 10–15 minutes when you first try it) each and every day will yield dramatic results if you stick with it.
- Don't think you can't do creative therapy because you 'aren't creative'. Nonsense. *Everyone* is creative. Some people just haven't developed their creativity as much as others, and creativity therapy is just as helpful (if not more so) for non-artists, who don't already have fixed ideas about how they are 'supposed to' create something.
- Most importantly, enjoy the process! Creativity therapy is illuminating, interesting and fun!

Keeping a Dream Diary

Keeping a dream diary is similar to creativity therapy in that your unmonitored creativity can tap your subconscious in the same way your dreams do. While the exact nature of 'the stuff that dreams are made of' is still a matter of controversy, many people believe that dreams access the subconscious mind's hopes, fears, goals, worries and desires.

We all dream, but it isn't easy to remember your dreams, and some people claim they never remember them. Keeping a dream diary is a way to begin identifying the images, themes, motifs and emotions in your dreams. It is a good stress-management tool because the mental training it involves helps the mind to become more stress-resilient. Also, the information you uncover through keeping a dream diary may help to root out and dispose of unnecessary stress in your life.

First, find a book that you will enjoy writing in. This could be your stress management diary or a separate notebook, which you keep by your bed. Then find a pen that is easy and pleasant to write with. Keep these items in a place that is easy to reach while you are lying in bed – a bedside table is ideal.

When you are in bed and ready to go to sleep, close your eyes and tell yourself: 'I will remember my dreams tonight'. This sets the intention in your mind. It may not work the first night, the second night, or even for a few weeks. But it should work eventually.

In the morning, the second you wake up, before you get up to do anything, as you are opening your eyes, reach for your dream diary and immediately start writing. If you remember a dream, write about it in as much detail as you can. Even if you don't remember a dream, just start writing down whatever impression is in your head. As you write, dream impressions, even full dreams with elaborate plots, may come into your head. If they don't, you'll still be writing from the subconscious, which is more accessible in the first few minutes after awakening.

Write until you've recorded all the dreams you remember, or until your awakening thoughts are exhausted. Then, the next night, repeat your intention to remember your dreams again, and record them again in the morning.

Dreams of flying may symbolize a feeling of freedom, power, success or a new perspective. Dreams of falling may symbolize a feeling of insecurity, anxiety, failure or the inability to control one's situation. Both flying and falling dreams are quite common. To learn more about what your dreams mean, have a look at *Everything You Need to Know About Dreams,* by Trish and Rob MacGregor, in the same series as this book.

As with creativity therapy, try not to read your dream diary for about a month. Then, after a month has passed, go back to it and see if there are any themes, motifs or recurring images. These are probably signals from your subconscious. Reflect on what they might be telling you about the direction your life is going in, your health, your relationships and your happiness. Your dream diary may give you clues about ways to reshape and de-stress your life.

Even if you don't find any obvious messages, persist in keeping your dream diary. As with meditation, this process helps you to focus and concentrate your thoughts, and will also help you to tap into your inner creativity and feel more connected to yourself. People who devote time each day to themselves, and engage in inner reflection, tend to feel better about themselves and are less likely to suffer from the negative effects of stress. Let your dreams lead you to a feeling of groundedness and connectedness with your inner self.

Flower Remedies

Flower remedies or flower essences are made from water and whole flowers, then preserved with alcohol. They contain no actual flower parts, but people who use and prescribe them believe they carry the flower's essence or energy and can promote emotional healing. The remedies are thought to work in a vibrational, rather than a biochemical, way on the body. The typical dosage is four drops of the flower remedy under the tongue four times per day.

Flower remedies are preserved with alcohol, and while the alcohol in the remedies is minute, it could be enough to trigger problems in anyone who is sensitive to alcohol or recovering from alcohol addiction. These people should not take flower remedies. Also, only choose flowers that you can identify, specifically those used in traditional flower remedies. You wouldn't want to drink a remedy made with mildly poisonous ragwort, even if the leaf didn't remain in the remedy.

Flower remedies are a non-invasive, safe, gentle way to balance the emotions. They are considered non-invasive because, although you drink them, no actual flower parts remain in the remedy. You are drinking spring water with a little alcohol for preservation and the vibrational energy of a flower.

Flower remedies directly address the emotional effects of stress in a lovely, natural way without any side effects. Different remedies address different emotional imbalances, helping to clarify the mind, 'unstick' the emotions when they get stuck in one place or mode, and helping to restore rational and productive emotions. Often several remedies are prescribed in combination. According to the *Illustrated Encyclopedia of Natural Remedies*, by C. Norman Shealy, MD, PhD (Element Books), flower remedies were created to be so easy to make and use that people could treat themselves.

There are complementary health practitioners who prescribe flower remedies, but you can also make and take them yourself. In fact, the actual process of making flower remedies can be a relaxing and enjoyable way to combat stress, and could even become a hobby, although many of the remedies that are effective for certain emotional imbalances will come from flowers that aren't available in your area.

If you would like to try making your own flower remedies, there are books that tell you about the processes, or you could talk to your complementary health practitioner. If you do not wish to do this, or if you need a remedy from a flower not available in your area, you can buy flower remedies from healthfood shops or complementary health therapists. Bach Flower Remedies are the most widely known, although other brands are available.

Flower remedies are often used to help pets overcome emotional imbalances, too. Pet shops and pet-supply catalogues often offer different complementary remedy mixes to help pets overcome separation anxiety, nervousness, hyperactivity, even depression. Always see your vet first, to rule out any other medical condition.

Find the emotional symptom of your stress in the table overleaf and see which flower remedy might benefit you.

SYMPTOMS	FLOWER REMEDY
Hiding problems behind a cheerful demeanour	Agrimony
Constant worry, anxiety, racing thoughts	White Chestnut Flower
Strong feelings of hopelessness and despair	Gorse
Inability to find a life purpose or direction	Wild Oat
Always on the move, can't stand to wait, rushing, can't slow down	Black-Eyed Susan
Resignation, passivity, apathy	Wild Rose
Selfish, sulky, self-pitying, ungrateful	Willow
Self-condemnation, disgust with self	Crab Apple
Self-obsessed, unable to listen to and share with others	Heather
Sensitivity to other people, obsessive worrying that something horrible will happen to loved ones	Red Chestnut Flower
Procrastination, exhaustion from work, inability to get motivated to work	Hornbeam
Compulsion to constantly give to others, disregarding one's own need, resulting in depletion	Centaury
Weak will, tendency to follow or imitate others	Cerato
Possessive, selfish, nagging, manipulative	Chicory
Excessive daydreaming, not living in the present, living in a fantasy world	Clematis
Nervous, stammering, intelligent but slow to learn	Bush Fuchsia
Being judgmental, overcritical, intolerant	Beech
Discouragement, despondency, and mild depression due to circumstances	Gentian
Intense fear, terror, nervousness, panic	Bach's Rescue Remedy, made from Rock Rose, Cherry Plum, Impatiens, Clematis, Star of Bethlehem
Obsessed with past, nostalgia, feeling that past was wonderful and future is bleak	Honeysuckle
Intense negativity, hatred, jealousy, suspicion, or revenge	Holly

Friend Therapy

Friend therapy is simple – let your friends help you to manage your stress. Research shows that people without social networks and friends, while feeling lonely, often won't admit it. Loneliness is stressful, and holding in your feelings is even more stressful.

Some people turn to friends automatically when things get tough. Others tend to isolate themselves during stressful times, just when they could most use a listening ear and a few words of encouragement.

Some people may already have a group of friends they can turn to, but when things get stressful it's easy to stop phoning. Do you stop replying to emails, phoning your friends or going out with them when you are feeling stressed? Engage in some friend therapy and give them a call. Warn them you are feeling stressed, and ask them to listen without offering advice if you don't want advice. Or perhaps you do.

If you don't have a ready-made group of friends or have lost touch with them, you may have to start from scratch. One of the easiest ways to make friends is to join something – an evening class, a club – or perhaps attend a church or find a support group. You might need to try a few different things before you meet people you really get on with, but keep trying.

Don't use the excuse that you can't fit anything else into your day. Set something up with a colleague you like, approach a parent at your child's school during a school event, or call a friend you haven't been in touch with for a while to meet for lunch. After all, you're going to eat lunch anyway, aren't you?

Treating stress with friend therapy doesn't mean sitting at home waiting for your friends to come to you. It means taking the initiative and going out there to make contact. Sometimes a few words are all that is needed to find someone who is in the same position as you and needs friend therapy, too.

Friend therapy isn't complicated. All it entails is human contact (not cyber-contact, although that's better than no contact). Phone contact can be helpful, but nothing beats the real thing. Just being with another person – talking (even if it's not about your problems), enjoying yourself, taking a break from the daily routine – is a great way to relax, raise your self-esteem and have the chance to be there for somebody else, too. You don't have to do anything in particular with your friends to make it friend therapy. You just have to have a social life.

Of course there are limits to what friends can and should do for you. Part of friend therapy is giving as well as taking. A productive friend therapy relationship should certainly be reciprocal. If you use your friends for constant offloading but never allow them to offload on you, they won't be your friends for long!

One way to start a friendship is to ask a favour. Acquaintances and neighbours are often hesitant to ask favours, but asking a favour starts a reciprocal relationship. If you ask your neighbour if you can borrow her snow shovel or the proverbial cup of sugar, your neighbour will feel easier about asking you for something later on. Asking a favour is more effective than offering a favour 'any time', because people are usually more willing to do you a favour than ask for one. Go ahead and ask for what you need – you may forge a friendship.

Hypnosis: Hype or Help?

People tend to have preconceptions about hypnosis: the swinging pendulum, the controlling therapist with the German accent, the hypnotized person running around on a stage clucking like a chicken. While hypnosis has certainly been used (or misused) by those seeking applause, hypnosis and hypnotherapy are legitimate tools for helping people put themselves into more positive mental states. Hypnosis is, in essence, deep relaxation coupled with visualization; it is *not* some mysterious state in which you are completely at the mercy of the hypnotist.

While hypnotized, you retain your awareness, but your body becomes extremely relaxed and disinclined to move. Your awareness becomes narrow, your thinking tends to become literal, and you become much more open to suggestion than you would be in a non-hypnotic state. This suggestibility is what makes hypnosis work.

During the course of our lives, we may often want to change things about ourselves – our habits, our reactions to stressful circumstances, our tendency to worry, our inability to sleep – but just telling ourselves 'Stop that!' or 'Just go to sleep!' doesn't often work. We have so much to do, we are caught up in patterns, our minds are uncontrolled and racing, we are tense. All these things keep us from doing what we know we should do, such as stopping smoking or worrying too much.

Hypnosis is a state similar to sleep. The body becomes so profoundly relaxed that it ceases to be a distraction. The mind becomes highly focused and, thus, more able to do what we want it to do. This focus makes the imagery we use to direct our behaviour and feelings seem more real; so real that our bodies respond to it. This is nothing new. When watching a film or even hearing a story, our bodies often respond as if we were part of the action – we may experience a faster heart rate at an exciting part, a surge of emotion at a poignant part, feelings of anger at an injustice. Hypnosis uses the body's ability to react to the mind by directing the mind in specific ways while the body is relaxed. That's all there is to it.

Hypnotherapy is the use of hypnosis by a trained therapist to, for example, help the patient heal from the trauma of a past event, reframe negative health habits or regain control over certain behaviour. Hypnotherapy is frequently used to help people stop smoking or overeating. It is a common therapy for people experiencing chronic fatigue. It is also effective for improving self-esteem and confidence.

 When you are hypnotized, you can't be made to do something that would harm yourself or others (unless you would do so anyway). You also can't be made to do things against your will. The hypnotic state is merely a highly relaxed state in which the mind is more open to suggestions from visualizations and verbal cues.

You can even hypnotize yourself, although not everyone is as open to this as to being hypnotized. You do have to be willing to try it and to follow the hypnotic suggestions. The following exercises, adapted from *The Relaxation & Stress Reduction Workbook*, by Martha Davis, PhD, Elizabeth Robbins-Eshelman, MSW, and Matthew McKay, PhD (New Harbinger Books), can be used to begin training your mind to respond to suggestion. You can also use these tests to see whether you would be a good candidate for hypnosis. If you don't respond to them after several tries, hypnosis may not be helpful for you.

EXERCISE 1

1. Stand with your feet about shoulder-width apart, your arms hanging loosely at your sides. Close your eyes and relax.
2. Imagine you are holding a small suitcase in your right hand. Feel the moderate heaviness of the suitcase and the way the suitcase pulls your body to one side.
3. Imagine someone takes the suitcase and hands you a medium-sized suitcase. This suitcase is heavier and bulkier than the small suitcase. Feel the handle in your hand. Feel the heaviness of the suitcase weighing down your right side.
4. Imagine someone takes the suitcase and hands you a large suitcase. This suitcase is incredibly heavy, so heavy you can hardly hold on to it, so heavy it pulls your entire body to the right as the weight of the suitcase sinks towards the floor.
5. Keep feeling the weight of this heavy suitcase for two to three minutes.
6. Open your eyes. Are you standing perfectly straight, or has your posture swayed, even a little bit, to the right?

EXERCISE 2

1. Stand with your feet about shoulder-width apart, your arms hanging loosely at your sides. Close your eyes and relax.
2. Imagine you are standing outside on a small hill in the middle of a wide, open plain. The breeze is blowing and the sun is shining. It is a beautiful, clear day.
3. Suddenly, the breeze begins to pick up and the wind starts to blow. You are facing into the wind, and as it blows harder and harder, gusting around you, you feel it pushing you back, blowing your hair back, even blowing your arms back a little.
4. The wind is now so strong you can barely stand up. If you don't lean into the wind, you'll be knocked backwards! You've never felt wind this strong, and each forceful gust nearly pushes you off your feet!
5. Feel the strength of the wind for two to three minutes.
6. Open your eyes. Are you standing perfectly straight, or leaning into the wind, even if only a little?

EXERCISE 3

1. Stand with feet about shoulder-width apart, both arms straight out in front of you, parallel to the ground. Close your eyes.
2. Imagine someone has tied a heavy weight to your right arm. Your arm has to strain to hold up the weight that hangs from it. Feel the weight. Imagine how it looks hanging from your arm.
3. Imagine someone ties another heavy weight to your right arm. The two weights pull your arm down and down. They are so heavy that your muscles have to tense and strain to hold them up.
4. Imagine someone ties a third heavy weight to your arm. The three weights are so heavy that you can barely keep your arm raised. Feel how the weights pull down your arm.
5. Now imagine that someone ties a huge helium balloon to your left arm. Feel the balloon pulling your left arm higher and higher, tugging it skywards.
6. Feel the weights on your right arm and the balloon on your left arm for two to three minutes.
7. Open your eyes. Are your arms still even, or is your right arm lowered and your left arm raised, even just a little?

If, after several tries, your body didn't respond at all to any of these exercises, hypnosis may not be for you. If you still want to try it, however, of course, do. The mind is powerful, and wanting it to work is half the battle. Many researchers believe that almost anyone can learn the process of self-hypnosis.

 Studies show that self-hypnosis is among the most effective methods of reducing migraine in children and teenagers.

While trained hypnotherapists and hypnotists may be able to hypnotize you straight away, with some practice and work you can learn to hypnotize yourself. This is done in a very similar way to hypnotizing somebody else. You'll need to decide exactly what you want to work on, for example, stopping smoking or not falling apart every time your mother-in-law comes to stay.

Then, self-hypnosis involves a detailed process of breathing, muscle relaxation and visualization, beginning with the descent down a staircase on a count from 10 down to one. After some detailed visualization to engage and focus the mind, the hypnosis session ends with a posthypnotic suggestion to trigger you to behave in the way you want to behave. Phrase the suggestion positively: 'I feel strong, confident and in control of the situation when my mother-in-law is in my house', not, 'I don't want to burst into tears every time my mother-in-law makes a comment about my housekeeping abilities.'

After the posthypnotic suggestion, you can bring yourself slowly out of the hypnotic state by counting to 10, telling yourself that at the number 10, you will be alert, refreshed and wide awake.

Books on self-hypnosis explain in great detail how to do it, but if you aren't comfortable doing it on your own, visit a qualified hypnotherapist. Whichever way you choose, hypnosis can be an effective deep relaxation technique that can help you to get a grip on the stress you thought was out of your control.

The National Register of Hypnotherapists and Psychotherapists (NRHP) keeps a database of hypnotherapists throughout the country and provides a free referral service for those seeking a reliable practitioner. Their address and website can be found in Appendix B.

Never practise self-hypnosis in a situation where you need to be alert, such as while driving. The deeply relaxed state could keep your body from responding quickly enough to stay safe.

Optimism Therapy

Do you think you are a confirmed pessimist? Optimism therapy is a form of attitude adjustment focusing on reframing responses as an optimist. Optimism may have a reputation as a deluded view in which the world is seen through rose-tinted glasses, but, actually, optimists are happier and healthier than pessimists because they tend to assume they have control over their lives. Pessimists tend to feel that life controls them.

Psychologists determine optimistic and pessimistic character from a person's explanatory style while describing an unfortunate event. The explanatory style has three parts:

1. **The internal/external explanation.** Optimists tend to believe that external factors cause misfortune, while pessimists tend to blame themselves (the internal factor).
2. **The stable/unstable explanation.** Optimists tend to see misfortune as unstable or temporary, while pessimists tend to see misfortune as stable or permanent.
3. **The global/specific explanation.** Optimists tend to see problems as specific to a situation, while pessimists tend to see problems as global – that is, unavoidable and pervasive.

How does an optimist's body differ from a pessimist's body? Profoundly. Studies show that optimists enjoy better general health, a stronger immune system, faster recovery from surgery and longer life.

tips

You can use a behavioural technique called 'thought-stopping' to counter your pessimistic tendencies and any other mental stress reaction. To practise thought-stopping, identify a negative thought you tend to have. Associate the thought with a clear image. Set a timer for three minutes, close your eyes and concentrate on the image. When the timer rings, shout 'Stop!' Repeat this process several times. Then whenever the image recurs, whisper 'Stop!' The interruption will stop the negative thought and give you the opportunity to consciously substitute it with a more positive one.

Because of their tendencies, pessimists may *feel* as if they are under more stress than optimists, even though both are actually under the same amount. How the stress *feels* may directly determine how the body reacts, making the stress response more severe in pessimists. Optimists are also more likely to engage in positive behaviour such as exercising and eating well. Pessimists may take the fatalistic view that what they eat or how much they exercise doesn't matter anyway, so they might as well do what is easiest. Pessimists also tend to be more socially isolated or lonely, or have friends with negative influences, such as other pessimists or people with habits that are destructive to health and wellbeing.

So if you are a pessimist, can you change? Of course you can – you just need some optimism therapy. Studies show that smiling, even when you aren't happy, can make you feel happy, but optimism extends far beyond a forced smile. Pretending to be an optimist can actually make you feel like one, and can also help your body to learn to respond like an optimist.

If your pessimism is temporary or recent, you can probably help yourself with personal optimism therapy sessions. At the beginning of each day, before you get out of bed, before you have time to become too pessimistic, say one of these affirmations out loud several times:

· 'No matter what happens today, I won't judge myself.'
· 'My life will improve from the inside out.'
· 'Today I will enjoy myself in healthy ways.'
· 'No matter what happens around me, this will be a good day.'
· 'This can be a good day, or this can be a bad day. I choose to make it a good day.'

Then choose a single area or part of your day and vow to be an optimist in that area only. Perhaps you'll choose lunchtime, or the staff meeting or the time with your children before supper. During that period, every time you begin to think or say something pessimistically, immediately replace the words or thought with something optimistic. Instead of responding to a spilled cup of coffee with 'I'm so clumsy!', respond with 'Whoops! That cup slipped right out of my hand'. Instead of responding to criticism of your work with the thought 'My manager always hates my work', change your thought and tell yourself 'She didn't like this part of this particular project, but the rest of it was great!'

You may feel forced and unnatural doing this at first, but like anything else, the more you do it, the more it becomes a habit. You can adopt the optimist habit – it's good for your health.

If you are a serious and fully committed pessimist, and/or if you suffer from depression, you could probably benefit from visiting a trained psychotherapist for cognitive therapy. In cognitive therapy, the therapist helps patients discover the effect of pessimistic or depressed thoughts on mood, and also helps them to discover the ingrained nature of these thoughts so that they can learn to catch themselves in the pessimistic act. Cognitive therapy can be very successful for depression, and some studies show it to be as effective as antidepressant medication. (For many people with depression, a combination of cognitive therapy and medication works best.)

Reward-based Self-Training

If you've ever trained a dog, you probably know about positive reinforcement training, because it is what most animal trainers use today. People (and dogs) do things for two reasons:

1. To benefit or be rewarded.
2. To avoid something negative.

The first reason is much more compelling and positive. Let's say you see a piece of chocolate cake. You know you shouldn't eat it because you could gain weight (negative reinforcement), but you want to eat it because it tastes good (positive reinforcement). Which is more fun, eating it or not eating it?

If you can frame your stress management in terms of positive reinforcement (not to mention other habits and the life changes you are trying to make), you are much more likely to succeed. If you are successful with negative reinforcement – not eating the cake – it won't be as enjoyable, and you may be less likely to keep it up. What if not eating the cake was rewarded with a stroll through the park on a nice day, or an afternoon matinee? That's far more inspiring than the mere promise of not gaining weight.

But who has time to go to the cinema every time they do something good? Your rewards don't need to be so time-consuming. They only need be rewards. Make a list of your own personal human treats, and every time you think you have a battle ahead in which you know you'll encounter stress, promise yourself a treat from your list. You'll get through the difficulty and stay on your best behaviour, and the promise of a reward will help to keep you thinking positive, feeling relaxed and enjoying the 'training session'.

Dog trainer Jean Donaldson lists the five things dogs consider most rewarding. How easily could you adapt this list to yourself?

1. Food
2. Access to other dogs
3. Access to outdoors and interesting smells
4. Attention from people and access to people, especially after isolation periods
5. Initiation of play or other enjoyed activity

Your personal treat list might look something like the one below, but of course these are just suggestions to get you started. Your list will be as individual as you are.

- Order a takeaway or eat out tonight instead of cooking.
- Have a massage (paid for, or ask a loved one).
- Go to a yoga class.
- Go to bed early.
- Watch your favourite film... again!
- Make time to call a friend and chat.

Continual rewards make life a lot more fun and a lot less stressful. They also help to boost and maintain your self-esteem because you are taking time for yourself and celebrating yourself by paying yourself (through rewards) what you know you're worth. So let yourself enjoy life with positive reinforcement!

CHAPTER 10

De-stressing the Nuts and Bolts

Stress-management techniques are great to add to your routine so that you can manage the stress of daily life. But what about that daily life? What about all those things you *have* to do? What about managing your money, your time, your work, your home – managing your *life*? There are many ways you can de-stress these daily obligations by making them simpler, easier, less time-consuming and even a bit more fun. In this chapter, you'll find ways to de-stress the nuts and bolts of your life so that you have more time for fun.

Your Money

On the list of things that stress you the most, how high is money? For many people, money is one of the primary causes of daily stress, usually because we don't think we have enough, and sometimes because we have enough but are worried about how we are managing it.

There is a lot more to managing your money than paying the bills with a bit to save or maintaining a profitable investment portfolio. Humans have lived with money in one form or another for thousands of years, and it has become deeply ingrained in our psyches. We have all kinds of hidden and not-so-hidden feelings about money, emotional blocks, obsessions and pretty strange ideas. The phrase 'It's only money' might be something you say sometimes, perhaps to justify an extravagant purchase or to make yourself feel better when you don't have any, but very few of us really believe that money is 'only' anything.

Studies show that income level has no apparent link with reported happiness or life satisfaction.

Money is important to us. It is important to our culture. Some might even say it rules the world. But it shouldn't rule you.

In *The 9 Steps to Financial Freedom*, professional financial planner and investment advisor Suze Orman lists 'Seeing How Your Past Holds the Key to Your Financial Future' as step number one. Money memories from childhood can hold the key to how we feel about money today, even if we don't realize it.

Perhaps you grew up knowing a family with a lot of money whose members weren't very kind to you. Did you learn to look askance at people with a lot of money, thinking they surely didn't understand the important things in life, such as love and family? Or perhaps you grew up in a family that didn't have to struggle for money and had contact with a less fortunate family whose members weren't trustworthy. Did you learn to be suspicious of people with low incomes?

Perhaps money was highly valued in your family, or not valued much at all. Perhaps you *were* taught to manage it, but many of us aren't given these skills, and as adults don't have the slightest clue what to do with the money we earn apart from paying the bills and buying the food.

Added to our personal experiences are cultural stereotypes galore. Television programmes, films and books often represent rich people as heartless snobs and poor people as work-shy thieves. Old misers who hoard their riches must be a bit mad. Generous souls who give all their money away must be angelic. Sometimes it seems like a sin to have or try to get money, yet it also seems to be a crime if you don't have enough.

One place to look for wasted money is in your own kitchen. How much food do you buy every week that goes uneaten? How much rotten produce do you throw out? How many plastic containers filled with unidentifiable leftovers are there? How many food items sit in your cupboard month after month – things you bought on a whim but can never quite bring yourself to eat? Planning your meals, avoiding impulse buys, and learning to cook an appropriate amount of food can save you hundreds of pounds a year.

In the West, the 'middle class' has been consistently held up as the ideal, and has become such a broad category that most people now consider themselves to be part of it. The majority of us don't live in poverty, but wouldn't call ourselves rich, either, and this is what makes us comfortable. Yet we remain obsessed with money – with wealth, with fear of poverty, with the material objects money can buy – which is what capitalism is all about.

If it's 'only money', why does it obsess us so? Money is not a simple matter, but that doesn't mean it has to be complicated for you. To de-stress your financial life, you need to do several things:

· Understand *exactly* how you really feel about money, including your prejudices and preconceptions.
· Continue to recognize with vigilance your financial preconceptions so that they don't control you.
· Have very specific financial goals, for both present and future.
· Have a very specific plan to meet your financial goals.

- Know *exactly* how much is coming in and how much is going out.
- Start by building a financial cushion.

Many excellent books are devoted solely to this subject and are worth reading. However, this book covers the subject only with stress relief in mind. I hope you'll start here, then be inspired to learn more from other sources. Let's begin by looking at these steps one by one.

How Do You Really Feel About Money?

To get you thinking about how you *really* feel about money (which may be different from how you *think* you feel about money), answer the following questions, either here or in your stress diary.

1. How do you feel, emotionally, when you think about your financial situation right now?

   _____

   _____

   _____

   _____

2. Examine any negative feelings you have about your financial situation. Why do you think you have these negative feelings?

   _____

   _____

   _____

   _____

3. How do your parents feel about money?

4. When you were a child, what was your family's attitude towards people who had more money than you did?

5. When you were a child, what was your family's attitude towards people who had less money than you did?

6. Describe an incident from your childhood that revealed your family's attitude to money.

7. Describe a specific book, film, television programme or other source that you think could possibly have affected your feelings about money in some way.

_____

_____

_____

_____

8. If you had all the money you could possibly ever spend, and you knew you would continue to be wealthy for the rest of your life, how would it make you feel?

_____

_____

_____

_____

9. List the things in life that you honestly believe are more important than money.

_____

_____

_____

_____

10. What, specifically, has to change in your life so that money no longer causes you stress?

_____

_____

_____

Continue to Recognize Your Financial Preconceptions

Now look back at your answers for clues to some of your financial preconceptions. Keep these in mind as you work on simplifying your financial life. If you have the preconception that there is something wrong with having money, you may have been sabotaging yourself your entire life, subconsciously keeping yourself from financial security. Perhaps you strongly believe that money shouldn't be important, but the lack of it in your life is controlling you, and now, in its absence, money has become the most important thing in your life. Perhaps you believe that self-worth is related to financial worth and that without money, you aren't worth much. Perhaps you believe that money can, indeed, buy happiness, or that it is, indeed, the root of all evil.

Whatever you believe, know that you believe it, and continue to question your preconceptions so that they don't sabotage your financial life. Your relationship with money should be completely clear and unimpeded by prejudice, otherwise your financial life will probably always be at least a minor source of stress.

Many people don't realize they are afraid to earn more money than their parents earned. This is natural, but something to be overcome. The fact that wealth is uncharted territory in your family doesn't mean you can't be a trailblazer.

Have Very Specific Financial Goals

If you don't know exactly what you want your money to do for you, it won't do much for you. No matter how much money you make, whether you dabble in the stock market or can't afford your monthly rent, you must have specific financial goals. If you know where you are heading financially, your life will be less stressful, even if it will take a long time to get where you are going.

How much money do you need to get by each month? (Most people underestimate this figure.) How much do you want to have saved by the time you retire? Do you need funds for your children's higher education? A deposit for a house? Would you like to have extra money for investing? How much do you need in savings to cover your expenses for six months if you should become unable to work?

Make a list of your financial goals, no matter how impossible they seem, on your own or with the help of an independent financial adviser.

1. _____
2. _____
3. _____
4. _____
5. _____
6. _____
7. _____
8. _____
9. _____
10. _____

It is said that a new car drops about 30 per cent in value the first time it is driven. Secondhand cars can save you money and, in many cases, eliminate the need for a credit agreement and extra interest charges. Many dealerships include guarantees with secondhand cars. Have your car checked by a reliable mechanic to ensure it doesn't have any major problems, and enjoy your savings!

Have a Specific Plan

It isn't enough just to have goals; you also have to have a workable plan to meet them. If this seems overwhelming, visit a good independent financial adviser for help. Anybody can work towards financial goals, and such financial advisers are trained to show you how, without being tied to any one financial product. If you aren't ready for that or feel you can work it out on your own, read books on the subject.

According to feng shui, the ancient Chinese art of placement, the upper right-hand corner of any room, as you enter from the door, is the prosperity corner. Keeping this corner clear, clean, uncluttered and decked in the prosperity colours of purple, red, green or gold will help to direct financial energy your way. (There's more about feng shui later in this chapter.)

Part of meeting your financial goals might be concerned with how to live on less rather than how to make more. Simplicity, frugal living and other downsizing trends have been popular in the last decade as people realize they've been making lots of money, and not getting much in return in the way of spiritual rewards. Books, websites, newsletters, and other sources are rich with information on this movement. Here are some tips for de-stressing your financial life by simplifying your financial needs:

·   Become aware of the way advertising works and how it tries to make you think you need things you really don't.
·   Every time you are about to spend money, stop for a moment, take a deep breath and ask yourself, 'Do I really want this, or do I just think I want this at this moment?'
·   Before you spend money, stop for a moment, take a deep breath and ask yourself, 'Is this item worth the time out of my life I took to earn the money I'll pay for it?'
·   If you decide you really do want something, that it really is worth the money for you, even if it would be frivolous to someone else (dinner at a restaurant when you can't face cooking, a special piece of early Coalbrookdale pottery you've been looking for for years, a pair of shoes that feels perfect), buying it will probably be less stressful than letting it go.

- Make a list of things you can do with your family and/or friends that don't cost any money. Be creative, then *use* the list!
- Slow down. You don't have to keep moving, going, spending. Why not relax at home with your family or friends and just do nothing for a change?
- Drive less. Walk, cycle or take public transport more.
- Do you really need all those extra satellite TV channels? Wouldn't basic TV be enough?
- Cooking can be fun, and home-cooked food is less expensive than the frozen convenience kind.
- How often do you go to the gym? Are you throwing away money on membership when you'd rather just go for a walk, a jog or a bike ride for free? For some people, the gym is really worth it. For others, it's a needless money drain.
- Establishing a garden requires an initial investment (small or large, depending on how frugally you go about it), but it yields free food and the opportunity for exercise and fresh air all spring and summer.
- Focus your energy on getting rid of the things you don't need rather than adding to them.
- Learn the joy and freedom of simple living!

Know *Exactly* How Much Is Coming In and Going Out

It isn't easy to keep track of every single penny that comes in and goes out, as many books on financial planning recommend that you do. However, if you don't do this for at least, say, a representative week or two out of each month, you will never know where your money is going. And *can* it go when you aren't looking! Just as with anything else, keeping track of your money is a matter of *habit*, and this is a good habit to get into. If you know where your money is going, you can make a realistic budget that works, not an example of an imaginative, fanciful dream budget you think should work but never does.

Plus, writing down every single penny you spend every single day has another surprising effect: major stress relief. Simply knowing where it is going is incredibly calming, because even when you know you don't have any money left, at least you have a feeling that you understand where it went. Have you ever spent an hour driving yourself mad trying to work out how that £20 you just withdrew from the cashpoint machine disappeared? Knowing is half the battle. When it comes to your money, knowledge really is power.

When you know how much you spend, you can also root out wasteful spending. Can you *believe* you spent £50 on caffeinated drinks last month? Isn't that ridiculous? If you think it is (perhaps you do believe such an amount is worth it, but if you don't...), then you know exactly what you need to change.

Financial stress is largely a product of not knowing, wondering, hoping, fearing – all because you have no idea what your money is doing (you'd almost think money had a life of its own). But if you know, you are in control – you say where it goes and where it doesn't go – and even if there isn't much coming in, that control still feels really good.

These days, many financial experts advise more conservative investing, such as in fixed-interest and corporate bond funds rather than the stock market, for example. The days of letting your investments save *for you* may be temporarily over, so save, save, save. Don't depend on investment gains to make up your savings.

Build a Financial Cushion

Financial stress is also largely caused by knowing that you don't have enough money in the bank if an emergency arises. What if your car breaks down, or you incur some major legal expenses, or the roof springs a leak or Uncle Jerry needs bailing out and you don't have any back-up cash? When events such as these occur, your stress level is likely to go soaring.

But if you have a cushion – many experts recommend six months' worth of monthly income stashed away in an easily accessible savings or money market account – you will rest easier, even when you don't need the money, just because you know it's there. Whenever you have to raid your account, make paying yourself back your first priority.

How do you get a cushion? It can be difficult if you think your salary barely covers your expenses, but successful savers say they put away 10 per cent or more of every single penny they earn before they ever have the chance to spend it. Setting up a system by which that 10 per cent is automatically deducted from your salary, just as it is for tax, is even easier. You don't ever get your hands on the money, so you won't ever miss it. You'll readjust to manage on just exactly what you earn, minus the 10 per cent. Then if things get really tight, you'll be OK for a while.

Make this your top priority – it's an easy way to give yourself financial peace of mind. Work out how much you need each month, then multiply that figure by six. That's your cushion goal. Put 10 per cent of your very next wage into that cushion fund.

If you put away just 10 per cent each month, you'll reach a six-month cushion in five years if you never use the money. To get there faster, put extra money in your cushion fund whenever it comes along – if you have a windfall of any kind, for example. Or put away 10 per cent this year, 20 per cent next year... some people make it their goal to be able to live on 50 per cent of their monthly income and save the rest. Now that is smart saving! This may not be a realistic goal for you if your income doesn't permit it, but the more you adjust and learn to live increasingly frugally, the more you'll be able to save, and the better and less stressed you are likely to feel.

What about the stress that comes from never being able to splash out or be financially frivolous and always feeling as though you have to save and budget?
It isn't fair! That's understandable. Many people on a tight budget describe how, when under financial stress, all they want to do is go out and spend money — but if they do, they dig themselves deeper into a hole. Just remember: you can get into the habit of enjoying rewards that don't cost money, and an occasional *controlled* splurge is both reasonable and safer than binge spending.

The Five Golden Rules of
No-Stress Money Management

Before we leave the subject of money, let's look at the five golden rules of no-stress money management. No matter what your tendencies, income, financial preconceptions or bank balance, these five golden rules will help to de-stress your financial life each and every day. Copy them out. Stick them on the wall. Live by them.

They aren't all easy to achieve straight away, so add them to your list of financial goals if necessary. Working towards these rules will put the money you (or do not) have in your life in its proper and rightful place: as a tool you use with total control and good sense to maintain and improve your life.

1. **Live within your means.** In other words, don't spend more than you earn each month. Don't use credit unless it is absolutely necessary. If you don't have the hard cash to go on a shopping spree, don't go on a shopping spree. Of course, to abide by this rule, you need to know exactly how much ready cash you do have available to spend each month (see the earlier section 'Know *Exactly* How Much Is Coming In and Going Out').

2. **Conquer your debts.** Make chipping away at any high-interest debts your top priority. Debt may not be something you can hold in your hand, but neither are a lot of the things that cause chronic stress. Just knowing you've got huge debts is enough to activate the stress response in some people. First, get rid of the debt, then start saving. As soon as you start to pay off your debts, you'll feel as though a black cloud is being lifted from your head. Don't listen to people who tell you that debt is necessary, that society runs on credit. Nonsense. A mortgage and payment for a car, perhaps. Other than these, pay them off, pay them off, pay them off and breathe more freely.

3. **Simplify your finances.** Set up a simple system for financial management. Use a single bank for all your transactions. If possible, have your salary paid automatically into your bank account, and use standing orders to make payments or online banking for regular

outgoings so that you don't have to run to the bank all the time. If you invest, go through a single broker. If the thought of investing stresses you, don't do it.

4. **Know your money.** Know how much you earn, how much you spend, where all your money is and how much your investments are earning. Know (and trust) your broker, or if you invest on your own, keep track of everything you do. Fill in your chequebook stubs, keep a running total of how much is in your account, and check your bank statements. If you do this, you will never be stressed because you don't know whether a cheque will bounce, if your investments are earning or losing, or how much you have saved.

5. **Plan for the future.** Save. Save. Save. The short-term sacrifice of not buying something you don't really need and probably won't use very much, the decision not to go ahead with expensive home improvement or buy a new four-wheel-drive, the decision to move to a smaller and more manageable house, to stop eating out so much, to spend more time at home – these are all in favour of saving, saving, saving, and well worth it all round. Your life will be simpler. It will be easier. You'll have a nest egg. All that adds up to a lot less stress.

Time Seems to Slip Away

Perhaps money doesn't cause you nearly as much stress as a basic lack of time. If you never seem to have enough time to finish anything, you might feel constant, chronic stress. But although, technically, we all have the same amount of time each day (24 hours), time is mysteriously malleable. Have you ever noticed how an hour can fly by like five minutes, or crawl by like three hours? Sometimes your working day is over in a flash, and sometimes it feels like 5:00 PM when it's only 11:00 AM. Can you make this malleability of time work for you? Yes, you can.

Although they say 'Time flies when you're having fun', time also flies when you are scattered and disorganized. If you have three hours in which to do something and you don't manage your time efficiently, those three hours will be gone in a rush of half-finished jobs and flitting from task to task with dispersed energy.

If, instead, you are organized and able to devote your full concentration to one task at a time, time seems to expand in quantity and quality. You get something – even one thing – finished and you feel a sense of satisfaction. The time won't crawl by, as it does when you are enduring something unpleasant. Time may seem to go fast, but because you have accomplished something, you'll enjoy a feeling of achievement, a boost in self-esteem and the relief of stress.

Time that rushes by seldom seems well spent, or sufficiently well spent. Time that expands, time in which something real is accomplished, seems more significant, more worthy of the ticks on the clock. The trick to making the most of your time is focus. Focus entirely on what you are doing, and time will be luscious and enjoyable, flowing smoothly along, each moment full and rich.

Learning how to manage your time efficiently takes some practice, but if you have a plan, time management is easy. There are many excellent books and websites to help you get organized and manage your time. Begin to free yourself from the unnecessary stress that comes with scattered energy and the inefficient use of your day by observing the Ten Commandments of Time Management:

1. **Start small.** If you start with too many goals, a too long to-do list or too high expectations of yourself, you are setting yourself up for failure. Begin with one single time-management step, such as laying out your clothes for the next day the night before, to save time in the morning, or by vowing that the sink will be free of washing up every single night, to ease the breakfast rush. As you master each step, you can add more.
2. **Identify your time-management issues.** Are you perfectly efficient at work, but your time management skills fall apart in the unstructured environment at home? Are you able to keep the house tidy, but when all the family are at home, life seems rushed and hectic, with no relaxed time together? Do you spend all day dealing with other people's crises

and taking care of business, but never having enough time to sit down and really concentrate on your job? Know your trouble spots – the places where time is being frittered away.

3. **Identify your time-management priorities.** Make a list ranking the things on which you most want to spend your time. Would you like to put family time first, then household organization, then some personal time? Would you like more time for work and less time for dealing with other people's crises? Would you like to make time for your favourite hobby, time for yourself or time for romance? Would you just like more time to sleep?

4. **Focus on your top five.** Look at the top five items on your Time Management Priorities list. Focus on these. Be very wary of taking on anything that uses your time if it isn't focused on one of your top five priorities.

5. **Have a strategy.** When the day starts, know where you are going and what you will do. Time unplanned is often time wasted. That doesn't mean you can't allow for spontaneity or a lovely, unplanned hour or two. Even a whole day of *purposefully* unplanned time is well worth it. But time unplanned in which you frantically try to accomplish ten different things is time wasted, and that's stressful. Resources abound for helping you devise a strategy that works for you (see Appendix B for some ideas).

6. **Just say no.** Your time is valuable, even more valuable than money. Why should you just give it away to anyone and anything that asks for it? Learn to say no to requests for your time unless the way that time is spent would be very important to you. You don't have to be on the committee, join that club, go to that meeting. Just say no and watch the stress that was waiting to descend upon your life float away in another direction.

7. **Let it go.** If you've already taken on too much, learn to cut back. Don't let anything waste your time. Time spent relaxing by yourself isn't wasted if it refreshes and rejuvenates you. Time spent pacing and worrying is wasted time. Time spent enduring a committee meeting you don't really enjoy is wasted time. Time spent actively engaged with a committee whose cause inspires you is time well spent. Cut out the dross and let go of everything that isn't really important.

8. **Charge more.** If you are self-employed, don't waste time on jobs that don't pay you for what your time is worth. (This is difficult until you are well-established.) And this rule doesn't just apply to work and actual money – everything you do takes time. Is the reward payment enough for the time spent? If it isn't, ditch it.

9. **Do it later.** Do you really need to clean the entire house every day? Do you really need to check your email every 10 minutes? Do you really need to change the sheets, clean the car and mow the lawn today? If doing it later is just procrastination, the time you saved will only be spent worrying. But sometimes, when time is at a premium, you can relieve stress and make life easier by postponing less crucial tasks. Even though many things do need to be done, they don't always need to be done right now.

10. **Remember that not having enough time is always an excuse, never a reason.** You can make time for anything if it's important enough, you just have to stop spending time on something less important. You have control over your time – it doesn't control you.

Stress-Proofing Your Work Life

For a few lucky people, work is a source of rejuvenation, personal satisfaction and stress relief. For many others, even though work is sometimes or often rewarding, it is also a major source of stress. The more work people do and the longer the working day becomes, the more we dream of being able to retire early. Who doesn't waste just a bit of time thinking about what they would do if they won millions on the lottery? Would we tell our bosses where to go? Leave with a flourish? *Would we never work again?*

Actually, research into the life satisfaction of lottery winners reveals that very few are happier and that many are less happy after leaving their jobs (winning the lottery brings its own kind of stress). Although any job can be stressful, and sometimes monotonous, our working time often brings us more than a salary. We gain self-esteem and a sense of purpose and worth from our jobs. We benefit from the social contact, the structure and the responsibility.

But perhaps your job doesn't give you these benefits, and perhaps you should consider a change. Nowadays people are likely to change careers more often than ever before, voluntarily or not. Is a change of job in order for you? Look at the following list – how many items apply to you?

- I dread going to work most days.
- I come home from work too exhausted to do anything but watch television or go to bed.
- I am not treated with respect at my work.
- I'm not paid what I'm worth.
- I'm embarrassed to tell people what I do for a living.
- I don't feel good about my job.
- My job doesn't allow me to fulfill my potential.
- My job is far from being my dream job.
- I would leave in a second if I could afford it.
- My job is keeping me from enjoying my life.

If two or more items on this list apply to you, you might want to consider a change of job. If you aren't qualified to do what you would like to do, you need a plan. Find out what would be involved in training in a field that holds more interest for you. Work on saving some money so that you can start your own business. If you aren't sure what you would really like to do, seek careers advice to discover what kind of work you might find more interesting and fulfilling.

The Health and Safety Executive defines stress as 'the adverse reaction people have to excessive pressure or other types of demand placed on them'. If you are experiencing an 'adverse reaction' to stress in your workplace, now may be the time to look for pastures new.

If you like your job but certain of its aspects are more stressful than you can comfortably handle, there are steps you can take to get the stress under control. Remember, some stress is good – it can motivate you and boost your performance. The important thing is not to exceed your stress tolerance level – at least not too often.

First, identify which areas of your work life are causing you the most stress. Perhaps the work itself is fine but your colleagues are difficult. Or perhaps it's the other way around. Think about each of the following aspects of your work life and write a few lines about how they make you feel. Writing about each aspect may help you to see more clearly where your stress lies.

Write your answers here or in your stress diary.

1. This is how I feel about the people I work with:

2. This is how I feel about my manager:

3. This is how I feel about the environment in which I work:

4. This is how I feel about the values and purpose of my place of employment:

_____

_____

_____

_____

_____

tips

Is your work environment ergonomic? If you are uncomfortable while doing your work, whatever it is, don't risk a lifetime of pain from repetitive strain injury. Talk to your employer about making ergonomic changes — for example, getting a new chair or keyboard, or changing tasks more often.

5. This is how I feel about the actual, day-to-day work I do:

_____

_____

_____

_____

_____

6. This is how I feel about the importance of the work I do:

_____

_____

_____

_____

7. My favourite thing about my work is:

8. My least favourite thing about my work is:

9. My work utilizes my skills in the following areas:

10. My work doesn't utilize my skills in the following areas:

11. My needs not met by work are, or aren't, being met elsewhere (explain):

12. I wish my job could change in these ways:

_____

_____

_____

_____

After answering these questions, it may be more clear where your dissatisfactions with your job lie, and where things are fine. Now make a list of the things about your job that cause you stress. After each item, circle O if you think you can live with this stressor, and X if you think you *can't* live with it:

1. _____ O X

2. _____ O X

3. _____ O X

4. _____ O X

5. _____ O X

6. _____ O X

7. _____ O X

8. _____ O X

9. _____ O X

10. _____ O X

Look at the items for which you circled X. If there aren't any, you're doing well. If there is one or more, there are the aspects of your work you need to manage.

A noisy work environment may be causing you stress, even if you aren't aware of it! A recent study showed that people whose work area was open, allowing them to hear the noises of other workers, showed higher levels of adrenaline in the blood than those whose work area was quiet, even though members of the group hearing the noise didn't necessarily report feeling more stressed.

How you manage the stressors at your job depends on what those stressors are. There are several different approaches:

· Avoid the stressor (such as a stressful colleague).
· Eliminate the stressor (delegate or share a hated task).
· Confront the stressor (talk to your manager if he or she is doing something that makes your job more difficult).
· Manage the stressor (add something enjoyable to the task and give yourself a reward on completion).
· Balance the stressor (put up with the stress, but practise stress-relieving techniques to balance out the effects).

Work is a big part of most people's lives. If you can do something to avoid, eliminate, confront, manage or balance the stress that comes from your work life, the rest of your life will be more balanced and less stressful. The key is to deal with the stressor in some way, rather than ignoring it and letting its negative effects build until you are so stressed that you begin to have time off work or find yourself putting your job in jeopardy, even though you know that really it is a good job.

Building a Personal Sanctuary

After a long, stressful, busy day at work, you come home to your castle, your home sweet home, your haven of peace and comfort and... there you are, faced with a pile of washing, a mound of washing up, one stack of newspapers and another of magazines waiting to be sorted for recycling, dirty footprints in the kitchen, a pile of boxes to inch around to get to the dining room (you'll go through those later), and, oh no, there are the videos you were supposed to return yesterday, and what on earth are you going to eat this evening.... Suddenly, it doesn't seem quite so relaxing to be at home – so you find the number of a takeaway and start rummaging around, looking for the cordless phone.

According to a television report in 1999, more than half of American workers are somewhat or extremely stressed at work. One in six workers reported being 'angry enough to hit a colleague'. One of the most common sources of stress was, ironically, that modern convenience that supposedly makes life easier: technology.

But coming home doesn't have to be like this. Coming home at the end of the day, or staying at home all day long, can be relaxing and peaceful, or even a positively exhilarating experience, if that's what you want it to be. It's your home and can be what you make it. It certainly shouldn't be just one more great big stressful burden. If your home isn't how you want it to be, it may require a little stress management.

Your Home and Office as Metaphor

According to feng shui, the ancient Chinese art of placement, our environment is a metaphor for our lives and the energy that comes and goes in our lives. Problems in your environment mean problems in your life.

Imagine for a moment that this is true. If your home is a metaphor for your life, what does it say about your life? Take a good look around you. Is your life cluttered with things you don't need? How does this affect the home's circulation? How long is it since you did any preventative maintenance on your life?

Your office, either at home or at work away from home, can also be a metaphor for your life. Is it scattered with unpaid bills, things waiting to be filed, scraps of information that take up energy but don't give anything back, faulty or non-functioning equipment, unstable piles of books, files, binders and folders?

If what you see in your home or office space is not exactly what you have in mind for your life, then take matters in hand. Let your home and office continue to be a metaphor for your life, but shape that metaphor in a way that suits your life. Remove the clutter and keep it clean. At home, build a relaxing, positive atmosphere in which to unwind and relax at the end of each day.

Once you're in the habit of keeping your house in order, you'll discover how calming and rejuvenating it is to be in. And whenever things begin to get out of order again, you'll have an immediate and visible clue that stress is creeping back into your life.

Changing your external environment seems to mysteriously and automatically change your inner environment. You may never realize how stressed you are because of the clutter in your environment until you get rid of it and experience the tranquillity of living in the home you knew existed beneath all the extra stuff. When you can see the things you love, find the things you need, and move unimpeded through your living environment, everything else seems easier.

1-2-3 Simplify

To make your home a less stressful, more tranquil place, one of the easiest things you can do is simplify. Spend some time in each room of your home and list all the things you do in that room. What are the functions of the room? Is anything impeding those functions? What would make each room simpler and its functions simpler?

Simplify the way you do your cleaning by creating a system for getting everything done a little bit each day. Simplify your shopping by buying in bulk and planning what you are going to eat a week in advance. There are many ways to simplify the way your home works and consequently reduce your stress while you are at home. Many excellent books, magazines and websites are devoted to simple living – see the resource list at the end of this book for further reading. Here are some more simplicity tips to get started:

· Wear your clothes a little longer (unless they get stained) to cut down on laundry.
· Have clothes that all match.
· Get rid of or pack away household items that complicate your life without giving you much back – for example, ornate objects that require frequent dusting, house plants that require constant watering, dishes you can't put in the dishwasher or are too delicate to be washed more than rarely, clothes you have to have dry-cleaned.
· Pay a student or local teenager to mow the lawn, sweep up leaves, run errands, or baby-sit. Consider getting a cleaning service.
· There are always more ways to simplify. Keep looking for them.

Making More Space

Some people feel comforted by a room full of possessions, but there is something relaxing and calming about clean, clutter-free surfaces, a wall with a single hanging, an expanse of floor free from toys, books or discarded clothes, even a room with just a few basic pieces of furniture – only what is necessary. Not everyone would like to live in a completely utilitarian home, of course, but the chances are that over the years yours has accumulated things you no longer need.

Why not pack away or give away some of those things and free some space? As you make space on your surfaces, floors and walls, and in your rooms, you'll feel as if you are making space in your mind. You'll feel calmer and more relaxed in a clean, organized, uncluttered space. If you donate things to charity, you'll also get the satisfaction of knowing that you've helped others. Or if you sell your surplus items at a boot or garage sale, you can make some extra money.

De-clutter, De-stress

Clutter does more than keep your home, desk or garage looking untidy. It keeps your mind untidy, too. The more things you have – especially disorganized, unmatched, lost or high-maintenance things – the more you have to worry about them, find them, maintain them, keep them and deal with them. Getting rid of the clutter in your home is the most important thing you can do to make your home a stress-free haven of tranquillity.

But getting rid of things can be hard, especially for those who can't bear to throw anything away. Are you a hoarder? How many of the following statements would you agree with?

· I keep a lot of clothes that I think might fit me one day.
· I have at least one drawer filled with spare parts and other odds and ends I might need one day, even though I'm not sure what most of them are now.
· I have at least a year's worth of magazines that I know I'll look at again eventually.
· All the storage space in my house is full to overflowing, but I'm not sure what with.
· I record more films, television programmes or music than I can watch or listen to, but I save all the tapes because I think I'll get round to them all... eventually.
· I buy more books than I can read, but I might just read them one day.
· I collect at least five different things.
· I think I need to move to a bigger house because the house I'm currently in is overflowing.

If you agree with more than one item on this list, you're probably a hoarder. This means that having a clear-out is trickier for you than for someone who doesn't mind letting go of things. If getting rid of clutter is actually *more* stressful for you than living with it, go with the least stressful option.

If you love your things and love being surrounded by them, the trick to keeping your home stress-free is to be well-organized. If everything is kept neat and you know where things are (so you aren't constantly in a panic trying to find them), then your various collections and other favourite items can bring as much joy, comfort and calm as a de-cluttered, pared-down space might bring to someone else.

Sometimes people are actually more comfortable with clutter – they seem to need extra things all around them. You may be one of them if you are a collector, you love bulk-buying or you save absolutely everything. If you love your things, that's fine – you probably wouldn't feel relaxed in a sparse environment. The trick is to organize what you have so that it is neat and accessible.

Stress-Free Feng Shui

In the last decade or so, feng shui has become a popular and influential trend in decorating in the West. Feng shui masters are widely available to advise those decorating homes or offices, or designing and building a house or office building. Feng shui classes are very much in demand, and there are many books on how to decorate or redesign your home using feng shui techniques.

Feng shui is a highly complex system that involves Chinese astrology, mathematical calculations and Chinese philosophy. There are several different schools of feng shui, each advocating different methods. But as with many things that come from the East to the West, feng shui has begun to be adapted for use by Westerners, and the methods are becoming simpler and more intuitive.

The basic premise of feng shui, particularly Westernized feng shui, is the one described earlier in this chapter: environment as metaphor. People who practise intuitive feng shui decorate according to what 'feels right' – what arrangements, objects, configurations and colours make the energy feel good and flowing in a room. If you've ever felt compelled to arrange your furniture in a certain way, or placed an object somewhere and thought, 'Oh yes, that's just right!', then you understand at least a little about intuitive feng shui.

Many feng shui experts use the bagua, an eight-sided shape that you imagine overlying your house. The corners are filled in to make a square. Each of the eight sides represents a different area of life, such as money, relationships, creativity, health and family, and is associated with different colours, shapes and elements (earth, air, fire and wood). Whichever part of the home falls in with a particular area of the bagua represents that part of your life.

But working with the bagua is just one way to apply feng shui to your home. It also uses light, movement (wind chimes, mobiles), water, plants, crystals and symbolic representations of positive things to activate and enhance the energy in different areas of the home.

According to feng shui, energy can get 'stuck' in corners and particularly in alcoves or other irregular shapes in rooms. Cobwebs in the corners of a room are a sign of stagnant energy. Keep corners dusted and areas of feng shui concern cobweb-free. Wind chimes or crystals hanging in corners are supposed to get energy moving out of the corner and into the main flow of energy through the room. Hanging bamboo flutes is also auspicious.

Feng shui should be personalized. Your date of birth, for example, can determine specific feng shui prescriptions, such as which way to position your bed, or even which direction to face if you want to appear more powerful during a meeting. (If you want to learn more about feng shui, consult one of the many excellent books on the subject.)

The list that follows gives general feng shui tips designed to enhance the positive energy and decrease the negative energy in any house. But remember, feng shui is most effective when used intuitively. Try any of these suggestions that appeal to you or feel 'right', but don't worry about following those that seem difficult, uninteresting or even silly. To be truly stress-free, feng shui should be fun and enjoyable. Choose from the following tips:

· Remember, symbolism is everything. Pictures of love birds or people in love encourage a romantic relationship, correctly placed coins or banknotes attract wealth, a picture of a far-away destination encourages the likelihood of travel. Use symbolism everywhere to attract the appropriate energy, and fix your intention firmly in your own mind. Arrange it, see it, think it... make it happen!

· A crystal, mobile, source of moving water (fish tank, small desk fountain) or wind chime will energize any area of your home you think needs it.

· Keep your cupboards and refrigerator well-stocked with fresh, healthy food, which represents abundance.

· Never leave your broom where you can see it. A visible broom symbolizes death or some other catastrophe.

· To increase energy for prosperity, keep your oven immaculately clean.

· If your toilet is in your prosperity corner – the corner to your upper left as you enter the room – your wealth could be getting symbolically flushed down the toilet. Keep the toilet lid down and the door shut, and hang a mirror on the outside of the door.

· Make sure you can't see yourself in a mirror when you are lying or sitting up in bed. If you can, cover that mirror at night. Seeing your shadowy image in the dark can be frightening.

· If you have a television in your bedroom, cover it at night. The energy it emits can negatively affect many areas of your life, including your health.

· Healthy living things add positive energy to any environment: a well-kept fish tank, dogs, cats, birds and healthy plants all improve your home's feng shui.

· Have fresh flowers in the living room, but not in the bedroom. Throw away flowers and plants as soon as they begin to die.

· Don't sleep with a beam on the ceiling crossing over you, or with a beam dividing your bed if you sleep with someone.

· Don't sit, stand or sleep with a corner or any sharp object facing you. Sharp objects send off 'poison arrows', or negative energy that can have a detrimental effect.

· Don't position your bed directly facing the door. Corpses are carried out feet first!

· Good hygiene, clean clothes, clean sheets and a healthy diet are all good feng shui.

To reiterate, feng shui is far too complicated to be explained fully here, but the most important way to use it to reduce stress is to have fun with it and not worry too much. Because feng shui works so well when used intuitively, don't worry if the things that feel right and good to you in your home don't match someone else's advice about furniture positioning, colour or anything else.

In Chinese, the word for the number eight sounds like the words for growth and prosperity. Eight is considered lucky, and in China wealthy people will pay huge sums of money to have an eight anywhere on their car numberplates.

Because the authentic, original version of feng shui is so complex, you have to take contemporary variations with a pinch of salt. Any easy-to-understand feng shui text is by necessity simplified and could easily be a misapprehension, so don't expect too much.

In other words, use advice from feng shui sources if you find it enjoyable and it results in a living environment that pleases you. If feng shui causes you stress, that's certainly not the point, so choose another hobby. If your home feels good and you feel good while at home, that's good stress management, and that's all that matters.

CHAPTER 11
De-stressing for Women Only

Stress comes in many forms, and it also comes in different ways, depending on who you are. Women have unique and particular symptoms of and reactions to stress because of their biology and because of culture. The ageing process is stressful for biological, psychological and cultural reasons, making stress for seniors another unique experience. In this chapter, we'll look at the way stress affects women throughout their lives so that you can map out a strategy for dealing with the stressors unique to your gender and your current stage in life.

A Woman's World of Stress

It has been only in the last century or so that research organizations have begun to pay more intention to health issues in women, but women have known all along that being a woman can be stressful – biologically speaking, and certainly culturally speaking as well.

Most women in Western society have an easier time, physically, than their grandmothers and great-grandmothers. For our grandmothers, managing a home, cleaning, cooking food and washing clothes were extremely labour-intensive. Now we have technology to help us with much of the housework. In addition, it has become both socially acceptable and expected that men will help out at home. So, why are we stressed, and what about?

Women may not have to do the laundry by hand anymore, but we do have plenty of other things to take up that saved time. We have jobs, often impossibly demanding ones. We have financial pressure, relationship pressure, pressure to look good no matter what our age, pressure to be fit, in charge, in control – pressure to be all that women have always been pressured to be and more. Many of us are also juggling homes, partners and children. If we have not acquired any of the 'requisite parts' – if we aren't married, didn't have children, decided not to work outside the home – we are bombarded with criticism. Sometimes the criticism comes from within, in the form of worry, anxiety, panic, guilt and fear. If the world doesn't expect us to do it all, we expect it of ourselves.

On top of everything else, women go through several intense hormonal changes during their lives and hormonal fluctuations each month. These hormonal fluctuations can compound feelings of stress, and stress can, conversely, affect a woman's hormonal levels. So what's a stressed-out woman to do? First, let's look at what we're dealing with.

Female Stress Mismanagement Syndrome

Studies show that, when under stress, women are more likely than men to communicate with others and talk through their problems. This is a healthy reaction to stress – remember friend therapy from Chapter 9 – and a tendency women should be proud of. However, the reliance on others for advice and opinion can easily turn into something that actually becomes a source of additional stress.

Even in the 21st century, women, more than men, tend to be more concerned with how others perceive them (there are, of course, many exceptions). Little girls are still encouraged (not necessarily by their parents but by others, including television) to be passive, to please others, to be helpful, polite and a team player, and to learn the rules of socially acceptable behaviour.

While little boys are in general also taught these things, society as a whole tends to be more accepting of, and more easily excuses, boys who bend the rules a little or who aren't always quiet and polite. 'Oh, boys will be boys. What are you going to do!' people are likely to imply with a knowing smile. Boys tend to get the message that independence, spirit, competitiveness and even aggression are appropriate. Girls are rewarded for docility and social compliance.

Even if you encourage independence and assertiveness in your daughter, watch for signs that she is getting another message from her environment, including the media. Stay aware and keep reminding her that she can excel at anything. Help foster her natural interests, whether they are traditional 'girl interests' or not.

Because women learn at such an early age that how they look and how helpful and agreeable they are will have an effect on how they are judged, they sometimes overemphasize the importance of appearance and socially acceptable behaviour, perpetuating the stereotypes of which they are the victims. Society continues to reward us for doing so. The price is an unreasonable level of stress if we: are seen not looking our best; do something outrageous; have a job in a traditionally male-dominated sector; have an untidy house; have unruly children; are an assertive and hands-on manager; or – believe it or not – are professionally successful at all! What will people *think*? What will people *say*?

To overcome female stress mismanagement syndrome, you don't have to start abandoning your good habits, but it is a good idea to practise doing things for yourself and the people you care about, rather than focusing on the judgments and opinions of people you hardly know. Whenever you feel stressed about what someone else thinks (or what you *think* someone else thinks), ask yourself these questions:

- Am I really bothered by what someone else thinks, or am I bothered because secretly I agree with them? (If this is true, reframe your worries from your own point of view.)
- Am I stressed about what others think *out of habit*? Do I really care?
- What is the worst thing that could happen if somebody doesn't approve of me?
- What do I really think is important in this situation, regardless of anybody else's opinion?

It's good to know how to be polite and how to help others. It's good to know how to keep your house tidy and cook a satisfying dinner. But it's also good to achieve career success, be independent and spirited, know how to get what you need in life, and not have to depend on anyone else to take care of you. People who don't see your positive qualities have narrow vision.

Panic disorder is twice as common in women as in men. It most often begins in young adults and is characterized by repeated, unexpected panic attacks with both physical and emotional symptoms such as fear, chest pain, racing heart, shortness of breath and abdominal distress. Nobody knows exactly what causes panic disorder, but it is treatable.

The Oestrogen Connection

One of the things that makes a woman a woman is the presence of the female sex organs and a particular cocktail of hormones that is heavy on oestrogen and light on testosterone. Oestrogen and related hormones govern an amazing number of bodily functions, from ovulation to the condition of your skin. By the time of the menopause, oestrogen levels in a woman's body have dropped by about 80 per cent, potentially causing many physical changes, from hot flushes to osteoporosis.

Oestrogen has a protective effect on the heart and is the reason why women tend to have a lower rate of cardiovascular disease than men. After the menopause, men and women have about the same risk of heart attack, and women are more likely to die from their first heart attack than men.

But during periods of stress, oestrogen levels drop temporarily because the adrenal glands are busy pumping out stress hormones instead of oestrogen. These oestrogen dips cause little windows of menopause-like cardiac vulnerability. Studies have shown that when subjected to stress, oestrogen levels drop. During this time, the arteries in the heart immediately begin to build up plaque, leading to a higher risk of heart disease. Stress may actually cause damage to the artery walls in addition to plaque build-up. Little nicks and tears caused by cortisol surges can speed up the accumulation of plaque on artery walls. Keeping oestrogen levels constant by keeping stress in check is just one more reason to manage stress during your childbearing years.

Which Came First, Stress or PMS?

That time of the month. Our monthly friend. No matter what we call it, menstruation is a potential source of monthly stress for almost half a woman's life. Menstruation is often accompanied by physical discomfort. PMS, or premenstrual syndrome, can cause additional physical problems, as well as emotional symptoms, such as irritability, sadness, depression, anger or exaggerated emotions of any kind.

Serious cases of PMS can be treated medically, but if you become just a little emotional, a little bloated, a little aching, or gain a little weight every month before or during menstruation, the best thing to do is increase your stress-management efforts in a few specific ways that focus on self-care. Many of these steps are basic stress-management strategies you can do at any time to help relieve stress, so if you've become forgetful for one reason or another, now is the time to reinstate your good habits:

· Be sure to drink eight glasses (2 litres) of water to combat bloating.
· Go to bed early – get plenty of sleep.
· Avoid caffeine, sugar and saturated fat.
· Eat plenty of fresh fruits, vegetables and whole grains. You need the fibre, and you'll feel more balanced.
· Drink extra milk and eat more yogurt. Studies show that calcium may be among the most effective treatments for the symptoms of PMS.
· Take it easy. If you really don't feel like staying out late or pushing yourself, don't.
· Relieve period pains by going to bed with a hot-water bottle, a cup of herbal tea and a really good book.
· Relax in a warm bath.
· Take ibuprofen to help relieve period pains.
· Meditate, focusing on relaxing and warming your abdominal area.
· Have a massage.
· Research women's history. What a good time to celebrate being a woman!
· A week after the end of your period, do a breast examination. Report any suspicious lumps, thickening or other changes to your GP. And don't forget that yearly cervical smear

One of the best ways to stay healthy is to catch health problems early, when they can be treated much more easily.

If you don't like taking pain relief or prefer a more natural treatment for the discomfort of PMS and menstruation, try remedies such as evening primrose oil, dong quai, blessed thistle, kelp, raspberry leaf tea or Siberian ginseng. (If you are taking any other medication, check with your doctor to make sure these herbs won't react adversely.)

Your Stress, Your Fertility

Deciding to become pregnant is incredibly exciting, but the excitement can quickly turn to confusion if your first few efforts don't result in pregnancy. Is stress the culprit?

Much recent research has helped to cement the connection between fertility and stress, and although there are still those who continue to assert that infertility causes stress, but stress doesn't cause infertility, more and more doctors are recommending stress-management therapies for patients struggling with fertility issues.

Although the possible or probable connection between stress and fertility is heartening (perhaps because it is easier to treat stress than a physical problem), it could have a downside, in that people might blame themselves for their inability to conceive, causing more stress and exacerbating the problem. There are many reasons why people aren't able to conceive immediately, or ever, and people who are already having difficulty shouldn't blame themselves or their lack of coping skills for their fertility issues.

However, stress-management techniques can help people feel better about themselves as they work on conceiving. If stress interferes with oestrogen production (it does) and testosterone production (it does), it is certainly reasonable to suspect that deep relaxation, meditation, self-care and other techniques that help to combat the stress response might help to balance your body and restore its equilibrium, which could help to promote fertility. Also, because mind and body are so inextricably linked, managing stressful feelings, especially those compounded by worry and anxiety at the inability to become pregnant straight away, may give fertility a boost.

If you discover that you have a specific barrier to fertility, whether it can or can't be treated, practise stress management for any of the following: speedier healing after surgery; to promote the effectiveness of your medication (try visualization – it isn't scientifically proven in such cases, but who knows?), or to help you help your partner with whatever treatment he is receiving.

For centuries, women have used herbal remedies to enhance fertility. Try a tea made from any one or a combination of the following: alfalfa, nettle, raspberry leaf, red clover, and rose hip. Women over 40 years of age can take 5–10 drops of dandelion root tincture before meals and add bitter greens such as dandelion and rocket to salads to aid the body's absorption of vitamins and minerals. Ragged robin may strengthen the uterus, and American partridgeberry may balance hormones.

Stress management can also help you to deal with the feelings of loss you will experience if you are told you will not be able to conceive. Give yourself time, attention and permission to mourn. Take care of yourself, or let others do it, too. Then let stress management help to ease your search for other options, such as adoption, or let it assist you in entering a new stage of life in which you construct a full and rewarding life as a child-free adult.

Stress During Pregnancy, Childbirth and After

Anyone who is or has been pregnant can probably provide a long list of specific stressors, from morning sickness to swollen ankles. This is in addition to the emotional stress of preparing to add a new little person to the family and all the changes that brings about in the life of an individual, the life of a relationship and the life of a family.

Childbirth itself is stressful in many ways. It hurts, for one thing! Your body goes through an amazing, but highly stressful, process. And your mind is adjusting to the drama of the situation in any number of ways.

The postnatal period, after giving birth, is fraught with environmental as well as hormonal adjustments. Postnatal depression can make even the simple chores of daily life seem impossible.

Managing stress is doubly important during this intense transitional period of life, because when you are pregnant, you are 'experiencing stress for two'. Although any of the techniques in this book are helpful during pregnancy, good health and self-care are crucial. When you are pregnant, it is essential to do the following:

- Drink eight glasses (2 litres) of water each day.
- Get enough sleep.
- Eat healthy, nutrient-dense food.
- Take some moderate exercise on most days of the week (unless your doctor recommends otherwise).
- Meditate or practise other relaxation techniques.
- Stop bad health habits such as smoking and drinking. Get help if necessary.

Also important during pregnancy is the support of your partner and/or friends and family. The worry and anxiety that comes with pregnancy will be much less intense if you know you have others to help you. Make sure you have support, and don't be afraid to ask for what you need. After all, you are doing it for your baby.

If you don't have any immediate support, find some fast. You aren't without options. Most communities have support groups for single mothers, or other kinds of activities through which you could make friends. Some people who find themselves pregnant and without support decide to move closer to family or helpful friends.

Whatever your situation, don't try to do it alone. You might be *able* to do it all, but the stress will be overwhelming, and that isn't good for your baby. Even if you feel able to deal with the situation now, you may well feel different about your abilities when the baby comes and you are overwhelmed with hormonal changes. Helping yourself helps your baby.

Having a birth plan in place for when you go into labour is also a great way to ease the pregnant mother's mind. Write down how you would like things to be, including how you feel about pain relief (allow for a change of mind on this one, just in case), what you would like to be able to do during labour (listen to music, take a shower, have friends or family present), whether you approve the use of a video camera during delivery, and anything else you consider a priority.

Managing the stress of childbirth can be an organized event. Classes in the Lamaze method and other techniques for easing childbirth are widely available, particularly through the Natural Childbirth Trust. Midwives and birth partners can ease the stress and fear of childbirth by being able to offer a voice of calmness and clear thinking. While birth partners should also be present to offer additional support, they may feel pretty stressed themselves and aren't always much practical help.

Birth partners can help to ease the stress of labour with some specific strategies. Ask your partner to look at the following list, memorize it and be ready to put it to use.

Ten Ways to Ease the Stress of a Mother in Labour

1. Follow her lead. If she wants you, be there. If she doesn't want you, have a break. Don't be offended.
2. Offer to massage her shoulders, neck, scalp or feet. If she doesn't want it or suddenly wants you to stop, stop. Don't be offended.
3. Stay calm. Practise deep breathing along with her. It will help you both.
4. Tell her how well she is doing.
5. Don't seem worried.
6. Hold her hand and try not to complain when she squeezes it really hard.
7. Redirect her to her point of focus during contractions, unless she tells you to stop.
8. Be her assistant. Go for magazines. Change the music. Fetch the water, wet flannel or whatever. Keep the relatives informed.
9. Be her advocate. If doctors or nurses are being unreasonable or doing things that are upsetting her or that go against her birth plan, be

assertive (not rude) and insist that the mother's wishes be followed (unless it is a case of the mother's or baby's health, in which case the doctors know best!).

10. Stay fully alert. You'll want to remember this experience, and the chances are that there will be parts of the experience the mother doesn't remember. You can fill her in!

Postnatal

The postnatal period is marked by drastic hormonal fluctuations that can leave you feeling like an emotional wreck. Irritability, sadness, intense joy, intense anger, intense frustration and sobbing at something as mundane as television commercials are par for the course.

In some cases, severe depression can occur, or even temporary psychosis. Make sure you have people around you to help when you can't handle things, and, if you have feelings of severe depression, feel unable to care for your new baby or are confused by irrational thoughts, please seek professional help. Postnatal depression and associated conditions are usually easy to treat.

Stress-management techniques are important during this time, especially techniques for self-care and relaxation. You need support and you need to take care of yourself. Postnatal emotional upheavals can happen when you least expect them.

Oh, Baby!

If you thought pregnancy was stressful, now you've got a baby, you know what real stress is! Parenthood has its own unique set of stressors. You aren't just responsible for your own life any more – you are directly responsible for the care, nurture, teaching and protecting of another human being for approximately 18 years.

This is a big responsibility, and the thought of it can be pretty daunting and, yes, stressful. Parents of new babies are generally unable to get enough sleep, and that makes everything else more difficult. But there are a number of things new mothers can do to manage the necessary stress of parenthood.

- Drink lots of water to stay well hydrated.
- Eat really healthy, soul-satisfying food.
- Take it easy. Let your body heal.
- Let people help you. You don't have to prove anything to anybody.
- Force yourself to make time for yourself, even if it's just 10 minutes each day alone in the spare bedroom breathing deeply.
- Sleep whenever the baby sleeps.
- Let yourself relish your time alone with your new baby.

Parents often have to make sacrifices – of time, money and autonomy. Of course, it's worth it, but to be a good parent you also have to manage your stress effectively. If you teach your children how to manage their stress as well, you'll be giving them a great gift. As children grow and encounter school, peer pressure, homework overload and the expectations inherent in our society, they'll also encounter plenty of stress.

Most teenagers probably experience at least as much stress as they cause their parents. If your family can learn how to manage stress together, you'll all have a stronger relationship. Teach your teenagers how to manage stress. You'll be giving them a gift for a lifetime.

If stress is to be well managed in family life, a sense of togetherness is most important. It doesn't matter how your family is made up – you don't have to be a husband, wife, 2.5 children and a dog. As long as everyone knows they belong, feels loved, and spends time together, it's a family. A weekly family night may be all it takes – play games, talk about world issues, watch films, take turns making dinner. Whatever you do, just being together will make the memories sweet.

Low-Stress Single Parenting

The fact that you don't have a partner doesn't mean you can't be a good parent. Forget all the statistics (even if it's hard to forget them when people keep quoting them to you) about children in single-parent families experiencing more problems and getting into more trouble.

Single-parent families are still families. If the people in your single-parent family share a sense of belonging, spend time together, have fun together and are open about their love and mutual caring, they will be an excellent family.

If your relationship is breaking up, you are probably experiencing many intense emotions, and inflicting these emotions on your children can increase their stress. Being strong, calm and happy with your children is important for them, and it can have a surprisingly positive effect on you, too. Acting as if you are calm and happy can actually make you feel calmer and happier. Don't bury your emotions, but do compartmentalize them and deal with them when your children aren't around.

Life is often pretty stressful for a single parent, who has to fulfill the role of both parents on a daily basis. It isn't easy to have to cook supper, wash up, sweep the floors, take out the rubbish and earn the money all by yourself – and then be relaxed and playful with your children! But you can do it, and it's worth the effort. If you put a degree of effort into stress management, it will make the rest of your life quite a bit easier:

· Get enough sleep! You may think it isn't possible, but it is *always* possible to rearrange your routines.
· Eat a healthy diet. Your children will learn from your example.
· Sit down with your children during meals and talk to them, even if you plan to eat later. Turn off the television!
· Don't let your entire life revolve around your children. Go out as a grown-up at least once a week.
· Pamper yourself – you deserve it.
· Meditate every day.
· Remind yourself every day that although, like any parent, you are bound to make mistakes now and again, overall you are doing an excellent job.
· Enjoy your time with your children – you'll never have it back again.

- If you have to choose between cleaning and being with your children, let them win out most of the time. Or involve them in cleaning and make it a family affair. (My children love to scrub the kitchen floor.)
- Try not to doubt yourself, but if you find yourself doing so, consciously replace your doubt with a vote of confidence in yourself.
- Teach your children to exercise. Learn a sport, or do yoga together. Children love yoga, and it's good for the whole family.
- Make it a family tradition to tell each other what you love about each other.
- Be silly!
- Be your own best friend. Nurture your inner confidence so that you'll have plenty of reserves when it seems as if no one else is on your side.

Childless by Choice

Women who choose not to have children or who, for whatever reason, find themselves towards the end of their childbearing years without having had children, can be subject to considerable social pressure. This is because society still expects women to have children, so surely there must be something wrong with those who don't?

If you feel you need to build up your reserves of confidence and courage, learn the yoga warrior pose. Stand with your feet about 1.2m (4ft) apart (further if you are tall). Turn your right foot to point to the right, and turn your left foot in slightly, by about 30 degrees. Hold your arms out straight at shoulder height, one hand pointing right, one pointing left. Then turn your torso so that you are looking straight out over your right arm. Your right arm, right foot and face should all be pointing to the right. Bend your right knee so that your thigh is parallel to the floor and balance your weight between your feet. Your knee should be directly over your ankle – if it isn't, adjust your stance. Hold your arms out strongly and feel the power of the warrior! Repeat to the left.

Of course this is not true! The world has plenty of people, and we have no obligation to procreate. Yet women who do not have children, whether or not they choose to marry, are often on the receiving end of constant well-meaning comments from relatives and friends. 'So when are you going to settle down and have children?' These thoughtless remarks can be painful for those who have tried and been unable to conceive, but they can also be painful for those who, even though they may sometimes regret the path not taken, have decided that parenthood is not for them.

How do you handle the pressure? By staying calm and having ready answers. While you may be tempted to snap back with a similarly intrusive response to unwanted questions about your procreative status, you'll just add to the tension and make yourself feel worse. Instead, try these comments to end the conversation (if that's what you want to do):

- 'Why do you ask?'
- 'That's a personal matter.'
- 'Children aren't in my plan at the moment.'
- 'That path doesn't interest me.'
- 'I have other outlets for my maternal instinct.'

Or, if you want a more humorous response:

- 'Oh, my goodness! I didn't realize there was a shortage!'
- 'Well, I didn't pass the test.'
- 'But it's the 21st century! Don't they have special equipment for that now?'
- 'They don't encourage undercover agents to procreate.'

Perhaps these answers don't make complete sense, but they may at least confuse people into silence!

The point is this: whether or not you choose to have children is nobody's business but your own. You aren't obliged to justify yourself to anyone (not even your parents). Don't let people make you feel guilty about your decision, just breathe deeply and let the comments go.

Stress and the Menopause

Stress doesn't cause the menopause; ageing causes it, and that's all there is to it. There is an adage about having the courage to change the things you can change, accept the things you can't change, and having the wisdom to know the difference. This is one of the things you can't change. If you are a woman, eventually you'll go through the menopause.

Stress is often about change, and they don't call the menopause 'the change' for nothing – it can be very stressful for both mind and body. The menopause is marked by plummeting oestrogen levels, and the results can be hot flushes, depression, anxiety, a feeling of flatness or loss of emotion, wildly fluctuating emotions, vaginal dryness, loss of interest in sex, loss of bone mass, increased risk of cardiovascular disease and stroke, increased cancer risk... and the list goes on.

Could there possibly be a positive side to the menopause?

The menopause is more than just a hormonal adjustment, and fortunately, many of the changes associated with it are temporary. While your risk of certain diseases will remain higher after menopause, the hot flushes, depression, mood fluctuations and even loss of sex drive are all temporary.

Stress-management techniques can help to alleviate or reduce many of the temporary side effects of the menopause. Meditation and relaxation, coupled with regular moderate exercise, including strength training, add up to just the two-pronged attack your uncomfortable symptoms need. Hormone replacement therapy (or HRT) may further alleviate many of the temporary symptoms of the menopause, too, freeing you to focus on the benefits: the new you!

You are still you after the menopause, of course, but there is something liberating about moving to the next stage of life, post-childbearing. Even if you have never had children, knowing you are past the stage in your life when people are likely to ask you when you are *going* to have them is a freedom in itself. You have also moved to a stage in life where you can be the centre of your universe again. This doesn't mean becoming selfish – you can still devote time as you wish to helping friends, family, children and grandchildren.

But for many older people, this isn't that easy. Just when your life was about to become your own again, you find yourself in demand: perhaps caring for elderly parents and/or the primary baby-sitter to your grandchildren. There is even the possibility that your own adult children may be moving back in with you. You may love helping your family, but as you enter the post-childbearing stage of life it is crucial, for your own happiness and sense of wellbeing, that you also devote time to yourself. This isn't selfish. If you are happy, calm and fulfilled, you'll also be more helpful to others in a productive (rather than a codependent) way. Make yourself your top priority, as you continue to love and support your parents and offspring. Appreciate what you've accomplished.

 The older you get, the more loved ones you will lose. With loss comes grief, and grief is extremely stressful. Keep in touch with your feelings of loneliness and sadness when you lose people you love. If you've lost a partner, try not to let yourself become isolated. Finding companionship and others to love is one of the most important things you can do to help yourself.

Stress and the Senior Woman

Once you've passed your childbearing years, life begins to open up. You feel more secure, you know who you are, you have time to yourself. But these 'golden years' can be stressful for women. Children move out and the house seems empty. Bodies become more prone to aches and pains, and less agile.

If you've worked most of your life and are now in retirement, you may find yourself suffering from stress just when you thought you were leaving it behind with your job. Jobs are often a great source of self-esteem as well as money. Now, money may be tight after retirement, and the house may seem tight, too, when you and your partner are suddenly at home all day together. Even if you have plenty to do, you may feel as if this work is less important because you aren't being paid for it, or perhaps because you aren't getting feedback from your manager – you aren't used to being your own manager.

If you are far from relatives and friends, life may get lonely. Health problems are stressful, and depression is common in older women. What can a senior woman do to combat the negative effects of stress?

- *Stay engaged.* Participate in activities outside your home, whether volunteering, exercise classes, art classes, language classes, book groups, church, cookery classes or social groups. You'll stay enthusiastic about what's going on around you, your mind will keep active, and this will help to keep you feeling young.
- *Don't lose touch with friends.* Make an effort to stay in touch. Have a mix of friends of your own age – and younger ones, too.
- *Consider getting a pet.* Pets are proven to reduce stress and can provide you with a lasting and satisfying relationship. Small dogs and cats are easy to handle, and give back tenfold what you give them. Birds can also be rewarding companions, and you can teach them to talk!
- *Stay active.* Take a walk or do some other kind of exercise every day. Walking alone, or with friends, is beneficial both physically and emotionally.
- *Pay attention to what's going on in the world.* Talk about events with your friends and/or partner. Work on being open-minded, and make sure you have a good case to back up your opinions.
- *Try yoga* to help keep your body flexible and less prone to injury.
- *Eat nutrient-dense foods* with plenty of calcium, protein and fibre. Soya foods may also help with the effects of the menopause. Try vanilla or chocolate soya milk.
- *Lift weights* to keep your bones strong and to combat osteoporosis.
- *Keep drinking lots of water* and getting enough sleep.
- *Consider seeing qualified complementary health care practitioners,* who may suggest putting you on less medication and helping you to adjust your lifestyle for better health.
- *Meditate daily* to explore the universe of the inner you. Get to know yourself all over again!

· *Keep your mind busy*. Take up a new hobby, learn a new language, read books in a different genre, do crossword puzzles, have intellectual discussions with your friends.

· *Do things for other people*. Service to others will make you feel good about yourself as well as helping other people.

· *Start writing your life history*. You'll enjoy sorting through the memories, and your manuscript will be a valuable family treasure.

· *Value yourself*.

A recent study described the differences in the way men and women handle stress. While men tend to react with aggression or by leaving the situation (a kind of 'fight or flight' response), women are more likely to 'tend and befriend', or protect their young and seek help from others. The hormone oxytocin, which helps to stimulate the maternal instinct in women, may be responsible.

CHAPTER 12
For Men Only

Like women, men have a much easier time than their ancestors did. Machines make life easier, and computers make life more sedentary. Men live longer than ever before, but the fact that you aren't ploughing fields by hand all day doesn't mean you aren't stressed. You *are* stressed, and it's no wonder. Men are expected to do more than ever before – to be both provider and nurturer, strong and emotionally available, independent and supportive. Men may feel stress if they aren't always confident and strong or willing to share their emotions.

Male Stress Mismanagement Syndrome

Studies show that men and women tend to handle stress differently. Women tend to talk about their problems with others, men don't. Instead, men tend to seek out the company of others, minus the sharing. Or they turn to physical activity.

Both methods can work well, but men's stereotypical reluctance to express feelings can lead to an increase in the negative effects of stress, including a sense of isolation, depression, low self-esteem and substance abuse. Men are four times more likely than women to commit suicide, and men are more likely than women to abuse drugs and alcohol and commit violent acts.

How can you help yourself manage your stress and combat your tendency to keep it all inside? Following are some tips for better male stress management:

·   Don't feel like talking about it? Write about it. Keep a diary as an outlet for your feelings. Even if you don't *feel* like writing about how you feel, once you get going, you may find it very therapeutic.
·   Exercise is an excellent way to release pent-up anxiety, anger or feelings of depression.
·   Drink more water – it makes everything work better.
·   Cut down on caffeine, which can make you feel more anxious and raise your blood pressure.
·   Try meditation or other relaxation techniques.
·   Use humour to diffuse tense situations.
·   If you feel as if your feelings are out of control, talk to a counsellor or therapist. Sometimes it's easier to talk to somebody who isn't part of your personal life.

Real Men Do Feel Stress

Men are taught to be independent and strong, to deal with things rationally and logically. Sometimes this approach can be an effective way to handle a crisis, get things done or let things go that aren't worth dwelling on. But sometimes rationality and strength don't address the real problem, which doesn't go away. Some men turn to drugs, alcohol or other addictions, such as gambling or sex, to numb the pain, sadness or anxiety that are the result of too much stress. Many men get depressed, but far fewer men than women are likely to admit it or to seek help for their depression.

Sometimes not acknowledging stress makes it worse, and eventually, the stress will take over and force you to feel it. The best way to ensure that you remain in control is to manage the stress as it comes. Let yourself acknowledge it so that you can deal with it.

Recognize that 'manliness', and everything that word implies for you, could be interfering with your ability to manage your stress. Life doesn't have to be a competition. Success isn't always measured in money and prestige. You don't have to survive on five hours' sleep or try to keep up with your mates in the pub after work. And you don't have to deny that you are feeling stressed.

You don't have to tell everybody you meet, but neither do you have to deny your stress to yourself. There are lots of ways to manage stress and make your life easier, and many of them can be practised alone in your own home. It's your business.

 A man is most likely to have a heart attack in the morning. Some experts believe that morning heart attacks could be related to typically higher blood pressure levels in the morning. Save your stressful moments – such as a meeting with a difficult client or checking your bank statement – for the afternoon.

The Testosterone Connection

Studies have linked both physical and psychological stress to a drop in the level of testosterone, the hormone that gives men masculine qualities such as facial hair growth, musculature and a deep voice. Testosterone is a hormone with a complex relationship to behaviour: behaviour can influence testosterone levels, and testosterone levels can influence behaviour. Historically, when men were castrated so that they could serve as eunuchs to royalty or become Italian castrati, with legendarily beautiful, high voices, they would tend to be more docile, have a reduced sex drive and develop more body fat.

Testosterone is linked to dominant behaviour in men. It is to a degree responsible for the male perspective and the feeling that control, rationality and the ability to dominate are desirable traits in men. Countless studies that assert the differences between the genders in communication style, learning style and even basic understanding of language, are exploring the differences between people who are more driven by testosterone and those who are more driven by oestrogen.

Studies have shown that women tend to be attracted to men with distinctly masculine features and who exhibit dominant behaviour – not aggressive behaviour, necessarily, but dominant behaviour. While cultural factors certainly modify biological impulses, and while there are many exceptions, masculine features and dominant behaviour are biological signals of reproductive fitness.

Traditionally, in Western culture, men went out to earn a living and support their families, fulfilling this urge to dominate. The oestrogen- and oxytocin-driven females were more likely to stay at home, nurturing children and looking after the domestic front. But in life today, things are very different (although surely we oversimplify the past). As society evolves, its members are less likely to be restricted to a certain role. Many women gain enormous satisfaction from earning a living and supporting their families. Many men gain immense satisfaction from staying at home to look after their children, and are excellent in this capacity. This so-called role reversal isn't really a reversal at all. Caring for a household and raising children can wholly fulfil a man's need to achieve something important. A stay-at-home father can be a dominant figure in a very positive way for his children. Looking after a home can be a matter of competition and pride.

Similarly, women tend to excel in the world of work by being communicative, empathetic and nurturing. In other words, both men and women can do any kind of job, but they will tend to go about it in different ways. You may not run the house or care for the children in the same way as your partner would, but that doesn't mean your way isn't just as good.

The point is that a man does not necessarily become frustrated or stressed just because he isn't doing traditional 'man' things. Rather, that stress sets in when a man isn't allowed to be who he needs to be. The inclination towards dominance can result in feelings of stress when dominant individuals are put in subordinate positions. If a man is forced to be subordinate when it isn't in his nature – even if that means having to be subordinate to a powerful managing director – the result can be lots of stress. If left unchecked, this stress can manifest itself as aggression or in other forms of antisocial behaviour. If a man isn't able to fulfill his need to control his own situation, to go out there and compete, and feel as if he is making an important contribution, he may feel frustrated and unfulfilled.

What happens when stress depresses a man's testosterone level? A lowered level of testosterone could result in a drop in self-confidence and feelings of control, which can be frustrating and provoke anxiety in men who are used to feeling dominant, thus exacerbating an already stressful situation. To maintain your health and confidence, it is crucial that you manage stress and keep it in check. If you keep your testosterone level in balance, you'll feel better – and you'll be more confident and more in control of your feelings and actions.

Both men and women have some oestrogen and some testosterone. In men, small amounts of oestrogen are beneficial to the brain and other parts of the body, but if a man becomes obese or drinks too much alcohol, the body can start producing more oestrogen than is healthy.

Your Stress, Your Reproductive Fitness

Stress can lower testosterone production, and lowered testosterone levels result in a lower sperm count, which drastically reduces a man's reproductive fitness. If you and your partner want to have a baby, stress management is equally as important for both of you. How do you improve your reproductive health? The same way as your partner. Do the following together:

· Take moderate daily exercise.
· Eat healthy foods.
· Get sufficient sleep.
· Drink plenty of water.
· Meditate or practise relaxation techniques daily.
· Practise breathing deeply.
· Make a conscious effort to have a positive attitude.
· If you really aren't able to control something, let it go.

Anger, Depression and Other Unmentionables

Stress can have specific effects on men, which, although they are often very treatable, can leave men feeling lost, frustrated or hopeless. Anger management is an important skill for men. Your naturally higher testosterone level makes you more prone to anger and aggression than women (although there are certainly exceptions). Suppressing anger can be just as dangerous as expressing it inappropriately. Both cause a surge in stress hormones that can be harmful to the body.

Frequent anger can also be a sign of depression. Depression is a very real problem for many men, who are less likely to admit they are depressed or to seek treatment. Here are the signs of depression:

· Feeling out of control
· Excessive irritability or anger
· Loss of interest in things that you previously enjoyed
· Sudden change in appetite (much higher or lower)
· Sudden change in sleep patterns (insomnia or sleeping too much)
· Feelings of hopelessness and despair
· Feelings of being stuck in a situation with no way out
· Anxiety, panic

- Frequent crying
- Thoughts of suicide
- Sabotaging success (such as leaving a good job or ending a good relationship)
- Substance abuse
- Increase in addictive behaviour
- Decreased sex drive.

If you are depressed, please seek treatment. Depression is easily treatable, through therapy, medication or a combination of both. Once you are over the first hurdle, you will feel better about yourself, and be more able to implement lifestyle changes, such as taking daily exercise, that will help to further alleviate depression.

Pressures Everywhere

Men often feel that asking for help is a sign of weakness, but in the case of depression (and in many other cases, for that matter), it is a sign of strength. The situation is never hopeless, so do ask for help.

Another area of concern for many men, and something that can be a direct result of even minor and/or temporary stress, is erectile dysfunction (ED), or impotence. Isolated incidents of being unable to maintain an erection adequately to complete sexual intercourse are normal. Being overtired, drinking too much, having a bad day or putting too much pressure on yourself to perform can all result in an incident. But if the condition persists – if you cannot maintain an erection at least half the time you try – then you could have erectile dysfunction, and erectile dysfunction can be caused by stress.

Other Causes

There are other causes, too. In men over 50 the most common cause of ED is circulatory problems such as hardening of the arteries. It isn't just the arteries in your heart that can harden with age; the ones to the penis can also get clogged, preventing a sufficient flow of blood for an erection. ED can also be a symptom of serious diseases such as diabetes, or kidney or liver problems. It can also be caused by nerve damage to the area as a result of disease or surgery, including spinal surgery or surgery on the colon or prostate. ED can be a side effect of many different medications, including antidepressants (very common), medication for high blood pressure, and sedatives. Excessive alcohol consumption can cause ED, as can smoking.

Do you need yet another reason to stop smoking? Studies show that erectile dysfunction is more than twice as common in heavy smokers as it is in non-smokers. Heavy smoking causes blood vessels in the body to shrink, which reduces blood flow all over the body, including to the penis... just when you need it most!

In many cases, people who experience ED for psychological reasons will still have erections during sleep or in the morning. See a doctor to make sure there isn't an underlying physical condition, but if it's clear that the cause is psychological, then you can focus on managing your stress.

Stress and ED do an insidious dance. You're stressed. You experience an incident of impotence. That makes you more stressed, increasing your chances of it happening again. It happens again. You get more stressed. So how do you break the cycle?

Begin by seeing if you can pinpoint the reason. The stress that causes erectile dysfunction can come from any source. It can certainly be overall life stress, but there are other kinds of stress to be considered as well, including the following:

- Stress in the relationship between sexual partners
- Stress caused by fear of poor performance
- Stress caused by a fear of intimacy or a sudden change in the nature of the relationship, such as becoming engaged
- Fear of disease
- Stress due to unresolved sexual issues, including sexual orientation
- Depression and its accompanying loss of interest in sex.

If you know, or suspect you know where your stress is rooted, you can begin to work on that area. Practise meditation and relaxation techniques. Take enough exercise. If you are afraid of something, talk about it, think it through, write about it or seek help so that you can work through it and get past it. If you are depressed, seek treatment. If you are having relationship problems, confront them and work through them together – sometimes all it takes is open communication.

Or perhaps your ED is a signal that you are having sex with the wrong person. Think about that, too. Whatever it is, in most cases the psychological causes of ED can be resolved and your function will return without any sign of having left you. When it comes to ED, 'don't worry, be happy' may be easier said than done, but it's still pretty good advice.

Should you try Viagra?

Men with erectile dysfunction may benefit from Viagra because it facilitates erection and can increase the desire for sex. However, all medication has side effects and risks, and Viagra shouldn't be used when it isn't needed. Your doctor can help you decide if it is appropriate for you, and explain the effects, the risks and how to use it properly. (While some men reportedly use Viagra occasionally for greater stamina, this medication is not for people with normal sexual functioning.)

The Midlife Crisis: Myth, Reality or Stress in Disguise?

While both men and women can experience midlife crises, the term is most often applied to men. The midlife crisis may or may not have a hormonal basis, but it is certainly real enough. During this period of their lives, typically in the late 30s to mid-40s, men begin to question the direction their lives have taken. They wonder if they've missed out on things. They may be tired of their jobs, feel their relationships have stagnated, and fear that they have lost interest in life generally.

What a man does in response to his midlife crisis depends on the man and the intensity of the feelings, but we've all seen the stereotypes on television and in films: the divorce, the 20-something girlfriend, the red sports car. Of course it doesn't always work out like this. Sometimes the response is depression, withdrawal, anxiety or an increasing dissatisfaction with daily life. Sometimes men change careers at this point and go after their dreams.

What does the midlife crisis have to do with stress? Years of chronic stress caused by unresolved relationship problems or job dissatisfaction can build up to the final breakdown that is the midlife crisis. In addition, the midlife crisis itself can become a source of stress because of the changes it has made to the individual's life.

There is nothing to stop you changing your career; just don't do it on a whim. Plan the change by thoroughly researching your chosen field, learning everything you can about it, obtaining any necessary qualifications, having a solid business plan, securing any necessary capital – then giving it everything you've got.

What can you do about a midlife crisis? First, learn to manage your stress before you get there. This can subvert a midlife crisis, because if your life is going just the way you want it, you won't have any reason for a crisis. If you're already heading full speed into yours, however, you can help to soften the blow by preparing for the stress to come:

· Make a list of all your unfulfilled dreams. Look at it and contemplate it. Which of the dreams are unrealistic – things you know you'll never do, but just like to dream about? You can cross those off for now (or put them on a different list).

Look at what's left. What have you really wanted to do, always intended to do, but haven't yet accomplished? Think hard about these items – are they things you really want, or things you just think you want? Relax, close your eyes, and visualize having these things. Sometimes we like the idea of something – being awarded a PhD, having a drop-dead-gorgeous partner, becoming extremely rich – but when we think about what it would actually be like to achieve it, we realize it isn't really worth it. Which of your items are probably not worth the effort of getting them? Cross them off (or move them to a different list).

Look at what's left. Why haven't you accomplished these dreams yet? What would make them happen? Start thinking about what you could do to make these dreams come true. Make a list of steps. If you have a partner, encourage her to make her own list, then talk about how you might both achieve your dreams together while you are still young (*young* is a relative term, after all).

· If your dissatisfaction lies with your relationship, this is the time to do something about it, and that doesn't necessarily mean leaving it. Take steps to revitalize your relationship: change your routine, go away together, do things differently in the bedroom, be romantic, pay real attention to and put focus on your sex life. If you aren't both ready for these changes, discuss the reasons why. If you have past issues to work out, work them out with the help of a professional therapist.

· Stop doing things you don't like and don't really have to do. If you really, truly can't stand your job, find a new one or start your own business. There are more opportunities to be self-employed these days, and more people prefer to work close to or from home, redirecting their energies to their personal lives and to living more in line with their dreams and desires. Can you manage on less money? If so, do it. If you cringe at the thought of the committee you are on, the group you joined or the club of which you are a member, then let it go. Don't waste your life doing things you don't like that aren't necessary.

· Give to others. Self-examination over a period of time can make you feel selfish, so balance it out with a conscious effort to give your time, energy or money to people who really need it. You could devote some time to a charity that has special meaning for you, or to a cause you believe in, or you could spend more time with your partner, your children or your grandchildren.

Stress and the Senior Man

It isn't easy when your body starts to betray you, and it can be hard to admit that you can't do all the things you once could. Getting older is stressful for men, and may sometimes seem fraught with loss: of muscle tone, stamina, sex drive, even hair. Some women may say that men get better-looking as they age, but men often don't feel better-looking as they recognize that they have gained weight and lost energy.

Retirement can also add stress in great heaps to your already full plate. The loss of a job, which you've relied on for a sense of identity and worth for years, can be devastating for men, who suddenly don't know who they are or what to do with themselves. Of course you aren't your job, and you probably know that, but after 50 years of working you may feel as if you've let go of a big part of yourself.

Although women typically live longer than men, men often lose their partners and are left living alone. It is difficult for many men to seek companionship elsewhere, and depression, loneliness and isolation are common problems for those who have lost their partners, especially if they are living far from close relatives. Making the effort to maintain social contact is extremely important.

What can a senior man do to feel strong, confident, and stress-free? Manage his stress, of course. Try some of these tips (they're similar to the tips for senior women listed earlier in this chapter):

· *Stay engaged.* Take part in activities outside your home, for example volunteering, playing on a sports team, taking painting or writing classes, joining a hobby group or church. Take up woodwork or cooking, fly fishing or ballroom dancing. Do whatever interests you – you finally have the time, so don't waste it! Perhaps you always wanted to study law, learn to speak Italian or be a bird watcher. Staying active will keep you enthusiastic about what's going on around you, as well as keeping your mind active, which helps to keep you feeling young.

- *Don't lose touch with friends.* Make an effort to stay connected. Maintain a mix of friends of your own age and younger ones. Take part in activities outside your home with these friends. You might even help someone else who really needs to get out of the house.
- *Consider getting a pet.* Pets have been proved to reduce stress and can give you a lasting and satisfying relationship. Dogs and cats give back all that you give them. Birds can also be rewarding companions.
- *Stay active.* Take a walk or do some other kind of exercise every day. Walking with friends is beneficial physically and emotionally.
- *Notice what's going on in the world.* Talk about events with your friends and/or partner. Work on being open-minded, and having opinions you can back up with good reasoning.
- *Try yoga* to help keep your body flexible and less prone to injury. More and more senior men are trying yoga and enjoying great benefits.
- *Eat nutrient-dense foods* with plenty of calcium, protein and fibre.
- *Consider taking a daily zinc supplement* to keep your prostate healthy. Pumpkin seeds are also rich in zinc. The herb saw palmetto may also be good for prostate health.
- *Lift weights* to keep your muscles and bones strong.
- *Keep drinking lots of water* and getting enough sleep.

More white men over the age of 85 commit suicide than any other group. Even though women report attempting suicide twice as often as men, more than four times as many men than women commit suicide.

- *Consider seeing qualified complementary health care practitioners*, who may suggest putting you on less medication and helping you to adjust your lifestyle for better health.
- *Meditate daily* to explore the universe of the inner you. Get to know yourself all over again!
- *Keep your mind busy.* Take up a new hobby, learn a new language, read books in a different genre from your usual one, do crossword puzzles, have intellectual discussions with your friends, make things.

- *Do things for other people.* Service to others will make you feel good about yourself as well as helping other people.
- *Start writing your life history.* You'll enjoy sorting through the memories, and your manuscript will become a valuable family treasure.
- *Value yourself.*

Whether you are a man or a woman, in your 20s or in your 90s, stress can disrupt your health and the way you function. But no matter your gender or age, you can always do something to lessen the effects of stress. Don't be a victim of your gender or age – it's your body, your mind and your life!

CHAPTER 13

Stress Management from Childhood to Forever

From the stress of being born to the stress of ageing, encountering and dealing with stress is a lifelong process. Although you may be coming to the idea of stress management as an adult, children today need stress management just as much as their parents. Teaching children stress-management techniques while they are still children gives them a gift that will last a lifetime.

Junior Stress

Adults sometimes have the misconception (or the not-altogether-accurate memory) of childhood as one long interlude of candyfloss and fairground rides. Perhaps it is the comparison with our adult lives that makes childhood seem so carefree. Yet children today are suffering the negative effects of stress in greater numbers than ever before. The causes of stress in children tend to be primarily environmental (family, friends, school) until puberty sets in and adds troublesome hormones to the mix.

Stress in children has been recognized and diagnosed only recently. Many children report having to deal with violence, peer pressure, underage drinking, drug use, and pressure to have sex, not to mention pressure to do well at school, be involved in back-to-back extracurricular activities, have a social life and keep all the adults in their lives pacified.

For kids dealing with learning disabilities such as dyslexia or barriers to success in traditional environments such as attention deficit hyperactivity disorder, school can be an unrelenting source of frustration and feelings of failure. If your child seems to be having problems succeeding in school, have him or her tested for learning or behavioural problems.

Even young children can experience stress. They, too, are sometimes faced with difficult family situations and relationships with peers, which may not seem challenging to adults but that can cause profound stress reactions in children.

Childhood experiences can affect the individual long into adulthood. One study demonstrated that children who were poorly cared for were less able to deal with stressful situations, more likely to react in an extreme manner, and maintained high levels of stress hormones in their bodies long after stress subsided, compared to those who were well cared for as children. The key to giving young children the tools for handling stress in the future is to provide a supportive, loving, caring environment. If you do so, you may be helping your child form the neural pathways necessary for healthy stress management.

High stress as a child, for example, that which would occur in situations of extreme neglect, may also actually destroy neural pathways already established. This could explain the higher incidence of learning disabilities in young children who have suffered from extremely high stress.

The chances are that your children don't experience the extreme stress of neglect, however. It is more likely to be the average stress that comes with childhood. Just as with adults, some stress is good for children. It can enhance performance when it is most necessary, whether for getting out of a dangerous situation fast or doing well in a dance performance. It can also teach children how to handle stress, since stress is an integral part of life.

 Suicide is the third leading cause of death in 15–24-year-olds and the fourth leading cause of death in 10–14-year-olds.

Teaching Children About Stress Management

If adults don't have to take stress lying down, why should children? If children learn that stress is a natural part of life and that they can do something about it, they won't have to wait until adulthood, when its negative effects are already compounded, to start feeling better. Children who understand stress management will be empowered to manage stress throughout their lives.

The first step to teaching children about stress management is to be aware of the stress they are feeling. You may not always know all the details of the causes of stress for your children, but if you live with them and pay attention, you can probably tell when your child's equilibrium is disturbed.

Signs of stress in children are similar to signs of stress in adults. Suspect that your child is suffering from stress if you notice any of the following:

· Sudden change in appetite that seems unrelated to growth
· Sudden weight loss or gain

- Development of an eating disorder
- Sudden change in sleeping habits
- Chronic fatigue
- Insomnia
- Sudden drop in achievement in school
- Sudden change in exercise habits (much more, or stopping completely)
- Withdrawal, sudden refusal to communicate
- Signs of anxiety or panic
- Frequent headaches and/or stomach aches
- Frequent frustration
- Depression
- Loss of interest in activities
- Compulsion to do too much
- Suddenly stopping participation in many activities.

Children of any age can learn stress-management techniques. Teenagers may be interested in reading this book, and any of the techniques included here will work for them as well. For younger children, certain stress-management techniques are particularly effective because children enjoy them and are motivated to try them.

Signs of stress in young children include increased whining, clinging and crying; intense separation anxiety from parents or carers; aggressive behaviour, such as yelling, biting, kicking and hitting; rashes and allergy symptoms; inability to concentrate, remember things, or pay attention; frequent forgetfulness and disorganization; impulsive or hyperactive behaviour; disassociation for surroundings; and sudden lack of creativity.

To help build a strong stress-management foundation for your children, and to teach them how to manage stress in healthy ways, consider the following strategies.

Soothing Infant Stress

For infants, try a daily infant massage. Gently and softly stroke your baby's legs, arms and body to improve circulation and relax muscles. Talk softly and sweetly to your baby as you massage her, sing to her and make eye contact.

New parents are often overwhelmed and find their energies scattered. Even so, make a commitment to set aside several 15-minute sessions each day during which you devote your full and total attention to your baby. Make eye contact, talk to her, play with her and don't do anything else; turn off the television or radio, put away the newspaper and stop cleaning. Make it all about baby. He will soon learn he is important and worth your attention. He'll learn that he is lovable and a priority. Eventually he'll learn to take care of himself as well as you took care of him.

If your child has a low stress tolerance, keep life moving at a slower pace, stay at home more, and don't force your child to take part in lots of activities. Studies show that children with a lower tolerance of stress actually have lower rates of illness and behaviour problems when put into low-stress settings than children with higher stress-tolerance levels. Just like adults, children with low stress tolerance thrive when life is low in stress, and, as a parent, it's your job to help keep pressure low and life at a leisurely pace.

Toddler Time

For toddlers, life is a big exciting adventure to be explored. How mysterious the behaviour of adults must be to a curious, enthusiastic toddler – the simplest efforts at fun can cause adults to shout, snatch things away from you, or behave in other strange and frightening ways. Even if your toddler can't always understand what you say, talking to her about what is and isn't allowed is much more effective than shouting. Firm but calm and, ultimately, consistent behaviour is paramount in raising a toddler who has self-confidence and doesn't fear or mistrust adults.

Notice your toddler's reaction to the world. Instead of forcing him to do something that makes him nervous, accept that he is nervous and take it slowly or put off the activity until later. Some toddlers are always ready to jump into new activities; others require more time to consider before trying new things. Respect your child's individual style. He'll learn that it's OK to be the way he is, and less likely, later in life, to blame himself for his stress. He will also be more likely to understand how to approach new things successfully.

Pre-school and Nursery School

Pre-schoolers and nursery-school children love to learn, but children learn in different ways. Some parents tend to direct their children too much. Try stepping back and letting your child explore, learn, question and discover on her own. Instead of constantly saying, 'Did you see this? What do you think of that? How do you think this works? What might you do with this?', let your child take the lead. She just might teach you something, and you'll be reinforcing her confidence in her own learning style.

School Daze

Once children start school, it's easy for parents to overload them, especially children with many interests. Music lessons, swimming lessons, football practice, babysitting, homework, extra tuition, gymnastics, Scouts or Guides, socializing with friends, family time, dance classes, home tasks – when do they have a chance to relax and do nothing? Free time (this doesn't include watching television) is actually empowering for children. During free time, children can organize their own activities. Overloaded children don't learn how to direct themselves. They spend years being told what to do, so when they are suddenly expected to behave independently, they're at a loss... and that's pretty stressful. Also, with too much to do, children necessarily have bodies and brains that are working overtime. Learning how to relax as a child makes adult relaxation a much easier process.

Children really enjoy yoga, and yoga classes for children are becoming more widely available; alternatively, look for one of the many books about yoga for children. Learning yoga as a child is an excellent way to form a lifelong habit of good health, strength, flexibility and mind–body integration.

 Encourage your children to take deep breaths from the stomach when they are starting to feel nervous, anxious or fearful. Deep breaths directly combat the stress response in children just as they do in adults. They signal to the body that everything is fine, returning heart rate, muscle tension and blood flow to normal.

Teenagers in Trouble

Being a teenager is always difficult because of the surge of hormonal changes experienced during puberty. But some teenagers seem to handle the intense feelings of adolescence better than others. Why? Some theories suggest a genetic factor, but the chances are that the answer is almost always at least partially due to external circumstances.

Many teenagers suffer from depression, self-doubt, anger, hopelessness and other intense emotions, even in response to situations that adults wouldn't necessarily consider stressful. Today, many teenagers also have to deal with extreme circumstances, such as a nasty divorce at home or the threat or actual occurrence of violence in or after school.

If parents don't want to acknowledge that their teenagers are in trouble, they increase the distance that often exists between teenagers and adults – the generation gap, or whatever we choose to call it these days. If they try too forcefully to intervene in their children's lives, they may push their children away even further. It's a tricky job, being the parent of a teenager, and many parents get by with their fingers crossed.

If you think your teenager is perfectly fine, you may be right, but even the most well-adjusted adolescent occasionally experiences overwhelming emotions. Even if your teenager resists sharing her intense emotions with you, make sure she always knows she can. Keep the lines of communication open and stay aware so that you'll notice when your teenager's stress level escalates. You'll be ready to do something about it, whether that means going for counselling together, seeking medical treatment, or simply sitting down for a serious heart-to-heart.

Here are some important things you can do for a stressed teenager:

- Be consistent.
- Don't lose your temper.
- Let your teenager know you are always there; be a solid foundation.
- Let your teenager know you love her, no matter what.
- Let your teenager know he can always count on you to help him if he's in trouble.
- Make it clear what behaviour you think is wrong, and why.
- Set a good example by practising stress management yourself.
- Provide opportunities for your teenager to practise stress-management techniques with you.
- Keep talking.
- Don't give up!

One theory about why children are more stressed than they once were is that they are overexposed to stimuli. In a media-intense culture, children can spend hours each day watching television, playing video games, surfing the Internet and listening to music. Encourage your children to spend some media-free time each day doing something relaxing, whether it's writing in a diary or taking a bike ride.

Stress-Management Tips for Children of All Ages

Healthy children are more likely to handle the average stresses of life with ease. Lay the foundation for healthy habits by teaching your children how to take care of themselves. Set a good example by practising healthy habits yourself. You might also try the following tips.

· Serve water instead of sugary drinks. Keep a jug of good-quality water in the refrigerator or buy bottled water that is as easily available as a fizzy drink.

· Keep healthy snacks in the house instead of junk food. Cheese cubes, carrot sticks, peanut butter, wholemeal bread, fresh fruit, whole-grain crackers, hummus, dried fruit and whole-grain cereal with milk are all healthy, high-energy choices.

· Encourage daily activity. If children aren't involved in school sports, look into other organized fitness opportunities, such as gymnastics, dance classes, swimming lessons or gym memberships.

· Make exercise a family affair. Walk, ride bicycles, jog or run around in the playground together.

· Encourage self-expression. Many children enjoy drawing, modelling in clay, making things or writing. These creative activities can also be excellent outlets for stress because they build self-esteem and develop artistic talents.

If your child is really stressed about an impending test, remind her to practise deep breathing, which will help to feed oxygen to the brain, making it work better. Taking a break during study time for a 20-minute nap can also help your child to feel refreshed and able to get back to the books in a more effective state of mind. To work well, a power nap should be between 20 and 30 minutes – no shorter, no longer.

Making time for family or for just doing nothing is an important way of teaching children that overachieving isn't always the answer. Reserve at least one evening each week as family night. Encourage a leisurely, relaxed time together with no organized activities. Play games, make a meal together, talk, laugh, take a walk or a bike ride. Your children will always remember this together time, and these sorts of evenings put a nice pause in busy routines.

Perhaps most important, keep the lines of communication open. This sounds obvious, but keep reminding your children they can talk to you, and keep talking to them. Let them know you are there to listen, and let them know what things are important to you. Discussions about smoking, drinking or drugs are important, but you can also talk to your children about other potential stressors, such peer pressure, how they are enjoying or not enjoying different subjects at school, how they feel about the various activities in which they are involved, who their friends are and how they feel about themselves.

Finally, never try to let your child feel responsible for your stress. Make sure your child knows that you are the adult and that she doesn't have to take care of you. Taking care of you is your job. If you are suffering from severe stress, caused by a divorce or depression, for example, it is essential to seek help from an outside source, not from your child. That kind of stress is too much for a child to bear. Do your best to keep your vulnerable moments to yourself. Set an example by showing your child you know how to manage stress in effective ways, including by asking other adults for help.

If your child does seem to be in trouble, take action. Take him for counselling if necessary, keep talking to him, and bring up subjects such as depression that he may be afraid or embarrassed to mention. Be an ally and an advocate for your child. If he knows you are on his side, he won't feel he is bearing all his stress alone. This can be a monumental relief to a stressed child.

Many teenagers engage in underage drinking, and the effects can be devastating. Underage drinking increases a child's risk of accidents, makes a child more vulnerable to dangerous situations, and puts physical stress on the body, especially in the case of binge drinking. Many teenagers have died from alcohol poisoning while trying to 'have fun'. Make sure your children understand the dangers of alcohol.

The Seven Steps to Stress Management for Children

Children can learn how to deal with stress on their own terms and in their own way. Memorizing a few stress-management strategies can give children access to help when they need it most – during an exam, on a night out, before a big performance. Show this list to your children, stick it on the fridge or push it under their bedroom doors. They might just read it, and they might even use it (whether they tell you about it or not).

1. **Talk about it.** Feeling stressed? Tell a friend. Call it letting off steam, a rant or a rage, but do it! Share your stress daily and you'll ease the burden. Listen to a friend with stress and ease your friend's burden.
2. **Go with the flow.** Things aren't what you expected? That friend isn't who you thought they were? That subject is harder than you thought it would be? Go with the flow. Move along with changes in your life rather than resisting them. Be like a river that finds the easiest way around obstacles and just keeps on flowing.
3. **Find a mentor.** Parents are fine, but sometimes you may feel more open to advice from a 'non-parent' adult. Teachers, counsellors, coaches, bosses, aunts, uncles, vicars, priests or other adult friends who have already been through what you are going through can make great mentors. Find a person you can relate to and let him or her help you when you need some advice or a good example.
4. **Get organized.** That exam wouldn't be so stressful if you hadn't lost all your notes. You might be able to relax more easily in your room if you could get from the door to the bed without stepping on piles of junk. Work out a system you can live with, and get yourself organized. It's a good project, a great hobby and a skill you'll value for the rest of your life.
5. **Establish healthy habits now.** You've probably seen adults who have obviously led a life of unhealthy habits and are paying for it now. This doesn't have to be you. If you start forming healthy habits while you are still growing up, you'll have a healthier life ahead of you. Try to exercise for about 30 minutes on most days, and eat lots of fresh,

healthy foods such as vegetables, fruits, whole grains and low-fat sources of protein such as lean meat, fish, beans, tofu and low-fat yogurt and milk. Drink lots of water, and get enough sleep – enough for you not to feel tired during the day.

6. **Adjust your attitude.** Sometimes it's easier to be cynical or to expect the worst, but studies show that people who have a positive attitude are less often ill, recover from illness and injuries more quickly, and may even live longer. Life is a lot more fun when you look on the positive side. It's a habit you can learn.

7. **See the big picture.** Life may seem to revolve around the humiliating thing you said in front of the whole class last week, or failing an exam or not being chosen for the team. Whenever things seem horrible or hopeless, remind yourself to step back and look at the big picture. How will you feel about this in a year? In five years? When you are an adult with a satisfying career and a fulfilling personal life? If you learn to look at temporary setbacks with an 'Oh well, moving right along' attitude, life will seem much less stressful.

Stress Management Forever

You have the tools. You have the knowledge. But the days go by and, somehow, there never seems to be enough time to do anything about it. Can't you start your stress management tomorrow... later... when you have time?

No, because you won't ever have time. Tomorrow will become today, later will become yesterday, and you'll still be just as busy as you are today, if not busier. If you don't start to de-stress now, none of it may never happen.

Perhaps you can't join a gym today, but can you go for a walk? Perhaps you can't overhaul your junk-food diet today, but can you order a chicken Caesar salad instead of a double bacon cheeseburger? Perhaps you aren't up for meditation tonight, but can you go to bed a bit earlier?

Any major life change starts with small steps, and you can weave stress management into your life one thread at a time. Luckily, you can work a daily antistress regime into your routine with very little effort, while enjoying a big payoff. Anything you do to help relax your body and calm your spirit is a positive step. To start establishing your new habits, try doing just four little things every day. That's only four, and they don't have to take very long. You can work them into your routine in any way that suits you – in fact, you may already be doing some or all of them.

1. Do something good for your body.
2. Do something to calm your mind.
3. Do something to feed your spirit.
4. Do something to simplify your environment.

Doing one thing each day to maintain your sense of wellbeing in each of these categories is all it takes to begin a lifelong habit of stress management. What will you do? All the techniques listed in this book will fit into one or another of these categories. You can even take care of two categories at once: meditate for mental and spiritual maintenance. Then add a brisk walk for physical maintenance and get rid of one stack of clutter you don't use or need.

Or perhaps you'll choose the body scan in the morning, yoga in the afternoon, 20 minutes of undisturbed quiet time listening to music in the evening, and dropping an activity that you no longer enjoy.

Still too complicated? Eat a salad (body), turn off the television (mind), tell a friend how much you appreciate her (spirit), and throw away one thing you've no reason to keep (simplify).

One of the best ways to reduce your stress is to help somebody else relieve his or her stress. Helping and caring for other people helps you to feel better about yourself. It also helps you regain a sense of purpose and direction, which makes it a great activity for people who have retired from a job that used to provide that purpose and direction. Most communities have many opportunities for volunteering in a variety of areas. Find something that interests you, and start helping yourself by helping others.

You probably already have some ideas about how you can work these four antistress steps into your day. You don't have to keep them the same each day, either. Changing them from time to time can be fun if you thrive on change. If you love your rituals, doing the same things each day is fine, too. There are many ways to keep your body, mind and spirit well fed that take only minutes. You can work in exercise time, meditation time and time for any of the other techniques listed previously in this book.

In the following sections are some quick, easy – practically effortless – ways to boost your daily antistress regime to new heights of effectiveness. You'll feel special implementing these small changes.

Open to Change

This is a good one if you are change-resistant. For some people, no change is ever a good change, but change is inevitable in life and is almost always stressful, even if it's stress that feels good. Becoming more open to change takes a shift in attitude. Start being aware of changes and then finding one good thing about every change you experience. Has someone parked in your usual space? You can get an extra few minutes of exercise by walking from a space further away – it's good for your body. Your favourite restaurant runs out of your favourite food? What a great opportunity to try something different. Has your favourite television show been cancelled? Another opportunity! Spend the evening reading a book, taking a walk or practising a new stress-management technique.

A recent study showed that stress-management programmes could reduce the risk of cardiac problems such as heart attacks by up to 75 per cent in people who already have heart disease. Another study demonstrated that stress management may be even more effective than exercise for reducing cardiac risk.

Major changes are even easier. Any change, no matter how disturbing, can have its positive side, even if you can't find it straight away. But even finding the positive side isn't the most important thing. The most important thing is a willingness to accept that things change, and that you can go with the flow.

Passive, Aggressive or Passive-Aggressive?

Some people tend to deal with stress passively, letting things happen to them without trying to control the situation. Others tend to be aggressive, taking stressful situations forcefully in hand. The passive-aggressive among us forcefully control stress in a seemingly passive manner. We do this by inflicting guilty feelings upon people, or by subtly implying what we want, while acting as though we don't care either way.

Each of these habitual methods of dealing with stress has its damaging effects. For the passive stress manager, stress can begin to feel like an uncontrollable force. While maintaining a passive attitude is sometimes recommended (in this book as well as elsewhere) for effectively managing the stressful changes inherent in life, too much passivity can engender a feeling of hopelessness. If you give up, if you are not in control at all, then what good is it trying to live how you want to live? If you are a hapless leaf being blown randomly about by the wind, what importance do you have? For the naturally passive, assertiveness training is in order. Chakra meditation (see Chapter 8) can be an effective way to regain control over the things you really can control. Meditation may also help to clarify the areas of your life over which you really are lord and master.

For the aggressive stress manager, stress can begin to feel like a formidable foe to be vanquished, and while a gung-ho attitude can certainly be helpful in some situations, eventually it is physically and mentally exhausting. It also puts you on the defensive. You begin to feel as though fate is conspiring against you, throwing you one challenge after another, and that if you don't whack them all over the boundary with your great big bat, you'll be a great big failure. For the naturally aggressive, meditation can be a healing tool as well as an enlightening exploration of the nature of reality. A Zen approach may be particularly helpful. If things simply are what they are, if right now is the only reality, and if there is nothing to be improved upon, what is there to be aggressive about? Learning to accept rather than attack is a valuable stress management skill for aggressive types.

For the passive-aggressive stress manager, stress is something to subvert with trickery. Even if you don't fully realize it, you don't approach stress directly. You manipulate your circumstances underhandedly so that you get what you need without feeling as though you've behaved inappropriately. This, too, can be an effective way to deal with certain kinds of stress. Sometimes the stress in life is best soothed into submission with flowers and chocolates. But sometimes the passive-aggressive way is simply indirect and therefore wholly ineffective. Like the mother who struggles into the house with bags full of shopping calling out, 'Goodness, this shopping certainly is heavy; if only someone would give me a hand', you don't ask for what you need – you just complain loudly and hope someone will step in and help you out. Like the stubborn teenager on the sofa, blatantly ignoring her mother's non-request, the stress in your life might just stay put. A direct acknowledgment of your stress and direct action to purge it from your life would be much simpler.

Only you can decide which, if any (or all) of these categories you fall into, and only you can begin to make the necessary changes to readjust your stress-management approach. But if you tend to be passive, aggressive or passive-aggressive, you may not be handling your stress as well as you might.

Do your feelings of stress go in cycles?
Some people are more easily stressed at some times and less easily stressed at others, no matter what is going on around them. On a calendar, keep track of how much stress you are feeling each day – just write *high, medium high, medium, medium low* or *low*. After three months, see if you can spot any patterns. If you know when you are more likely to be stressed, you can be prepared and take precautionary measures by cutting back on your commitments and stepping up your relaxation efforts.

Stay Inspired

When life is stressful, the stress always seems easier, more manageable, if the circumstances surrounding it lift you to heights of positive feeling. Staying inspired is essential for maintaining the necessary energy, enthusiasm and motivation to keep your life on track, your stress in check and your goals in sight.

Staying inspired might mean a commitment to a hobby about which you are passionate, starting your own business, learning something new, taking up some form of art, writing a novel, volunteering or keeping in touch with inspiring friends. Whatever keeps you excited about the day, glowing with anticipation and happy to be alive should be a priority. If you make time for the source of your inspiration, you'll be happier and better able to handle the pitfalls along the way.

The Daily De-clutter

Whether your house contains mountains of clutter or one untidy surface in a spare room out of sight, clutter attracts stress. Just looking at clutter suggests clutter to the mind. While de-cluttering your entire garage, attic or wardrobe may be too big a task to tackle all at once, any big de-cluttering job can be accomplished in small steps. Every day, spend five or 10 minutes – no more, unless you plan ahead to spend a greater length of time – de-cluttering something. Perhaps it will be the table by the front door where absolutely everything seems to gets dumped, or the forgotten pile of laundry on top of the dryer, or a corner of your desk. Clear something out once a day and feel your mind let out a sigh of relief.

The Weekly Spa

Women don't have to go to an expensive salon or health farm to enjoy a luxurious beauty treatment – you can do it yourself every week in the privacy of your own bathroom. Give yourself a manicure, a pedicure, a facial and a hair conditioning treatment. Soak in the bath with a splash of lavender oil, then moisturize from head to toe. While you relax, play tranquil music, soak by candlelight, burn incense in a scent you love and think about things you love, beautiful places and calming images. You'll feel pampered, relaxed and energized, and your skin will look great.

Family Time

Nothing restores you like time with the people you love, even if that time can also be stressful. People with strong family ties have a much larger base or foundation on which to rely in times of stress. Start building that foundation with regular family gatherings. The family that spends time together grows stronger together. Let family time be an important component of your stress-management plan.

Quiet Time

Family is important, but time spent alone with yourself is equally important for physical, mental and spiritual renewal. Let yourself reflect on you – who you are, what you want, where you are going. Spend at least 10 minutes each day in quiet reflection, with nobody else in the room. This healthy habit is an incredibly powerful stress-management tool.

Loneliness is bad for your health! Loneliness and lack of social support trigger the release of stress hormones that suppress the immune system and, according to some experts, a lack of social support is as bad for you as smoking, obesity or not taking any exercise. Lonely people are less able to fight off infections and may be more susceptible to serious diseases such as cancer.

Be Your Own Best Friend

Only you really know what you need, and only you can make it happen for yourself. Only you can decide what is good for you, what is bad for you, what can make your life better or what will make it worse. Be an advocate for yourself. Stand up for what you need. If you don't manage your stress, who will? A best friend should know you as well as he knows himself. Be your own best friend, and that's exactly what you'll have.

Antistress Breaks

It's holiday time. Do you know what you are going to do? Will it be another visit to see relatives? Another trip to France with six people in the minivan? Another slog from one tourist attraction to the next?

If just the thought of a holiday stresses you, you are missing the point. Holidays are for relaxation and renewal; they should be a deliberately fulfilling break from your regular routine. Make the most of your holiday time to supercharge your stress management. Consider any of these antistress holiday ideas:

- **One man's cruise...** Some people live for their next cruise. For others, being stuck on a boat with a bunch of strangers sounds anything but relaxing. But today's cruises come in all shapes and sizes. Check with your travel agent if you like the idea of being on the open sea.
- **The spa.** If you want to be treated to a truly tranquil experience and you don't mind the price tag, visit a spa. Spa holidays are very luxurious and offer healthy cuisine and everything from massages to meditation sessions, spirituality programmes, yoga classes, to walks to breathtaking vistas.
- **The nature experience.** If nature relaxes and renews you, consider going on a holiday that involves any of varying levels of physical activity in interesting natural places. These can be found all over the world, from California to Tibet, from Australia to the Alps.
- **The tropics.** If relaxing on the beach is your idea of a stress-free holiday, then go for it. Visit the Caribbean, the Mediterranean, Bali, Java or Lombok... the list is endless, and fares and accommodation are no longer just for the richest.
- **The extreme holiday.** If basking is not your style, extreme holidays are becoming increasingly popular. The concept involves the training in and execution of some kind of extreme sport, such as sky-diving,

parasailing, hang-gliding, or mountain-climbing. If this is your idea of a good time – and intense athletic activity is certainly an excellent way to learn mental focus – then go for it. (Just be careful!)

· **The don't-tell-anybody-but-we're-staying-at home holiday.** Who says you have to leave the comfort of your own home just because you aren't going to work? Sometimes the most relaxing holiday is the one that you *don't* take. Staying at home means you can catch up with all those nagging, stress-inducing chores you need to finish; you can sleep in longer than usual; you don't have to spend the money associated with a holiday; and you won't have to deal with travelling, time zones, bureaux de change, traveller's cheques or not being able to speak the language. If you don't tell anybody you're staying at home, you'll have more freedom than ever. You may come to appreciate your own home more than ever if you spend your holiday in it. It's not against the rules!

Stress Management for Life

You can change your life for the better simply by clearing out the stress that doesn't have to be there and managing the stress that does. You can feel better today, and you can feel even better in a few days, a few weeks, a few months, a few years. Stress management is for life, and with little changes here and there, with vigilance, with monitoring and with a continued commitment to maximizing your individual potential by minimizing the things that are holding you back, things can only look up.

I'll leave you with ten final tips for managing the stress in your life for the rest of your life. You can do it! Put a stop to wasting your time and letting the best part of you drain away because of a lack of energy. Let yourself be strong, energized, and in control of you.

1. **Know thyself, know thy stress.** You are worth your own time. The more you know about yourself, the more you'll understand what stresses you and what you can do about it.

2. **Stay tuned in.** Notice how you feel. Write it down. Keep track, and you'll understand more about what needs to be done and why you do the things you do when life gets stressful.

3. **Keep building your stress-management network.** Nobody can do it alone. Let your friends and family help you, and be there to help them, too.

4. **Believe in yourself.** If you break past your barriers, you can be the person you know you are inside. Trust in yourself and have confidence in yourself, even when it seems as if nobody else does. Only you know your true potential.

5. **Keep your perspective.** When things seem out of control, step back to gain a perspective. What does this mean in the grand scheme of things? What are your options? What are the alternative strategies? Is it worth letting go of this one?

6. **Don't worry, be happy!** Trite, perhaps, but it's a catchy song and even catchier advice. If you find yourself worrying, stop. Do something that makes you happy instead. It's good medicine.

7. **Accept what you can't control.** You have control over what you say, do and, in some cases, feel. You don't have control over what other people say, do or feel. You don't have control over many of the things that happen to you or affect you in life. If you can't control it, you might as well accept it. Anything else is just a waste of energy.

8. **Control what you can control.** You don't have to accept the negative effects of stress on your body, mind and spirit. You don't have to agree to do everything you are asked. You don't have to be overwhelmed, overcommitted or overworked. If it can be controlled, work out a way to control it. It's your life. Nobody else is in charge but you, so start being in charge.

9. **Live, love, laugh.** Those three things make it all worthwhile and put stress in its proper place.

10. **Always take care.** Take care of yourself – you are worth caring for. You deserve to love yourself and feel good about yourself, no matter what your imperfections. If you take care of yourself, you'll be in the best possible state to take care of others. It's all connected, after all.

Stress is just something that happens to us. It doesn't affect who you are inside, and its presence in your life says nothing about you except, perhaps, that you are human. But if stress is hurting you, you can make it stop. Commit to yourself, commit to stress management, commit to being happy, and you'll discover that the future's looking bright on the road ahead.

Good luck to you as you go along your way.

Stress Management
Tools Reference Guide

Here is an alphabetical listing of tools, techniques and therapies for combatting the stress in your life. Try a few, or try them all – you'll be managing your stress in no time.

Alexander technique: The Alexander technique is movement instruction in which clients are taught to hold and move their bodies with full consciousness in a way that releases tension and uses the body as well as possible. People say that practising the Alexander technique makes them feel lighter and more in control of their bodies. The Alexander technique is popular with actors and other performing artists.

Applied kinesiology: This is a muscle-testing technique that determines where in the body a person is experiencing an imbalance or problem. Massage as well as movement of certain joints, acupressure and advice on diet, vitamins and herbs are then offered as treatment.

Art therapy: In art therapy you can use any art form as an expression of creativity to help release stressful feelings.

Assertiveness training: Assertiveness training helps you to be direct and assertive rather than indirect. It helps to combat the tendency to internalize stress, anger, disappointment, fear and pain by teaching techniques for acknowledging and expressing these feelings in effective and appropriate ways.

Attitude adjustment: Being negative is a habit, and adjusting your attitude to be more positive can be a habit, too. Just as with any habit, the more you get used to halting your negative reactions and replacing them with neutral or positive ones, the less you'll find yourself reacting negatively. Instead of 'Oh NO', react with silence and take a wait-and-see attitude. Or react with an affirmation: 'Oh... I can learn something positive from this!'

Autogenic training: Autogenic training, or autogenics, was designed to reap the benefits of hypnosis without the need for a hypnotist or the time typically involved in a hypnosis session. Autogenics uses a relaxed position and the verbal suggestion of warmth and heaviness in the limbs to induce a state of deep relaxation and stress relief. Autogenics has been used to treat muscle tension, asthma, gastrointestinal problems, irregular heartbeat, high blood pressure, headaches, thyroid problems, anxiety, irritability and fatigue. It can also be useful in increasing your stress resistance.

Ayurveda: Ayurveda (pronounced I-YOUR-VAY-DA) is an ancient Indian science of living a long and healthy life through a variety of practices. It defies disease and ageing, and promotes wellbeing and good health. Ayurveda may be the oldest known health care system, being probably over 5,000 years old, and it is still widely practised today.

Biofeedback: This high-tech relaxation technique, designed to teach the body how to directly and immediately reverse the stress response, puts you in control of bodily functions once considered to be involuntary. A biofeedback session involves being hooked up to equipment that measures certain functions, such as your skin temperature, heart rate, breathing rate and muscle tension. A trained biofeedback practitioner then guides the subject through relaxation techniques while the subject watches the machine monitors. When heart rate or breathing rate decreases, for example, you can see it on the monitor. You learn how your body feels when your heart and breathing rate decrease. Eventually, after a number of sessions, you learn to lower your heart rate, breath rate, muscle tension, temperature and so forth, on your own.

Body scan: This is a relaxation technique involving a systematic scan of the body and conscious relaxation of tense areas.

Breathing exercises: These exercises involve any of various techniques for infusing the body with oxygen and energy. The purpose is to improve health and relaxation.

Breathing meditation: This meditation involves any of various techniques for measured, controlled breathing to relax the body and improve health.

Chakra meditation: This involves meditation on the seven chakras, or energy centres, in the body. Meditating to open and energize the chakras is an effective technique for freeing the body to do the work of extinguishing the negative effects of stress.

Conscious moderation: Conscious moderation involves making a conscious effort to consume food, drink and other resources, including money, in a moderate way for greater inner and outer balance.

Creativity therapy: In this therapy, you use creative expression, such as painting, writing, poetry or playing music, as a way to release stressful feelings.

Dance: Whether you go to an organized class – ballet, jazz, tap, ballroom dancing, swing dancing, country dancing, square dancing, Irish dancing, to name a few – or go out dancing with your friends every weekend, dancing is great cardiovascular exercise and also a lot of fun.

Exercise: Exercise involves moving the body to improve health, mood, strength, flexibility and cardiopulmonary function, and to release excessive energy such as that generated by the stress response.

Feng shui: The ancient Chinese art of placement is used in the 21st century to help people enhance the flow of positive energy through their homes and properties.

Flower remedies: Flower remedies or flower essences are made from water and whole flowers, then preserved with alcohol. They contain no actual flower parts, but people who use and prescribe them believe they contain and carry the flower's essence or energy and can promote emotional healing.

Friend therapy: Friend therapy is simple: let your friends help you to manage your stress. Research shows that people without social networks and friends, while feeling lonely, often won't admit it. Loneliness is stressful, and holding in your feelings is even more stressful. Sharing your feelings with your friends helps you to experience them and move on.

Gym/health club: This is a good way to have lots of fitness options in one place.

Habit restructuring: Habit restructuring involves working to consciously eliminate or redirect habits that are having a negative effect on the body or mind.

Herbal medicine: Herbal remedies are taken for better health and stress resistance. Practise with caution or under the guidance of an experienced and qualified herbalist.

Homeopathy: Homeopathic remedies are taken for better health and stress resistance. They are highly diluted substances that counteract the symptoms of certain diseases.

Hypnosis: Hypnosis involves deep relaxation coupled with visualization, and is achieved through a systematic process. When hypnotized you retain your awareness, but your body becomes extremely relaxed and disinclined to move. Also your awareness becomes narrow, your thinking tends to become literal, and you become much more open to suggestion than you would be in a non-hypnotic state. This suggestibility allows for hypnosis to help relieve stress and correct undesirable behaviour.

Imagery meditation: This is a meditation technique that helps you imagine yourself in a different place or circumstance in order to induce relaxation.

Keeping a diary: Writing in a diary is a way to release stressful feelings.

Keeping a dream diary: Keeping a dream diary means recording the dream images you remember every morning, then looking back at them periodically to detect recurring themes.

Lifestyle management techniques: This term covers any techniques for improving and easing daily life, including practices for simplicity, de-cluttering, organizing, time management, relationship management, family dynamics and self-improvement.

Light therapy: This is a treatment for Seasonal Affective Disorder (SAD) that involves exposing the skin to full-spectrum light for extended periods of time to improve mood and symptoms of depression.

Mandala meditation: This is a significant kind of meditation in Tibetan culture, where the focus of the meditation is a mandala, or circular picture, sometimes very plain, sometimes highly ornate, containing designs that draw the eye to the centre of the mandala, helping the mind to focus on that centre point.

Mantra meditation: Any concentrated focusing while repeating a sound can be called a mantra meditation, whether it's Sufi chanting or the recitation of the rosary prayer. Some people believe that the sounds of a mantra actually contain certain powers; others believe that the key to mantra meditation is the repetition itself, and that any sound would work.

Massage therapy: In massage therapy, any of various massage techniques are used to relax the muscles and free blocked energy in the body.

Meditation: Meditation is focused concentration to gain control over the wayward mind and enhance relaxation.

Mindfulness meditation: This is a type of meditation in which the meditator maintains a 'mindful', highly observant state. Mindfulness meditation is different from other meditations because it can be practised anywhere at any time, and no matter what you are doing. It is simply focusing on total awareness of the present moment. Mindfulness meditation is inherent in many other forms of meditation, but it can also be practised while walking, running, playing football, driving, studying, writing, reading, eating. Whatever the activity you are doing, you can do with mindfulness.

Nutrition: You should eat a variety of fresh, natural foods in moderate amounts to improve health and the body's ability to handle stress.

Optimism therapy: So you think you are a confirmed pessimist? Optimism therapy is a form of attitude adjustment focusing on reframing responses as an optimist. Studies show that optimists enjoy better general health, a stronger immune system, faster recovery from surgery and longer life than pessimists.

Pain centring: This is a pain-management technique that focuses on pain as an experience separate from suffering and negative associations.

Passive attitude: Having a passive attitude can be a good way to manage stress. By having an 'Oh well' attitude to stressful events that you can't control, you give yourself permission to let the stressful feelings go.

Pilates: This consists of specific core-muscle-strengthening exercises performed on a mat or special machines that concentrate on the abdominal and back muscles.

Polarity therapy: Polarity therapy is a little like Reiki in that it is designed to free and balance the body's internal energy, but it is more of a combination of Eastern and Western approaches. It includes massage, dietary advice, certain yoga exercises and psychological counselling for a full mind–body approach to energy balancing.

Pranayama: Pranayama describes the specific breathing techniques of yoga.

Prayer: Prayer is focused, concentrated communication, a statement of intention or the opening of the channel between you and divinity, whatever divinity means to you. A prayer can be a request, thanks, worship or praise to God. It can be an expression of gratitude directed to the universe. It can be used to invoke divine power, or to attempt to experience divine or universal energy directly. Many different traditions have many different modes and types of prayer. Prayer can mean whatever you want it to mean.

Reflexology: Reflexology is a little like acupressure, except that all the pressure points are in the hands and feet. According to the theory, the entire body, including all the parts, organs and glands, is represented in a 'map' on the hands and feet, and that pressure applied to the right area of the 'map' will help to balance the problem in the associated area of the body. Once you know the map, you can work on yourself by massaging your hands or feet in the appropriate area.

Reiki: Reiki (pronounced RAY-KEY) is an energy healing technique based on ancient Tibetan practices. Practitioners of Reiki put their hands on, or just above, the body in order to balance energy by acting as a sort of conduit for life force energy. Reiki is used to treat physical problems as well as emotional and psychological ones, and is, more positively, also a tool for supporting and facilitating positive changes.

Relaxation techniques: These include any of many techniques for relaxing the body and mind.

Reward-based self-training: This training involves choosing behaviour you want to establish, then rewarding yourself for your improvements and successes rather than punishing yourself for your slips and failures.

Rolfing: Rolfing is a type of deep massage designed to restructure the body's muscles and connective tissue to promote better alignment. If you like your massages hard, this one's for you. Some people claim that the deep tissue massage actually releases deeply buried emotions and that emotional outbursts are common during the course of the 10-session programme.

Savasana: Savasana, or corpse pose, is a yoga position that involves complete relaxation of the body.

Self-care: In self-care, you make a conscious effort to care for yourself regularly and attend to your physical, emotional and spiritual needs.

Self-esteem maintenance: This requires working consciously to maintain and protect self-esteem for better physical and mental health and performance on all levels.

Self-hypnosis: This is a technique for hypnotizing oneself to achieve positive goals and to stop negative behaviour.

Self-massage: If you learn about acupressure, Swedish massage, reflexology and many other techniques, you can perform massage on yourself. You can massage your own neck, scalp, face, hands, feet, legs, arms and torso. Many yoga positions also result in internal and external massage. By bending the body in certain ways against itself, or by using the pressure of the floor against certain parts of the body, massage takes place.

Shiatsu and acupressure: *Shiatsu* is the Japanese word for 'finger pressure' and is related to acupressure. Shiatsu is an ancient form of massage, still widely practised, that involves the application of pressure through fingers, palms, elbows or knees to pressure points in the body.

Sleep: Most adults need about eight hours' sleep a night, although some need even more. Getting enough sleep is an important step towards being able to manage stress.

Swedish massage: This common form of massage involves the practitioner applying oil to the body and using certain types of massage strokes – namely, *effleurage* (gliding), *petrissage* (kneading), *friction* (rubbing), and *tapotement* (tapping) – to increase circulation in muscles and connective tissue, help the body to flush out waste products and heal injuries.

Swimming: Swimming is especially good for people who can't take much stress on their joints, who are overweight and just beginning to exercise, or who enjoy being in the water.

Tai chi/Qigong: Tai chi and its precursor, Qigong, (sometimes called chi kung), are ancient Chinese Taoist martial arts forms that have evolved into a series of slow, graceful movements, in concert with the breath. It is designed to free internal energy and keep it flowing through the body, uniting body and mind, and promoting good health and relaxation. Tai chi is sometimes called a moving meditation. Qigong involves specific movements and postures, as well as other health-maintenance procedures such as massage and meditation, to maintain and improve overall health and balance the body's internal energy.

Team sports: For people who like to play on a team and are motivated and energized by the energy of others, team sports can be an excellent way to get exercise and enjoy a social life at the same time.

Thought stopping: Thought stopping is the practice of noticing destructive or obsessive thoughts and telling yourself to stop, then re-directing your thoughts in a more positive way.

Visualization: This is the technique of imagining something you want, or a change you would like to see in yourself, so that you mentally set your intention and help to effect the changes.

Vitamin/mineral therapy: This therapy involves taking vitamins and minerals to cover your nutritional bases and protect against deficiencies for better health and a more stress-resistant body.

Walking: A versatile exercise choice for people of any fitness level, walking is excellent for boosting mood and reducing stressful feelings as well as improving physical fitness.

Walking meditation: This is a form of meditation that is practised while walking.

Water: To keep the body well hydrated and properly functioning, drink 2–2$\frac{1}{2}$ litres each day.

Weightlifting: Lifting weights is great for any adult. It builds bone mass and can reverse osteoporosis. It also increases muscle tone and helps your body to burn more calories – the more muscle you have, the more calories you burn during the aerobic portion of your workout.

Worry control: Worry control involves learning to recognize obsessive worrying and re-direct that energy in more positive ways.

Yoga: Yoga is an ancient Indian method of exercise designed to 'yoke' body and mind through specific postures, breathing exercises and meditation.

Yoga meditation: This is a form of meditation designed to help the meditator to recognize ultimate oneness with the universe. It can result in a state of pure, joyful bliss called samadhi.

Zazen: Zazen is the sitting meditation of Zen Buddhism, although many non-Buddhists practise zazen. It involves just sitting and is not affiliated with any religion or philosophy. When practised regularly, just sitting becomes a mental discipline that results in a greater ability to manage stress.

APPENDIX B

Stress Management Resources for Easier Living

When it comes to stress management, knowledge is power. These resources will help you to further your knowledge about stress, good health, good nutrition and yourself. I've also listed organizations that you can contact for more information, therapy, or relaxation and websites for stress-free Internet surfing. Happy explorations!

Note: Inclusion of resources in this book does not necessarily imply endorsement of these resources' health-related content, products or services.

Organizations and Websites

International Stress Management Association
 PO Box 348
 Waltham Cross
 Herts EN8 8ZL
 07000 780 430
 www.isma.org.uk

The UK National Work-Stress Network
 9 Bell Lane
 Syresham
 Brackley
 Northants NN13 5HP
 01280 850 388
 www.workstress.net

The Mental Health Foundation
 83 Victoria Street
 London SW1H 0HW
 020 7802 0300
 www.mhf.org.uk

Stressbusting.co.uk
 www.stressbusting.co.uk

The British Sleep Society
 PO Box 247
 Colne
 Buntingdon PE28 3UZ
 www.sleeping.org.uk

The Sleep Council
 01756 791089
 www.sleepcouncil.com

Eating Disorders Association
 103 Prince of Wales Road
 Norwich NR1 1DW
 0870 770 3256
 www.edauk.com

FlyLady
 www.flylady.net

Cruse Bereavement Care
 Cruse House
 126 Sheen Road
 Richmond
 Surrey TW9 1UR
 0870 167 1677
 www.crusebereavementcare.org.uk

The British Wheel of Yoga
 25 Jermyn Street
 Sleaford
 Lincs NG34 7RU
 www.bwy.org.uk

The National Register of Hypnotherapists and
 Psychotherapists (NRHP)
 12 Cross Street
 Nelson
 Lancs BB9 0DD
 01282 716839

Complementary Healthcare Information Service –
 UK
 www.chisuk.com

British Complementary Medicine Association
 PO Box 5122
 Bournemouth BH8 0WG
 0845 345 5977
 www.bcma.co.uk

Complementary Medical Association
    The Meridian
    142A Greenwich High Road
    London SE10 8NN
    www.the-cma.org.uk

Foundation for Integrated Medicine
    12 Chillingworth Road
    London N7 8QJ
    020 7619 6140

Institute for Complementary Medicine
    PO Box 194
    London SE16 7QZ
    020 7237 5165
    www.icmedicine.co.uk

Confederation of Healing Organizations
    The Red and White House
    113 High Street
    Berkhamsted
    Herts
    HP4 2DJ

Council for Complementary and Alternative
    Medicine (CCAM)
    Suite D
    Park House
    206/208 Latimer Road
    London W10 6RE
    0208 968 3862

Books

Benson, Herbert, M.D. *The Relaxation Response*, Updated and Expanded Edition. Avon Books, 2000.

Budilovsky, Joan, and Adamson, Eve. *The Complete Idiot's Guide to Yoga*, 2nd edition. Alpha Books, 2001.

Budilovsky, Joan, and Adamson, Eve. *The Complete Idiot's Guide to Meditation*. Alpha Books, 1999.

Budilovsky, Joan, and Adamson, Eve. *The Complete Idiot's Guide to Massage*. Alpha Books, 1998.

Butler, Gillian, and Hope, Tony. *Manage Your Mind: The Mental Fitness Guide*. Oxford Paperbacks, 1995.

Cameron, Julia. *The Artist's Way*. Jeremy P. Tarcher/Putnam, 1992.

Chopra, Deepak, M.D. *Ageless Body, Timeless Mind*. Harmony Books, 1993.

Chopra, Deepak, M.D. *Creating Health*, Revised Edition. Houghton Mifflin Company, 1991.

Chopra, Deepak, M.D. *Perfect Health*. Harmony Books, 1991.

Epstein, Mark, M.D. *Going to Pieces Without Falling Apart*. Broadway Books, 1998.

Farhi, Donna. *The Breathing Book*. Henry Holt & Company, 1996.

Fontana, David. *The Meditator's Handbook*. Thorsons, 2000.

Hall, Alvin. *Your Money or Your Life*. Coronet, 2003.

Hanh, Thich Nhat. *Peace Is Every Step*. Bantam Books, 1992.

Harrar, Sari, and Altshul O'Donnell, Sara. *The Woman's Book of Healing Herbs*. Rodale Press, Inc., 1999.

Johnson, Don Hanlon (editor). *Bone, Breath, & Gesture*. North Atlantic Books, 1995.

Kabat-Zinn, Jon, Ph.D. *Full Catastrophe Living: Using the Wisdom of Your Body and Mind to Face Stress, Pain, and Illness*. Delta, 1990.

Lacroix, Nitya. *Relaxation: 101 Essential Tips*. DK Publishing, 1998.

Linn, Denise. *Sacred Space: Clearing and Enhancing the Energy of Your Home*. Ballantine Books, 1995.

Milner, Marion. *Eternity's Sunrise: A Way of Keeping a Diary*. Virago Press, 1987.

Monro, Robin, Nagaranthna, R. and Nagendra, H.R., *Yoga for Common Ailments*. Simon & Schuster, Inc., 1990.

Morgenstern, Julie. *Organizing from the Inside Out*. Henry Holt and Company, 1998.

Mumford, Susan. *The Complete Guide to Massage*. Hamlyn, 2000.

Northrup, Christiane, M.D. *The Wisdom of Menopause: Creating Physical and Emotional Health and Healing During the Change*. Bantam Books, 2001.

Orman, Suze. *The 9 Steps to Financial Freedom*. Crown Publishers, Inc., 1997.

Richardson, Cheryl. *Life Makeovers*. Broadway Books, 2000.

Schiffman, Erich. *Yoga: The Spirit and Practice of Moving into Stillness*. Pocket Books, 1996.

Shurety, Sarah. *Feng Shui for Your Home*. Rider, 1997

St. James, Elaine. *The Simplicity Reader*. Smithmark, 1998.

Tirtha, Swami Sada Shiva. *The Ayurveda Encyclopedia*. Ayurveda Holistic Center Press, 1998.

Van de Castle, Robert L., Ph.D. *Our Dreaming Mind*. Ballantine Books, 1994.

Weil, Andrew, M.D. *Eight Weeks to Optimum Health*. Alfred A. Knopf, 1998.

Whitaker, Julian, M.D., and Colman, Carol. *Shed 10 Years in 10 Weeks*. Simon & Schuster, 1997.

Index

to stress, 18
Nettle, 256
Nicotine, 105
Nirvana, 171
Niyamas, 171
Noise habit, 108–109
Noise pollution, 16
Noise stress and, 239
Noradrenaline, 10, 11
Nutrient-dense foods, 151
Nutrition, 308. *See also* Diet
   in stress management, 56, 58

O
Obesity, stress and, 12
Obsessive behaviour, 26
Obsessive news watching, 107
Obsessive worrying, 63–64
Oestrogen, 75, 252–253
   menopause and, 264
Omega-3 fatty acids, 152
Optimism therapy, 193,
   212–215, 308
   in stress management, 57,
   212–215
Osteoporosis, 144
Outdoor exercise, 142–143
Overeating, 105–106
Oxytocin, 267

P
Pain, 90
   back, 88
   chronic, 17, 22
   endorphins and, 11
   indirect stress and, 17
Pain centring, 308
Panic disorder, 252
Parasomnia, 96
Parenthood, stress in, 259–262
Partridgeberry, 256

Passive-aggressive stress manager, 298
Passive attitude, 308
   stress and, 49
Passive stress manager, 297
Perfection meditation, 68
Peripheral vision, focusing on,
   127
Personal eating plan, 154–156
Personal habits, 104
Personality
   effect on behaviour, 103
   stress and, 60–61
Personal sanctuary, building,
   239–247
Personal stress, 57
   management of, 57
Personal stress profile, 39–70
Personal stress test
   stress response tendencies in,
   50–51, 68–70
   stress tolerance point in,
   45–47, 52–55
   stress triggers, 47–48, 56–59
   stress vulnerability factors in,
   48–49, 60–68
Petrissage, 146
Pets, in stress management, 37,
   266, 281
Physical stressors, 16
Physiological stress, 17, 57–58
Physiological stressors, 16
Pilates, 141–142, 308
Pineal gland, 10
Pittas, 196, 197
Placebo, 22
Plaque, 75
Polarity therapy, 148, 308
Pollution
   air, 16
   environmental, 16

   noise, 16
   water, 16
Polyunsaturated fats, 152
Porridge, in stress management,
   123
Positive affirmations, 187
Postnatal depression, 259
Postnatal period, stress during,
   256, 259
Pranayama, 171, 309
Pratyahara, 171
Prayer, 184–185, 309
   practising, 185
Pregnancy, stress during,
   256–258
Premenstrual syndrome (PMS),
   16, 117, 253–254
Pre-schoolers, stress in, 288
Procrastinating, 109–110
Protein, 151, 281
Protein Power diet, 150
Psoriasis, 22
Pumpkin seeds, 281

Q
Qigong, 142
Quiet time, 300

R
Ragged robin, 256
Raspberry leaf, 254, 256
Red chestnut flower, 206
Red clover, 256
Reflection walk, 31–33
Reflexology, 146–147, 309
Reiki, 147, 309
Relaxation
   balancing stress with, 121–124
   in stress management, 57, 58
Relaxation techniques, 124–129,
   309